Democracy and t[illegible]

Is shame dead? W[illegible]ly available, an eroding public/private [illegible]urn in public discourse, many seem to think so. People across the political spectrum have criticized these developments and sought to resurrect shame in order to protect privacy and invigorate democratic politics.

Democracy and the Death of Shame reads the fear that "shame is dead" as an expression of anxiety about the social disturbance endemic to democratic politics. Far from an essential supplement to democracy, the recurring call to "bring back shame" and other civilizing mores is a disciplinary reaction to the work of democratic citizens who extend the meaning of political equality into social realms. Rereadings from the ancient Cynics to the mid-twentieth century challenge the view that shame is dead and show how shame, as a politically charged idea, is disavowed, invoked, and negotiated in moments of democratic struggle.

Jill Locke is Professor of Political Science at Gustavus Adolphus College.

Democracy and the Death of Shame

Political Equality and Social Disturbance

JILL LOCKE
Gustavus Adolphus College–St. Peter, MN

CAMBRIDGE
UNIVERSITY PRESS

CAMBRIDGE
UNIVERSITY PRESS

University Printing House, Cambridge CB2 8BS, United Kingdom

One Liberty Plaza, 20th Floor, New York, NY 10006, USA

477 Williamstown Road, Port Melbourne, VIC 3207, Australia

4843/24, 2nd Floor, Ansari Road, Daryaganj, Delhi – 110002, India

79 Anson Road, #06–04/06, Singapore 079906

Cambridge University Press is part of the University of Cambridge.

It furthers the University's mission by disseminating knowledge in the pursuit of education, learning and research at the highest international levels of excellence.

www.cambridge.org
Information on this title: www.cambridge.org/9781107635906

First published 2016
First paperback edition 2017

A catalogue record for this publication is available from the British Library

Library of Congress Cataloging in Publication data
Names: Locke, Jill, 1969– author
Title: Democracy and the death of shame : political equality and social disturbance / Jill Locke.
Description: New York, NY: Cambridge University Press, [2016] | Includes bibliographical references and index
Identifiers: LCCN 2015039552 | ISBN 9781107063198 (hardback)
Subjects: LCSH: Democracy. | Shame – Political aspects. | Shame – Social aspects. | Equality. | Political participation. | Political sociology. | Political science – Philosophy.
Classification: LCC JC423.L5933 2016 | DDC 321.8–dc23
LC record available at http://lccn.loc.gov/2015039552

ISBN 978-1-107-06319-8 Hardback
ISBN 978-1-107-63590-6 Paperback

For Eric

Contents

Acknowledgments

The opportunity to acknowledge in writing the countless people who have supported this project and made it possible for me to write it has carried me through the most difficult parts of the writing process. On more than one occasion, I reminded myself that if I didn't finish this book I wouldn't have the opportunity to say thank you publicly. All errors, shortcomings, and confusions in the book are, of course, mine.

I want to begin by thanking my editor, Robert Dreesen, and the staff at Cambridge University Press for taking on this project, finding such excellent reviewers, waiting patiently, and shepherding the book through the stages of review, revision, and production. I appreciated Robert's gentle pressure both to "take your time" and write "the best possible manuscript."

It was possible both to take my time and make the manuscript the "best possible" thanks to the extraordinary gift of a year of membership at the Institute for Advanced Study in Princeton and participation in Danielle Allen's Egalitarianisms seminar, where I presented and received excellent feedback on Chapter 5. Danielle generously read and commented on the full manuscript, and my reading and understanding of the Greeks and the concepts of equality and egalitarianism are much richer for having worked closely with her this year. Her generosity of spirit and commitment to historically sensitive and politically engaged theorizing is inspiring. While at the Institute, I also benefited from Brady Brower's help with the European context of Arendt's views of children, Michael Hanchard's insights into Arendt's blind spots about political children and ideas about how I might situate my own voice vis-à-vis hers, and Charles Payne's expertise on the role of children in the civil rights movement. Sophie Rosenfeld read my Introduction and two chapters; her specific comments as well as many "teatime" conversations about work at the intersection(s) of political theory and history helped me to clarify several parts of this project. Brian Connolly's careful reading of Chapter 4 and our talks on the patios of Oppenheimer Lane helped me to better appreciate the debates among historians about how best to characterize the Jacksonian era of US democracy (and the eighteenth-century dynamics that preceded it). I cannot thank Jennifer Morgan enough for the solidarity and intellectual engagement, reading suggestions, and conversations about historical writing and writing about sensitive material, in particular. Her friendship helped to sustain me through the final push of revising. Stimulating conversations and general encouragement from Manduhai Buyandelger, Anver Emon, Didier Fassin, Gary Fine, Julilly Kohler-Hausmann, Nan Koehane, Anandi Mani, Mara Viveros Vigolla, Joan Scott, and Michael Walzer also supported my writing and revising.

It was fitting to bring this book to a close in New Jersey, as the inkling of an idea for it began at Rutgers University nearly twenty years ago. I am grateful to Linda Zerilli, Benjamin Barber, and the late W. Carey McWilliams for believing in both that project and my ability to execute it. Sue Carroll pushed me to think about the gendered dimensions of shame before I was ready to do so. I think I finally figured out that piece of the story – or at least have done better justice to it. I was also extremely fortunate to receive a Charlotte W. Newcombe Fellowship to support this early work. Fellow travelers from Rutgers have nourished my mind and spirit from the beginning. Thank you, especially, to Cristina Beltrán, Mark Button, Mark Brown, Richard Boyd, David Gutterman, Jennet Kirkpatrick, Laurie Naranch, Karen Shelby, Rose Sarja, Claire Snyder-Hall, Liz Swanson, Matt Voorhees and Karen Zivi.

In the intervening years, I put this manuscript away and came back to it several times. During my 2006–2007 sabbatical at the Center for Ethics and Public Affairs and 2007–2008 visiting position in Political Science at Tulane University, I reconceptualized it and began working on the material that comprises the book you hold in your hands. Richard Teichgraeber and Meg Keenan graciously invited and welcomed me to Tulane. Susanne Sreedhar and Dana Zartner were essential sounding boards and soul-sustaining company in the early stages of the book planning.

I was able to continue working on this book upon my return from New Orleans with the support of many colleagues at Gustavus Adolphus College. Elizabeth Baer and Linnea Wren were model senior colleagues. Priscilla Briggs, Betsy Byers, and Audrey Russek listened to me sort out the argument and the logistics of executing it as we drove to campus together. Eric Dugdale, Séan Easton, and Yurie Hong helped me to navigate the Classical texts and references I rely on so heavily. My colleagues in Political Science, Mimi Gerstbauer, Chris Gilbert, Asli Ilgit, Lori Carsen Kelly, Kate Knutson, and especially Alisa Rosenthal, who as my office neighbour often got blow-by-blow reports of chapter progress and kept me laughing through some of the difficult periods, made being a scholar-teacher in Political Science a possibility and a pleasure. Janine Genelin helped me stay on top of logistics, especially during my six years as Chair and Program Director; Peg O'Connor pushed me to keep writing when I needed her to; and finally, Kate Wittenstein and Greg Kaster have been anchors throughout my time at Gustavus, generous with their historical knowledge, senses of humor, and company both on and off campus.

One of the pleasures of teaching at Gustavus has been getting to work through so much material directly with my students. I have learned an incredible amount from their candid reactions and questions. Many of the sources that I engage in this book have appeared on my course syllabi. Students in Political and Legal Thinking, Ancient Political Thought, Modern Political Thought, Democracy and Citizenship, Politics and Sexuality, Sex, Power, and Politics, the Politics of Race and Racism, and the senior seminar on the Political Theory of Hannah Arendt: Thank you for bringing so much life to the course material and for caring about politics and political ideas. Rebecca Knudson, Reid Foster, Heidi Hope, Kristen Nelson, Leslee Mahoney, Kelly Dumais, Ashley Steinberg, and Mashal Sherzad helped with research support. And finally, at the institutional level, sabbatical support, travel support, and Research, Scholarship, and Creativity funds from the Provost's Office, the Kendall Center, and the Gustavus office at the American Swedish Institute provided the time, space, and resources to renew my investment in this project, present parts of it at conferences, and bring it to completion. I would be remiss if I did not also thank the librarians at Gustavus and other institutions, especially Tulane and the Institute for Advanced Study, whose help with interlibrary loan, in particular, made it possible for me to access necessary research materials. Kathie Martin and Sonja Timmerman at Gustavus warrant special mention.

Thank you, also, to the communities of political theorists beyond the walls of my home institutions. The annual Feminist Theory Workshop at the Western Political Science Association has been a godsend of like-minded scholars and feminist friendship. I first tested out my ideas about "unashamed citizenship" there nearly a decade ago. The workshop is where I first met Lori Marso and Joan Tronto, both of whom gave me excellent feedback on an early version of the full manuscript. I was fortunate to present some sections of the project at colloquia and seminars at Gustavus Adolphus College, the Institute for Advanced Study, University of Minnesota, University of Wisconsin, Rockefeller College at SUNY-Albany, Tulane University, Union College, Whitman College, and Willamette University and on panels at the annual meetings of the American, Midwest, and Western Political Science Associations. At critical junctures, I benefited from conversations with and the insights and encouragement of Paul Apostolidis, Lawrie Balfour, Jane Bennett, Eileen Botting, Susan Burgess, William Connolly, Barbara Cruikshank, Mary Dietz, Andrew Dilts, Lisa Disch, Tom Dumm, Kennan Ferguson, Jason Frank, Vicki Hsueh, Steven Johnston, Tim Kaufman-Osborn, Chris Lebron, Patchen Markell, Jeanne Morefield, Ella Myers, Melvin Rogers, Mort Schoolman, Torrey Shanks, Christina Tarnopolsky, Darren Walhof, Liz Wingrove, Lena Zuckerwise, and the insightful and generous reviewers for Cambridge University Press.

I was very lucky to be writing my first book alongside close friends. Karen Zivi, Michaele Ferguson, Nancy Luxon, and Holloway Sparks have been the backbone of my writing support. Weekly – and sometimes daily – contact with each of them, exchanges of work, help with strategic decision making, and unalloyed solidarity have made it possible to research or write nearly every day for the past seven years. Karen's insights into the politics of "claims-making," her nuanced accounts of stigmatized subjectivity in her work on HIV and AIDS, and her wry and sardonic wit have been essential. Michaele's wide-ranging knowledge in democratic and feminist theory, her keen editorial eye, and her gentle prods to *keep going* helped me to do just that. Nancy, with whom I have shared many strong coffees and Minnesota winters, read and commented on the full manuscript at least twice (and bits and pieces at other times) and helped me to find intellectual resources I did not know I had. Holloway, with whom I share an appreciation for unruly and disrespectable forms of citizenship and the juggling act of scholarly life and parenting young children, has been a voice of calm and comfort amidst some of the more difficult moments in the writing process. Although his own first book was done quite a while ago, David Gutterman graciously and generously commented on portions of this manuscript, has believed in this book more than I have, and has always helped me to see the political and social stakes of the project as a whole.

A network of friends outside of the academy have been essential providers of everything from food to child care to writing and publishing advice. Gena Camoosa, Dennis Cass, Michael Gillespie, Annie Howell, Amy Jamieson, Matt Sewell, Jennifer Thompson, and Pam Wood have been lifesavers. I am relieved to report that the moment is here! The book is done!

Portions of Chapters 4 and 5 appeared previously as parts of "Aristocratic Mourning: Tocqueville, John Quincy Adams, and the Affairs of Andrew Jackson" and "Little Rock's Social Question: Reading Hannah Arendt on School Desegregation and Social Climbing." Thank you to Pennsylvania State University Press and the journal *Political Theory*, respectively, for permission to use sections of those chapters here.

My parents, Jack and Louise Locke, encouraged me to care about politics, the "authentic" self, and the world. They have supported me in ways large and small throughout the researching and writing process, from care packages to emergency childcare and meal-preparation and notes about shame and politics in the media. I owe special thanks to Jennifer Locke, whose generosity, humor, and reminders to *have fun* are unparalleled, and to Robert Farver, whose thoughtful hospitality always puts me so completely at ease. My family-in-love, Sally Vrooman, Peter Vrooman, Johnette Stubbs, Bruce Vrooman, and my late-father-in-law David Vrooman, thank you for sharing your love of books and ideas with me. And thanks, too, to my own children, Maxine and Felix, who came on the scene just as I was figuring out what I wanted this book to be about. Although at times it seemed that parenting and book writing were fundamentally at odds, in the end I think I finished this book and wrote it the way I did in part because of them and their own emerging curiosities about ideas, justice, and care for the world.

Eric Vrooman has been living with me and various incarnations of this project for a very long time. A book dedication is a small gesture to acknowledge all that I have learned from him about generosity, humor, care, and how to write a sentence (paragraph, chapter, and book). But it is where I will start. This book is for him.

Note on the Cover Art: *Sleeping Venus* (1944) by Paul Delvaux

I am grateful to the Tate Modern and the Artists Rights Society that manages the Paul Delvaux estate for permission to reproduce *Sleeping Venus* for the cover of *Democracy and the Death of Shame*. I came across Delvaux's 1944 painting of the *Sleeping Venus* before I had completed a full draft of this book, yet I knew instantly that I wanted to use it for the cover. The stunning painting with its sumptuous palette and evocations of feminine embodiment, *pudeur* (and its lack), death, Victorianism, supplication to the heavens, and neoclassical architecture has been an inspiring, visual reminder that the tropes of the story I wanted to tell resonated beyond my own thinking and writing. My interest in including the painting as a character in my story is not unique. As I learned by reading about Delvaux and his work, his paintings appear with some frequency in French novels of the 1950s.[1] Although he insisted that his paintings had no narrative structure but were rather figures in a composition, French novelists used them to construct their own.[2]

In keeping with Delvaux's own understanding of his work, I do not want to map my own narrative onto the *Sleeping Venus* but rather present it as a set of images for meditation. The figures in Delvaux's composition conjure ambivalence about the "death of shame." On the one hand, there is a naked and unashamed female body – Venus, no less – who is at ease. And on the other hand, there is death, Victorian mores cloaked in black as if in mourning, Furies-like supplication by other nude women, and vacant buildings that suggest they used to contain the bustle of activity and politics. The images conjure threat, stasis, and possibility. The stories people tell about democratic politics do much of the same.

[1] Gavin Parkinson, "The Delvaux Mystery: Painting, the Nouveau Roman, and Art History," *Nottingham French Studies* 51, no. 3 (2012): 298–313.

[2] Ibid., 306.

PART ONE

SHAME'S ALLURE

Introduction

The Mythology of Aidōs

I would die of shame to face the men of Troy and the Trojan women ... if I would shirk from battle now, a coward.

– Hector, *Iliad*, Book VI

A death of shame! Ah woe on woe! A treacherous hand, a cleaving Blow.

– Chorus, *Agamamenon*

Aidōs ... was hallowed in tradition as a necessary mark of civilized life.

– Anthony Long

"You'll hang your head in shame [*aidōs*] – every day of your life – if the Argives strip my armor here at the anchored ships where I have gone down fighting. Hold on, full force – spur all our men to battle!" So says king of Lycia, Zeus's son Sarpedon, on his deathbed to motivate his comrade Glaucus to keep fighting in the name of Troy.[1] The cry of *Aidōs*! *Aidōs*! appears and reappears in the *Iliad* to prompt Homer's armies on to the battlefield. Its message is clear: Be courageous, do what you must to protect the honor of yourself, your family, your city, and your manhood. Spurred by the threat of shame to put aside fear, Homer's men are commanded to do what is agreed-upon to be right, and consider the disgrace that would come to one's city, wife, children, and reputation were they to lose this war. Homer's heroes soldier on – often to death and self-destruction.[2] Even in the face of bodily harm, the heroes and their families take comfort in knowing that they have fought honorably to preserve their city

[1] Homer, *The Iliad*, trans. Richmond Lattimore (Chicago: University of Chicago Press, 1951), Book XVI, lines 588–591.

[2] Douglas L. Cairns, *Aidōs: The Psychology and Ethics of Honour and Shame in Ancient Greek Literature* (Oxford: Oxford University Press, 1993), 68.

and their family's reputation. *Aidōs* linked Homer's men and women to each other, the city, and divine forces beyond themselves.

The ancient Greek emotion of *aidōs* – translated as shame, although generally understood to encompass more emotions than the modern English term – clarifies the individual's sense of him or herself and what he or she must do in relation to others. It connotes a sense of obligation – a sense that I cannot live with who I am unless I act in a particular way. *Aidōs* is therefore an ethical code of conduct that relates the individual to others, an emotion that grounds one's identity and links correct action to it, and a prescription that instructs people about the contextual elements of that action, specifically how they should act with respect to the particularities of identity and place.[3] *Aidōs* makes different demands in the city than on the battlefield. The consistency across these places derives from who the subject is. This "agency" of the *aidōs*-heeding subject is both enabled and constrained by its demands, but *aidōs* is generally theorized as an inhibitory brake: "*Aidōs* ... involves a check of some kind; it modifies the conduct of those affected."[4] *Aidōs* is universal in the sense that all of Homer's characters have the capacity to feel it, but its directions and obligations vary based upon the social location and standing of the particular actor. That is, *aidōs* motivates differently depending on one's city, gender, social class, family of origin. This is part of its appeal, as it serves the work of providing social order without requiring everyone to act in the same way. In the gloss of recent work on the concept, *aidōs* operates as an ethical emotion that both grounds one's particular identity and allows one to be true to him or herself as understood through difference (from others) and deference to the gods and forces beyond the self.[5] Whereas in the modern and contemporary landscape people often think of escaping social identities in order to be true to real, authentic selves, the Homeric world has no conception of the "authentic" self beyond one's particular station and the obligations that come with it.

Homer's people, by and large, appear to understand what is required by the social codes of their time, and draw strength from respecting these codes and their broader cultural authority. This does not mean that Homer's characters implement the demands of *aidōs* automatically. They agonize and weigh

[3] Ibid., 48.

[4] Ibid.

[5] Bernard Williams, *Shame and Necessity* (Berkeley: University of California Press, 1993); Cairns, *Aidōs*. My use of "difference and deference" as essential to the regulative work of *aidōs* that many political theorists, philosophers, lawmakers, and ordinary citizens long for is not the same conjunction of "difference and deference" located in Jacques Derrida's concept of *différance*. I am using the ordinary meanings of the terms: difference as relational segmentation and differentiation (which is consistent with Derrida's use) and deference as reverence and obeisance to some higher force, which may be mortal or immortal in character. (Derrida's use of deference refers to the deferring – as in delaying – of linguistic meaning.) See Jacques Derrida, *Of Grammatology*, trans. Gayatri Chakravorty Spivak (Baltimore: Johns Hopkins University Press, 1998).

outcomes before they act, sometimes choosing to resist *aidōs*. And even when Homer's characters are negatively affected by *aidōs* – for example, when potential disgrace prevents Odysseus, traveling as a beggar, from asking for help, its power remains strong as an emotional experience and threat with which the subject must reckon.[6] That is, Homer's characters understand *aidōs* to be "disadvantageous on certain occasions" and to be overcome in particular situations, yet they nonetheless remain aware of its requirements.[7] In spite of the agony and equivocation that respect for *aidōs* involves and the occasional refusal of its dictates, the power and consistent presence of *aidōs* in Homer's world remains intact. In the *Iliad*, when "Agamemnon urges Diomedes to ignore any feelings of *aidōs* which may lead him to consider status before merit in 'choosing an accomplice,'" the decision to overcome *aidōs* confirms its force.[8] To be shameless is to reject the code of *aidōs* on its face. To decide to be unashamed in a particular moment because other factors outweigh the value of *aidōs* still acknowledges its legitimacy.

The people in Homer's world appear never to have grappled with the problem or threat of widespread shamelessness. By way of contrast, lamentations about the death of shame, calls for "more shame" or a "return to shame," typologies of "good" and "bad" shame that will resolve our problems, shaming punishments and debates about their effectiveness, and so on mark the modern and late-modern eras. These cries about the death and decline of shame and how it might be revitalized appear in popular magazines as well as in political theory, moral philosophy, and the discourse of criminal justice. Each reflects an often well-intentioned effort to shame the polity back into a just moral and political order by identifying both individual practices and collective attitudes that have prioritized the self against the public good. In his work on the moral complexity of *aidōs*, Bernard Williams has argued that the ancient conception of shame is not as far gone as we imagine. His point, therefore, is not that we ought to *revive* something we have *lost*, but rather see how something like *aidōs* still operates today.[9] But much of the Western tradition of political theory and philosophy, extending into the contemporary landscape, has explicitly and implicitly wrung its hands over the putative fact that "shame is dead."

Political theorists have worried that the democratic promise of self-determination and popular sovereignty has disregarded an ancient ethic of shame as a brake against individuals rewriting social codes in keeping with their particular desires or self-expression. Many look with nostalgia for the civilizing morals of the ancients, most specifically the virtue of shame.[10]

[6] Cairns, *Aidōs*, 48.
[7] Ibid., 48–49.
[8] Ibid., 49.
[9] Williams, *Shame and Necessity*, 7.
[10] Jean Bethke Elshtain, *Democracy on Trial* (New York: Basic Books, 1995); Arlene W. Saxonhouse, *Free Speech and Democracy in Ancient Athens* (Cambridge: Cambridge University Press, 2006).

"I readily concede that shame has few defenders as we near the end of the twentieth century in the West," begins one political theorist's account that asks readers to recall the insights (of Tocqueville and Arendt) that "democracy is about not only constitutions, rules, public accountability, and deliberation but also everyday life, habits, and dispositions," and instructs us "to think about shame and shamelessness" as we confront contemporary democratic crises.[11] The refrain is similar in popular media where pundits and public intellectuals lament the death of shame and catalogue the myriad ways in which shame has died and needs resurrection. The refrain goes something like the following: There's is too much personal information in the public square; people are rude and uncivil; no one respects personal space; everybody is expected to share their own personal information; people and corporations are mean-spirited.[12] These lamentations indict both moral and spatial confusion.

Philosophers have also worried about spatial confusion and its moral implications. One account offers the media portrayal of the Lewinsky scandal of the Clinton presidency as evidence that we need the brakes of shame and restraint – "selective reticence" – to check the culture of public confession.[13] The media, in this account, disrespectfully forced confessions from the president of the United States. Another philosopher fears that the postwar Western conception of "self-fulfillment" and "authenticity" is in danger of drifting too far and must be constrained and recalibrated.[14] In each case, the shameless subject is figured as an *invader* who indecorously and uncivilly bombards unsuspecting citizens, (who would otherwise either mind their own business or pursue a legitimate common good), with highly personalized confessions and testimonies of "private" or otherwise "nonpolitical" ideas and activity. Liberals, conservatives, republicans, and communitarians alike have constituted a chorus of "civilitarianism" as they meld together their laments about the death of shame and civility, the decline of the public/private distinction, the loss of privacy, the preponderance of ethically outrageous behavior, and the general rise of selfish individualism and self-fulfillment against a lost tradition of respect for authority, borders, boundaries, humility, and shame.[15] Anxieties of contamination and loss abound.

[11] Elshtain, *Democracy on Trial*, 55.

[12] Christopher Hitchens, "The Death of Shame," *Vanity Fair* (March 1996) 68–72; Mark Shields, "Does Wall Street Know No Shame?," 2009, http://www.creators.com/opinion/mark-shields/-does-wall-street-know-no-shame.html; "Shields, Brooks on Gates' Legacy, Gingrich Campaign 'Meltdown,' Weiner Fallout, PBS NewsHour, June 10, 2011." http://www.pbs.org/newshour/bb/politics/jan-june11/sandb_06-10.html.

[13] Thomas Nagel, "Concealment and Exposure," *Philosophy & Public Affairs* 27, no. 1 (1998): 3–30.

[14] Charles Taylor, *The Ethics of Authenticity* (Cambridge, MA: Harvard University Press, 1992).

[15] Randall Kennedy, "State of the Debate: The Case against 'Civility'," *The American Prospect* 9, no. 41 (1998), http://prospect.org/article/state-debate-case-against-civility.

The targets of these late-twentieth- and early-twenty-first-century jeremiads?[16] Feminism, liberalism, identity politics, multiculturalism, gay liberation, and the "therapeutic turn" toward a culture of self-esteem. Although the birth of social media amplifies concerns about the death of shame and the rise of a culture of shamelessness, these concerns predate its arrival. As I will go on to show, earlier lamentations involve similar concerns about ideologies, movements, and the actors attached to them charting their own way against a receding status quo.

This chorus of nostalgic complaints has emerged alongside a rise in shaming punishments that are motivated by similar anxieties. These new, "alternative," and creative forms of punishment force criminals to publicly announce their crime and their shame. A Texas judge, who has since become a Congressman, became nationally known in the 1990s for his public punishments, such as requiring shoplifters to carry signs and asking abusive men to apologize in front of their partners on the courthouse steps while television cameras broadcast their apologies. He explained his rationale as follows: "The people I see have too good of self-esteem. I want them to feel guilty about what they've done."[17] Shaming punishments are highly specific to the individual and the act: "I have been convicted twice for shoplifting at J.C. Penney. I am truly sorry for what I did" was on the placard a North Carolina judge required of a twenty-one-year-old woman who pled guilty to stealing a $38 pair of jeans.[18] All of this has been part of a broader cultural trend in crime and punishment that turns on narratives of personal responsibility that romanticize bad feelings like shame – both for their punitive and for their potentially reintegrative power.[19] The punishments and their popularity have drawn scrutiny from legal scholars, but nonetheless persist today. One Ohio judge recently sentenced a man who harassed his neighbors and their children with disabilities to hold a sign on the corner of their neighborhood. The sign read, "I AM A BULLY I PICK ON CHILDREN THAT ARE DISABLED AND I AM INTOLERANT OF THOSE THAT ARE DIFFERENT FROM MYSELF MY ACTIONS DO

[16] The Lament fits squarely in the jeremiad tradition so keenly analyzed by Sacvan Berkovitch, David Gutterman, and George Shulman. Sacvan Bercovitch, *The American Jeremiad* (Madison: University of Wisconsin Press, 1978); David S. Gutterman, *Prophetic Politics: Christian Social Movements and American Democracy* (Ithaca: Cornell University Press, 2006); George Shulman, *American Prophecy: Race and Redemption in American Political Culture* (Minneapolis: University of Minnesota Press, 2008).

[17] Kate Shatzkin, "Judges Hope Public Humiliation Succeeds Where Jail Fails," *Toronto Star*, April 30, 1998: D9.

[18] Cory Reiss, "Shoplifter Must Sign Her Regrets," *Wilmington Morning Star*, Saturday, October 30, 1999: B1.

[19] This is not to say that shame's relationship to punishment is new, rather that there has been a resurgence of preoccupation with shaming punishments in the past twenty years. Martha Nussbaum notes that shame has been a part of punishment throughout history because it is a way of measuring an individual against a norm. Martha Nussbaum, *Hiding from Humanity: Disgust, Shame, and the Law* (Princeton, NJ: Princeton University Press, 2004), 174.

NOT REFLECT AN APPRECIATION OF THE DIVERSE SOUTH EUCLID NEIGHBORHOOD THAT I LIVE IN."[20] The idea behind shaming punishments is that shame does not denigrate but "*requires* self-regard as its essential backdrop."[21] That is to say, the defense of shaming punishments – by legal scholars, judges, and legislators – turns on the idea that the experience of shame is not an affront to dignity, but essential to it. Self-respect in this view requires that one has the capacity to feel ashamed when one has failed to live up to some necessary and agreed-upon social standard. If one does not feel appropriately ashamed of unethical behavior (bullying or stealing) or "immoral" nonnormative "sexual" behavior (public displays of gay liberation, gender nonconformism, nonmonogamy), one is *asking* to be humiliated and shamed.[22] In this account, the shameless subject always "fired the first shot" and therefore *deserves* – even invites – whatever public humiliation she or he receives. The state or the shaming party within civil society can behave in ways that are as unchecked, immoderate, and "shameless" as they wish.

Thus even as most political theorists, philosophers, and legal scholars of various orientations have rejected (or would reject) shaming punishments per se and the more draconian variants of the politics of shame, they nonetheless continue to theorize felicitous connections among shame, self-respect, and respect for others.[23] These works defend the ethical character of certain forms of shame and shaming, argue that shame is a suitable emotion to cultivate in a democracy, and hold some faith that shaming might have a progressive quality to it by which the politically weak may shame the strong.[24] Not all of these

[20] "Ohio Man Ordered to Hold Sign Saying He Is a Bully," *USATODAY*, accessed January 25, 2015, http://www.usatoday.com/story/news/nation/2014/04/12/ohio-bully-sign/7635449/.

[21] Nussbaum, *Hiding from Humanity*, 184. Emphasis added.

[22] Jean Bethke Elshtain's defense of shame supports this point: "When one's intimate life is put on display on television or the streets or in other public spaces, *one not only invites but actively seeks the exploitation of one's body* to a variety of ends not fully under one's control. For one has then withdrawn the body's intimacy from interpersonal relations and exposed it to an unknown audience. Thus one may become an occasion for scandal or abuse or *even violence toward others* through one's relentless self-exposure." Elshtain, *Democracy on Trial*, 55. Emphasis added.

[23] In addition to works already mentioned, see Jennifer C. Manion, "The Moral Relevance of Shame," *American Philosophical Quarterly* 39, no. 1 (2002): 73–90; Jennifer C. Manion, "Girls Blush, Sometimes: Gender, Moral Agency, and the Problem of Shame," *Hypatia* 18, no. 3 (August 1, 2003): 21–41; Gabriele Taylor, *Pride, Shame, and Guilt: Emotions of Self-Assessment* (Oxford: Clarendon Press, 1985); Christopher J. Lebron, *The Color of Our Shame: Race and Justice in Our Time* (New York: Oxford University Press, 2013); Farid Abdel-Nour, "National Responsibility," *Political Theory* 31, no. 5 (October 1, 2003): 693–719; Christina H. Tarnopolsky, *Prudes, Perverts, and Tyrants: Plato's Gorgias and the Politics of Shame* (Princeton, NJ: Princeton University Press, 2010); Jennifer Jacquet, *Is Shame Necessary?: New Uses for an Old Tool* (New York: Pantheon, 2015).

[24] On this point, Nussbaum notes that liberal defenders of shaming tactics and punishments seem to dwell on "examples in which the humiliated person is a powerful person" rather than acknowledge the social status of those most likely to be on the receiving end of the political and legal programs designed to incite shame. Nussbaum, *Hiding from Humanity*, 175.

accounts are necessarily nostalgic in the sense of looking to resurrect a past conception of shame that has historically regulated and lubricated social and political life, but each in its own way suggests that contemporary ethical and democratic life would benefit from an invigoration of healthy and respectful forms of shame and that our valuing of shame has regrettably diminished over time. One model for democratic deliberation is "respectful shaming," which is a form of ethical instruction designed to trigger reflection and self-awareness in one's interlocutors.[25] Another argues that Socrates' shamelessness – his flagrant disregard for the social norms and values of Athens – rendered him incompatible with the city and democracy, in general. Socrates, by this account, died because of his failure to feel shame in the face of Athens's elders and institutions, refusing to pay his respects to the institution of the jury, which made it possible for him to speak freely in his own defense. That is, democracies promote shamelessness and therefore *need* shame as a check.[26] Another study acknowledges the ways in which some forms of shame can be stultifying and self-negating, but calls for a feminist ethics of shame that reorients the experience of shame in favor of feminist principles: "Shame can play an important positive role for the ashamed person despite its negative and potentially debilitating effects."[27] The task, the author continues, is to weight our reasons for shame correctly.[28] Others call for collective shame as a response to national crises of state power, racial inequality, and environmental devastation.[29]

In *Democracy and the Death of Shame: Political Equality and Social Disturbance*, I argue that much of Western political thought can be read as a lamentation for a fantasy of what we believe *aidōs* secured: social regulation and lubrication across difference(s). The clear-eyed Homeric representation of shame – the sense of right and wrong, appropriate and inappropriate, the relationship to oneself as a particular individual and one's relationship to both specific and generalized others – has tremendous appeal. The mythology of *aidōs* speaks to conservatives who fear the death of moral standards; liberals committed to individual responsibility; democratic theorists attuned to the emotions; and poststructuralist and perspectivist accounts of ethics and politics as antiuniversalist and always embedded in particular social locations. Homeric shame presents a picture of a subject who finds both agency and humility in the demands of *aidōs*; and so it provides an ethical framework for intersubjective relations in both the personal and collective or public relationships. As it empowers people to act in these relationships, it also cements – rather than provides grounds to transcend – the particular social locations that the gods or other larger forces have dealt them.

[25] Tarnopolsky, *Prudes, Perverts, and Tyrants*. See especially Chapters 3 and 4.
[26] Saxonhouse, *Free Speech and Democracy in Ancient Athens*, 116–117.
[27] Manion, "The Moral Relevance of Shame," 73.
[28] Manion, "Girls Blush, Sometimes," 33.
[29] Abdel-Nour, "National Responsibility"; Lebron, *The Color of Our Shame*; Jacquet, *Is Shame Necessary?*

The alleged death or lack of *aidōs* as a governing ideal has direct relevance for discussions of democratic citizenship. To put it in Tocquevillean terms, most democratic theorists would agree that democratic citizenship requires specific mores and manners that connect citizens to one another, the polity, and something greater than themselves. Part of the Tocquevillean "ongoing, extremely arduous 'apprenticeship in liberty'" that prepares citizens for self-governance involves cultivating moral habits and sensibilities that will prepare them for democratic governance.[30] This is the allure of civil society, the mediating sphere between public and private in which citizens-in-the-making learn to deal with others different from themselves and orient themselves around common goals. In this Tocquevillean frame, shame has an essential role to play. Citizens need restraints, prods, and ethical commitments with respect to themselves and others.

But democratic citizens also – and Tocqueville appears to have understood this – orient themselves in the world in direct opposition to what they perceive to be the requirements of shame. Against the dictates of *aidōs*, the *people* rule themselves. Who constitutes this people and how it comes into being is a longstanding question in political theory, one far beyond the scope of this study.[31] But even if we bracket the question of who comprises the people, we can still say with confidence that part of the power of the democratic commitment to popular rule is the turn away from aristocratic deference to claims of religion, identity, and tradition. As Athens became democratic, for example, the prescriptions of *aidōs* lost their salience and significance. Compared with anger, desire, and pity, *aidōs* is conspicuously absent from Athenians' deliberations about obligation and punishment. To the extent that it *is* present, as seen, for example, in Socrates' dialogues, *aidōs* and its requirements are up for public contestation. Socrates' *parrhesia* takes up the question of whether shame ought to be heeded, what it requires, and what ends it serves.[32] This contrasts sharply with how Homer's characters perform the *internal* (rather than publicly debated) agonizing about whether or not to heed *aidōs* in particular circumstances. Homer presents *aidōs* as a force that prods people to do what they are meant to do, yet it also presumes, prescribes, and reinforces particular social identities that are in turn justified in the name of some higher order that must be heeded. Once both the value of *aidōs* and the activity it prescribes

[30] Benjamin R. Barber, *A Place for Us: How to Make Society Civil and Democracy Strong* (New York: Hill and Wang, 1998), 58.

[31] For two excellent recent treatments of this question, see Paulina Ochoa Espejo, *The Time of Popular Sovereignty: Process and the Democratic State* (University Park: Pennsylvania State University Press, 2011); Jason A. Frank, *Constituent Moments: Enacting the People in Postrevolutionary America* (Durham, NC: Duke University Press, 2009).

[32] See, for example, Socrates' dialogue *Crito*, which reflects Socrates' general skepticism about *aidōs* as a guide to action. *Aidōs* is also largely absent from Danielle Allen's discussion of the emotions in Athenian punishment. Danielle S. Allen, *The World of Prometheus: The Politics of Punishing in Democratic Athens* (Princeton, NJ: Princeton University Press, 2000).

and proscribes are up for discussion, *aidōs'* force has already been diminished. Early democratic citizens, speaking frankly in the Assembly and on the street as they forged a polis ruled by the people, understood the tension between *aidōs* as a governing emotion and political equality and democratic rule.[33]

Indeed, as I will go on to argue in the chapters that follow, much of the fear about shame's death and the desire to restore or recuperate its regulative characteristics reflects a fear about ordinary, nonelite democratic citizens fashioning themselves and the world without regard for the anchoring and governing traditions and institutions of the past. I do not mean to diminish the significance of the exclusionary character of Athenian citizenship. As has been well documented, women, enslaved people, and foreigners were debarred from the category of citizen and the "equality" on which it rested. But the extension of political equality to poor and unpropertied men marked a radical break with the rule by elites in the predemocratic eras. This tension between popular rule and traditional forms of authority like *aidōs* lingers on and intensifies in modernity. As Charles Taylor has noted, modern democracies and democratic ideas are entangled with the ideal of "authenticity," the late-eighteenth-century Romantic view "that each one of us has his/her own way of realizing our humanity, and that it is important to find and live out one's own, as against surrendering to conformity with a model imposed on us from outside, by society, or the previous generation, or religious or political authority."[34] Democratic Athenians did not have a concept of "authenticity," per se, but they expressed something like it in their skepticism about the religious and traditional customs, debts, and reverence required in the past. And this relationship between democracy and the calling into question of past hierarchies and the ideas that legitimate them produces a fair amount of anxiety, even among defenders of the authentic ideal, like Taylor himself.

Intervening in this conversation about shame, authenticity, ethics, and politics, this book offers an extended analysis and discussion of a phenomenon I term *The Lament That Shame Is Dead. The Lament*, I argue, is a nostalgic story about the ways in which shame used to regulate or at least soften the more difficult aspects of life in the world together. It emerges as a way of figuring changes in the social order as threats to civilization in need of restraint. So fixated on the salutary and essential work of shame, The Lament obscures and pathologizes radically democratic political activity that challenges the virtue and value of shame and calls for "authentic" and unashamed ways of being in the world. I want to recuperate this radical activity by way of theorizing a form of democratic action that I call "unashamed citizenship." Unashamed

[33] Alex Gottesman has written an excellent account of the Athenian "street" and the democratic negotiations therein. Alex Gottesman, *Politics and the Street in Democratic Athens* (Cambridge; New York: Cambridge University Press, 2014).

[34] Charles Taylor, *A Secular Age* (Cambridge, MA: The Belknap Press of Harvard University Press, 2007), 475.

citizenship is the work of courageous and unapologetic people who may or may not have the status of formal citizen.[35] These unashamed citizens interrogate and denaturalize the terms of shame and shaming, dethrone the arbiters of what counts as officially political, claim space for themselves in the world by whatever means available, and fight for a reconstituted social order that gives real meaning to democratic commitments. They refuse to hide their bodies and their objections to the social, economic, and political regimes that shame and blame them. To be sure, there are other ways to theorize and practice radically democratic citizenship. Much of this involves the work of activists whose identities and lives may not be so directly linked to the practices and regimes they strategically oppose. But I focus on "unashamed citizens" and the political work they perform because I fear they are both misunderstood and undertheorized in contemporary political theory. The force of The Lament blinds us to their democratic legitimacy.

The Approach

Democracy and the Death of Shame is best understood as a genealogical effort to understand the context in which The Lament That Shame Is Dead emerges and the phenomena to which it responds. The late-twentieth and early-twenty-first-century anxieties about "gay liberation," the obliteration of public and private, feminism, the "Me Generation," moral relativism, the "therapeutic turn," and the rise of shaming punishments are typically framed in terms of a loss of shame, reticence, concealment, and civility. As I have considered these late-modern anxieties, I have been struck by how familiar they seemed. Digging deeper, I confirmed my sense that the death of shame as it was so confidently pronounced by liberals, communitarians, and in a related way the "tragic" political theorist who also resists the discourse of "authenticity," was not an especially new phenomenon. The chapters that follow tell part of this reiterative story and its significance. Taking a historical tack, I look at moments of democratic expansion in the modern West with respect to how ideas of political equality open up doors for social transformation, specifically with respect to class, gender, race, and age. These social transformations, often authorized through the language if authenticity and "being true," seem to be a natural development in a democratic moment, yet they are met with cries about civilizational decline, taking things *too far*, needing brakes and containment, and triggering a cataclysmic death of shame.

To this end, paying attention to the inter-relationships among sexuality, gender, race, and class, I work through ancient, modern, and contemporary democratic texts and contexts to look at how subjects and citizens seek to expand

[35] On the significance of people who are legally noncitizens making political claims in the name of the citizen, see Melvin L. Rogers, "David Walker and the Political Power of the Appeal," *Political Theory* 43, no. 2 (April 1, 2015): 208–233.

the meaning of democratic equality to disturb the social order. They do so by invoking a language of "nature" and "authenticity" against the requirements of "convention" and "shame" in light of relatively new democratic commitments. That is, preoccupations with "authenticity" or a "life that is true" (rather than beholden to an artificial social order) circulate in moments of democratic expansion, specifically the extension of the category of citizen to persons previously denied its protections and privileges and the extension of the context of "the political" beyond formal politics. These moments and practices are routinely disciplined and forestalled through a naturalized appeal to the necessary brake of shame, which is supposedly put in jeopardy by this radical social reorganization.

To convey how unashamed self-fashioning, self-expression, and social disturbance done in the name of egalitarian ideals triggers The Lament as a panicked narrative of civilizational decline, I have immersed myself in the historical literature of periods concerned with the question of democracy and the expanding demos. These are periods during which "the people" struggled with the relationship among democratic self-governance, the experience of shame (especially as it relates to social and political exclusion), and the power and appeal of the ideal of the authentic life as a life that is "true" to oneself and not beholden to artificial or external mores and norms. My focus is primarily on modern democratic expansion in the eighteenth, nineteenth, and twentieth centuries, but it also looks back to the disruptive and self-consciously shameless practices of Diogenes the Cynic, the exile in Athens. Diogenes and the radical and unashamed cosmopolitanism with which he is associated worked as ciphers through which Enlightenment theorists navigated the degrees of their social criticisms and project of critical unmasking of artificial hierarchy.[36] He is essential to any study of shame and shamelessness regardless of its specific period of focus because he lives on for millennia as a representation of shame's death.

Within the modern contexts, I look at the broad appeal of a discourse of authenticity and the corresponding anxieties about the death of shame in the period before and immediately after the French Revolution; the Jacksonian era; and the US civil rights movement, specifically the effort to desegregate the schools. These are periods of democratic and popular unrest and self-fashioning, during which a politics that called attention to the disturbing requirements of an ethics and aesthetics of shame thrived. Each period involved radical demands to rework the social order and expand what counted as "political" in light of a nascent national commitment to egalitarianism. And each is met with cries of civilizational decline relayed through repeated appeals to shame

[36] Louisa Shea, *The Cynic Enlightenment: Diogenes in the Salon* (Baltimore: Johns Hopkins University Press, 2009); Sharon A. Stanley, *The French Enlightenment and the Emergence of Modern Cynicism* (New York: Cambridge University Press, 2014); David Mazella, *The Making of Modern Cynicism* (Charlottesville: University of Virginia Press, 2007).

as a regulative ideal that is necessary to make democracy "safe" and civil. By looking to democratic eras with which political theorists are acquainted, yet where the actual on-the-ground struggle for what political and social equality means is less familiar, I seek to challenge the general terms in which political theorists so often speak. More specifically, I challenge the portraits painted of democracy and democratic requirements put forth in Rousseau, Tocqueville, and Arendt. This book can thus be read as a work of intellectual history, attentive as it is to the development and deployment of an idea (the idea that "shame is dead") during periods of increased egalitarianism or democratic expansion.

Yet this book is also an explicit work of political theory that intervenes in debates within contemporary democratic and feminist theory, specifically with an intention to illuminate the critical significance of historical context analyzed through the questions and frames of gender, sexuality, race, and class. The book is concerned with how "established codes of behavior" like shame and civility "have often served," as historian John Kasson points out, "in unacknowledged ways as checks against a fully democratic order and in support of ... domination."[37] Political theorists may find it helpful to think of this book as a genealogical conversation among Rousseau, Tocqueville, and Arendt about the relative benefits and hazards of both the egalitarian impulses toward the ideal of authenticity and the braking force of the negative emotion of shame. Looking to these theorists while also moving past them, *Democracy and the Death of Shame* illuminates the limitations of theoretical accounts of both *shame* and *authenticity* to explore how experiences of shame and negative emotions shape the actual bodies and persons making the kinds of claims that inspired and troubled these theorists and their disciples. Along these lines, the book is also a tracing of how political outsiders participate in political life when they are expressly or implicitly debarred from it, and what to make of the ways in which criticisms that deem their activities and speech antipolitical police nascent citizenship. With these concerns about access to and the reorganization of political life in mind, I shine a bright light on the politics of The Lament and ask for a reappraisal of shame, the authentic ideal, the "therapeutic turn," and all of their entailments.

How the Book Proceeds

Chapter 1 provides a detailed account of the phenomenon I call The Lament That Shame Is Dead and reviews how political theorists, feminist theorists, queer theorists, and philosophers of varying persuasions have engaged the idea of shame and other restraints on the self with respect to democratic politics

[37] John F. Kasson, *Rudeness and Civility: Manners in Nineteenth-Century Urban America* (New York: Hill and Wang, 1991), 3; See also the classic study, Norbert Elias, *The Civilizing Process, Volume One: The History of Manners* (Oxford: Blackwell, 1978).

and democratic life. The chapter also maps out the concept of "unashamed citizenship," which circulates throughout the book and is the focus of Part II (Chapters 2 and 3).

In Chapter 2, "A Socrates Gone Mad: Plato's Lament and the Threat of Cynic Shamelessness," I read Diogenes and the Cynics as unashamed citizens who invoke the language of "nature" against "convention" and explicitly attack the requirements of shame (*aidōs*) in order to make a larger argument about the ways in which shame (and the restraint and reticence it involves) secures difference and deference through deep disparities in wealth and xenophobic orientations toward Others. Against those who read the Cynics as apolitical, individualistic moralizers or clear-eyed, ethical cosmopolitans, I draw from work in Classics and Rhetoric to argue that the Cynics authorized an unruly and indecorous democratic politics that deployed the ideal of authenticity and politicized the experience of shame. Just as The Lament pathologizes unashamed citizens today, Plato and other arbiters of elite social power also disciplined the Cynics with their own lamentations about the death of shame in Athens and the ways in which its death could explain the problems of Athenian politics. This Platonic residue lives on in the work of many contemporary democratic theorists who fear the death of shame.

Chapter 3, "Rousseau's Pariahs, Rousseau's Laments: *Pudeur* and the Authentic Ideal in Revolutionary France," turns a critical and historical eye toward Rousseau's Romantic invitation to live an authentic life in accordance with nature to show how his readers took up the promise of a life free from shame. Specifically, I am interested in the ways in which Rousseau's authentic ideal opened up the prerevolutionary public to an unruly and indecorous cast of political pariahs who sought to radicalize the meaning of eighteenth-century French republicanism by extending its antiaristocratic critique and commitment to self-rule to realms beyond the formal public sphere. These Rousseauean outcasts who dreamed of a life that was "true" triggered more than their share of lamentation and moral panic. Rather than being read as citizens struggling over the weighty questions of the personal, political, and social meanings of equality vis-à-vis the past, present, and future, they were cast by their enemies as threats to everything from gender difference to the republican ideal, God, the Church, and "nature." My reading recuperates these moments of "unashamed citizenship" that are opened up by Rousseau's Romanticism and then disciplined and closed down by The Lament – including Rousseau's own highly-gendered version of it.

Chapter 4, "Furious Democracy: Nineteenth-Century 'Slut Shaming,' Indian Removal, and the Ascent of the 'Ill-Bred' Man," focuses on how John Quincy Adams and other founding aristocrats deployed The Lament as they figured Jackson and his wife Rachel's sexual morality and the populism it represented as a threat to the newly constituted republic and the morals on which it rested. Given the extent to which Jackson both owned and traded enslaved people as well as his massive campaign to destroy Native Americans, Adams perhaps made a legitimate point that Jackson's moral compass and lack of shame warranted attention. This account of Jackson needing restraint found a sympathetic ear in Tocqueville, whose account of democracy and democratic mores canonized Adams's anti-Jackson lament. I use this chapter as a hard case to take up the question of whether in fact some forms of shame ought to be defended and cultivated because they protect against heinous crimes. I argue that Jackson's project of Indian Removal and the massacres it engendered were not constructed *against* aristocratic civility and shame per se, but shaped by a desire to speak in the language of shame and civilizational preservation – a language Jackson had inherited from the nation's founders who shamed him for his nonaristocratic background and the uncivil manner in which he married. Preoccupations with the checks of shame and civility, I argue, were part and parcel of Jackson's moral crimes and not fetters against them.

Chapter 5, "Arendt's Lament: The Death of Shame and the Rise of Political Children," considers Arendt's lament about the decline in adult authority in US education, specifically with respect to the NAACP strategy to focus on schools. I argue that while Arendt's call for a return to strict borders between public and private to protect African American children from the violence and judgment of the political sphere may have been well intended, the separate spheres and the boundary of shame would not deliver the protection she imagined. To the contrary, at least since the Reconstruction era, the traditional meaning of shame and the boundaries of public and private in the United States have been framed in favor of white supremacy and protected, rather than minimized, anti-Black violence. Hence just as "civilizing" brakes abetted rather than quelled Jackson's racial violence, they also fueled the segregationist movement and authorized the violence that was so essential to it.

The conclusion, "Is Shame Necessary?" gestures toward the implications of my historical argument for contemporary egalitarian movements, most specifically the emerging coalition, led by young activists, to politicize and abolish systematic police violence. The young people organizing through groups like Black Lives Matter are part of the tradition of "unashamed citizenship," and the anxieties about disrespectability and civilizational decline that their movement encounters are new iterations of The Lament That Shame Is Dead. This particular contemporary case highlights the democratic ambivalence about the legitimacy of "unashamed citizenship" and the tendency to focus on the shameless and uncivilized behavior of people involved in these movements rather than the violent and pathologizing ideas, policies, and practices that animate them. In this context, I revisit the Greeks' concept of *aidōs* and the extent to which it can be reimagined as part of the intersubjective relations within practices of unashamed citizenship, rather than securing the braking and containment defenders of shame often wish to guarantee. I contrast this already-present intersubjective work of *aidōs* with nostalgic appeals to *lost* shame and the fantasy of shame as an emotion that can address and resolve the crises of our time. I close by revisiting the anxiety about the "therapeutic turn" to say that practices of "unashamed citizens" suggest that political work can be therapeutic in character – not in the sense of being completely healed from one's agony and suffering, but in the sense that politics, political consciousness, and political activity can be subjectively and psychologically transformative – capable of reparative work in their own right.

1

The Lament That Shame Is Dead

> Among all the ancient civilized peoples [women] led very retired lives; they appeared rarely in public; never with men; they did not go walking with them; they did not have the best places at the theater; they did not put themselves on display; they were not even always permitted to go; and it is well known that there was a death penalty for those who dared to show themselves at the Olympic games.... If, on occasion, women stepped out of the bounds of this modesty, the public outcry showed that this was an exception.... Everything is changed.
>
> – Jean-Jacques Rousseau

> Intellectual and artistic elites have been searching for the authentic way of living or expressing themselves throughout the 19th Century. What is new is that this kind of self-orientation seems to have become a mass phenomenon.
>
> – Charles Taylor

> How we mourn is a deeply political issue.
>
> – Bonnie Honig

This is a book about a phenomenon I call *The Lament That Shame Is Dead. The Lament* is a nostalgic story of an imagined past that represents a longing for a mythical place and time when shame secured and regulated social life. It operates as a narrative of civilizational decline that expresses a fear of untethered, autochthonous, self-fashioning and self-authenticating subjects who wreak havoc on the social order and status quo. These subjects are named and disciplined as "shameless" threats who operate with an unfettered and unregulated desire to fulfill their own needs above and beyond any concern for others. They are positioned as lacking reflection, judgment, and regard for others, and characterized as natural forces – rushing rivers and raging seas that need civilization's dikes, levees, and canals to harness their nonreflective and uncivilized urges and passions.

And what do I mean by shame? I understand shame in this context as a *felt* ethic of obligation and regulation that involves an actual or internalized audience that judges one's thoughts and acts in terms of their relationship to norms or standards that one shares (or is expected to share) with others. Shame thus involves a social script, the departure from which occasions a set of negative feelings about oneself – feelings that most people seek to avoid. It is also corporeal – felt as the red on the face and ache in the gut. It is much deeper and more self-lacerating than embarrassment, the transient blush that occurs when one does something (either intentionally or accidentally) outside of particular social expectations. The unzipped pants, the shirt on inside out, the spilled coffee in the meeting, the forgotten lecture notes, the child's unpacked lunch, or for that matter the unexpected public praise and recognition – these are sites of embarrassment that people with relatively stable social standing often experience as fleeting sensations.[1] Contrast this with what Homer's people know: shame often gives a sense that one would *rather die* than have to face it. Because of the felt experience of shame or the fear of feeling it, people act in particular ways to avoid it. And sometimes the feeling of shame or the desire to avoid experiencing it publicly leads to a closing in on the self – a kind of stasis or paralysis that involves wishing one could disappear from the surface of the earth altogether.[2]

But I also want to argue that even as shame involves a set of generally agreed-upon psychological and bodily sensations, it has no clear ontology. Rather, shame is discursively and corporeally produced through lamentations about its death, conversations about what it involves, disavowals of its requirements, and tactics of its deployment. That is why shame is not at all *dead* in the

[1] There is no such thing as an essentially embarrassing or shameful act. Acts that might cause simple embarrassment among some (e.g., the forgotten lecture notes, failing to pack a child's lunch) can be debilitating in others whose standing is less secure.

[2] The reading I have done over the years of researching and writing this book has deeply influenced my formulation of the concept of shame. I am especially indebted to the following works: Sandra Lee Bartky, *Femininity and Domination: Studies in the Phenomenology of Oppression* (New York: Routledge, 1990); Simone de Beauvoir, *The Second Sex*, trans. Sheila Malovany-Chevallier and Constance Borde (New York: Alfred A. Knopf, 2010); Jennifer C Manion, "The Moral Relevance of Shame"; Manion, "Girls Blush, Sometimes"; Nussbaum, *Hiding from Humanity*; Jean-Paul Sartre, *Being and Nothingness*, trans. Hazel E. Barnes (New York: Washington Square Press, 1993); Michael Warner, *The Trouble with Normal: Sex, Politics, and the Ethics of Queer Life* (New York: Free Press, 1999); Williams, *Shame and Necessity*; Kathleen Woodward, "Traumatic Shame: Toni Morrison, Televisual Culture, and the Cultural Politics of the Emotions," *Cultural Critique* no. 46 (October 1, 2000): 210–240.

moments I explore in this book. Rather, it is generated and enforced through The Lament – the declaration of its fragile, moribund, or decimated status – as well as the unashamed disavowals that name and politicize what shame is invoked to conjure, discipline, and secure.

Accordingly, I focus on preoccupations with "the shameless" or "shame*lessness*" rather than "shame*ful*" behavior. This distinction is significant. Identifying something as "shame*ful*" marks it as a transgression against largely agreed-upon social codes of conduct. The person who commits shameful acts is not a threat to the social order. When we express that something is shameful, we state what we believe is already known: There are certain norms and rules of conduct, a given action falls outside their bounds, the person who commits it knows, and will feel shame – either through hiding or atonement (or both). In fact, the performance of hiding and shame about a particular transgression ultimately shores up the social codes that were breached. The charge of "shamelessness," which is my focus, calls a person, a people, or particular behavior or practices shameless as a way of noting they are outside of the bounds of the agreed-upon social codes rather than in violation of them. With the calling of "shame*less*," the assumption is that the person either does not know (having come from the "wrong" place) or does not care that what she or he does violates agreed-upon codes of conduct. The shameless person flaunts the requirements of shame and is therefore constituted as a threat to the social order.

The Lament That Shame Is Dead, I argue, emerges most pointedly when ordinary people, especially those lacking significant political power and status, resist and refashion the demands of shame and its requirements. It marks as civilization-destroying all political action that self-consciously disavows the terms of shame and reimagines who counts as a citizen and what counts as a civic practice. I argue that The Lament responds to both moments and movements of increased egalitarianism, periods during which ideals about equality extend into the realm deemed "social" and expose the borders between political and personal, public and private as protective cover for the status quo. That is to say, The Lament is preoccupied with what happens when an acceptable level of democratic skepticism toward hierarchy breaks out of the narrow category of formal politics and makes its way into what it deems nonpolitical (i.e., private/familial and social) spheres. The Lament pathologizes these ruptures in the borders among putatively "natural" spheres of personal/social/political by identifying them as evidence that shame – a good upon which all presumably agree as necessary for people to live together – is dead and needs resurrection.

Finally, The Lament has an inscriptive dimension to it, as it melds the collective proclamation that "shame is dead" to the identities and practices of particular bodies. Publicly mourning the death of shame as an anchoring sensibility that enforces a common set of values, The Lament frames new and nascent forms of citizenship and the subjects who enact them as disorderly threats to civilization that must be managed and contained. It positions shameless people as threats to the political order. Critiques of shame's requirements and the social regimes it guarantees are read as necessarily *against shame*, and therefore out of the bounds of reasonable and civil discussion.

Once upon a time, the story of The Lament goes, shame worked the magic of prodding relative strangers to interact with each other in respectful ways – the learning of manners, the paying of respect to elders, the customs of social grace and courtesy that remind the individual and her audience of a particular social order and make it feel natural. Shame, by this account, minimized the work of figuring out how to behave in the world, instructing people as to which words and actions are appropriate to reveal and which to conceal in particular times and spaces. Shame, operating as both a brake and prod, restrained individuals and the social and political organizations they comprise from their more selfish and self-serving tendencies; it directed them toward the "common good" and something beyond themselves. This is the work that Homer's *aidōs* performs. It secures the links among self, other, and community by telling people both who they are and what they ought to do in particular circumstances – how to interact both across lines and within the overlapping categories of ethnicity, status (adult/child; master/slave), and gender. *Aidōs* tells one how to be an Athenian; a woman; a slave; a master. Living up to the demands of *aidōs* is not easy. It often involves agonizing and deliberation (alone or with others), but the Homeric world is nonetheless anchored by the force of *aidōs* and the social regulation its mythology guarantees.[3] Under *aidōs*, people have a sense of who they are, the reputations they ought to maintain, and their place vis-à-vis the city, the gods, and the world. The Lament expresses a longing for this mythical form of social regulation. It functions as ideology, speech act, and shaming practice all at once.

In the alleged absence of shame as a civilization-preserving ethic of social obligation and regulation, The Lament targets an excessive, irreverent ideology of the "authentic" or "nature" against "convention." The Lament warns that when ordinary people – alone or in concert with others – deign to ignore the general script of shame, they do so because they are beholden to an ideology that is suspicious of any tradition or custom that requires them to conceal or moderate who they believe they "truly are." The promise of this ideology of "nature" and "authenticity" is a false promise, The Lament warns, as it leaves the political community – and civilization itself – without any of the anchoring traditions that make life together in the world possible. Examples of these warnings about the dangers of authenticity are widespread and intellectually ecumenical, present, for example, in the works of communitarians, feminists, critical theorists, political theorists, and cultural studies scholars who worry about a culture of self-fulfillment, the "Me Generation," and a "therapeutic turn."[4] The Lament

[3] Williams, *Shame and Necessity*, 21–49.

[4] Taylor, *The Ethics of Authenticity*; Taylor, *A Secular Age*; Christopher Lasch, *The Culture of Narcissism* (New York: Warner Books, 1979); Eva Moskowitz, *In Therapy We Trust: America's*

figures claims that call into question the value of shame and its requirements as enamored of an impossible ideal – the ideal of the authentic self who is detached from custom and convention, forging its way in the world without boundaries or banisters to guide it. Although the ideal of "authenticity" and living a life on one's own terms in a way that "feels true" emerged contemporaneously with democratic ideals, The Lament registers a panic that the democratic polity may not survive in the face of these claims and practices. In the age of authenticity that is enthralled by the ideology of self-fulfillment and self-expression, people are told they need shame or some cognate brake. In the logic of The Lament, they are free to reject the specifics of Homeric *aidōs*, but must embrace its central truth: Communities need some forms of shame to survive and thrive. The populist sea must be dammed with restraints; without them, democratic peoples will take democracy *too far* in the direction of calling every hierarchy into question; the traditions of the past become entirely up for grabs.

At first glance, The Lament appears to be the wail of royalists, aristocrats, patriarchs, and their sympathizers – the cry of Joseph de Maistre or Edmund Burke as they bemoan rising social equality and the death of *politesse* and *honnêteté*. Indeed, The Lament's most obvious manifestations involve straightforward elite nostalgia for political hegemony and the social order on which it rests. The imperial phrase "beyond the pale," expresses the ideology of The Lament especially well.[5] To call something or someone's behavior "beyond the pale" is to conjure an image of deviance that is moral, aesthetic, and spatial in its characteristics. To be shameless is to be (from) "beyond the pale." It suggests

Obsession with Self-Fulfillment (Baltimore: Johns Hopkins University Press, 2001); Wendy Brown, *States of Injury* (Princeton, NJ: Princeton University Press, 1995), see especially "Wounded Attachments"; Wendy Brown, *Edgework: Critical Essays on Knowledge and Politics* (Princeton, NJ: Princeton University Press, 2005), see especially "Freedom's Silences"; Theodor W. Adorno, *Jargon of Authenticity* (Evanston, IL: Northwestern University Press, 1973); Eva Illouz, *Saving the Modern Soul: Therapy, Emotions, and the Culture of Self-Help* (Berkeley: University of California Press, 2008); Mike W. Martin, *From Morality to Mental Health: Virtue and Vice in a Therapeutic Culture* (New York: Oxford University Press, 2006). Among the thinkers listed here Taylor is clearly the most sympathetic to the "therapeutic turn" or the "age of authenticity," as he names it. But even Taylor – perhaps because he wants to defend its democratic and moral legitimacy – wants to contain the more selfish and individualistic practices authorized by authenticity. Taylor's examples of authenticity going too far are directly related to gender and sexuality. See his discussion of self-help, choosing career over family, divorce, and abortion with respect to the dangers of "untrammeled freedom" from obligations to others. Taylor, *The Ethics of Authenticity*, 17, 44, 57, 75, 76, 116.

5 "Beyond the pale" refers to the Jewish lands in Imperial Russia and also the seventeenth-century British settlements that contained the Irish under the auspices of protecting Britain from Irish rebels. It recurs throughout British postcolonial literature as a spatial marker that justifies ghettoization and segregation in the name of aesthetic, political, moral, and security imperatives for the empire. Mechthild Nagel, "Beyond the Pale: Reflections on the Vulnerability of Black Life in the United States," in *Diversity, Social Justice, and INclusive Excellence: Transdisciplinary and Global Perspectives*, ed. Seth N. Asumah and Mechthild Nagel (Albany: SUNY Press, 2014), 69–70; Benjamin Nathans, *Beyond the Pale: The Jewish Encounter with Late Imperial Russia* (Berkeley: University of California Press, 2004).

bodies out of order, not in the right place, not behaving in agreed-upon ways. And who suffers when someone or something is "beyond the pale?" The entire social order; that is, all who are constituted in relation to "the pale" – the paradigmatic metaphor of the empire, the sphere past which the "uncivilized" cannot cross. These newly or seeking-to-be enfranchised bodies who are struggling for citizenship and political recognition or fighting to preserve the political equality on which their presence turns, do not typically comport with received mores. They look and sound unfamiliar; they act, by definition, inappropriately; they are often too loud; they eat unfamiliar foods; they wear the wrong clothes; they appear to have and live by their own social rules.[6] They are outsiders whose proper place lies "beyond the pale." They are uncivil. They are shameless. The world in which shame is dead is therefore the world *engulfed* by those beyond the pale, de-civilizing the empire and its standards of morality and decency. Given this fear of engulfment, of decivilization, those bodies must be marked as shameless or seen as evidence that "shame is dead." And yet – even with this banishment – they are everywhere, drawn into the fold of the public world in democratic moments.

These aristocratic and imperial residues of The Lament notwithstanding, what is especially interesting to me – and the focus of this book – is the ways in which theorists and citizens largely committed to democratic practices and principles also take up versions of The Lament as they, too, seek to quell the social disturbance that meaningful democratic ideals of equality and self-fashioning necessarily bring about. A refrain throughout the cases I examine in this book is that someone or some movement has taken the ideal of self-representation, self-fashioning, or a healthy democratic skepticism toward tradition and custom or hierarchy – the requirements of *aidōs* and shame – *too far*. These democratic thinkers also look back to a fantasy about the governing mores of the aristocracy (sometimes unselfconsciously) and seek to carry them over or recultivate them for the democratic polity. This more democratic iteration of The Lament helps to explain the revitalization of a discourse of shame in the United States alongside the increased attention to gender parity, multiculturalism, sexual rights, and the diversity of values that count as "American" or "Western." Perhaps to assuage anxieties about the tension between a culture of shame and a multicultural polity, General Colin Powell once explained that he wanted to run for US president to "restore a sense of shame in our society."[7]

Investments in reading shame as an essential component of a democracy also help to explain the proliferation of scholarly work that focuses on types of shame and which are worth cultivating or, alternately, disavowing or abandoning altogether. Over the past twenty years, various typologies have emerged in

[6] On the connection between proper food and modest, civilized living, see Chapter 2, "She Made the Table a Snare to Them": Sylvester Graham's Imperial Dietetics, in Kyla Wazana Tompkins, *Racial Indigestion: Eating Bodies in the 19th Century* (New York: New York University Press, 2012).

[7] Christopher Hitchens, "The Death of Shame," *Vanity Fair* (March 1996), 68–72: 72.

response to the tension between political claims and demands framed in opposition to shame – Women's Liberation, Gay Pride, Black Power, for example – and the nagging, Homeric sense that some forms of shame might help to secure full recognition and the inclusion of women, gays, and people of color. Clarifying that they are not *against shame*, political theorists and philosophers have sought to elucidate the particulars of the kind of shame they are opposing and retaining, believing that contemporary problems and dilemmas are still best understood and framed in terms of our collective failures to live up to common ethical standards. These typologies often look forward to a *new* form of shame (rather than back with nostalgia to a traditional order), but they share the faith evident in The Lament that a common set of moral principles could be leveraged through the negative emotion of shame as solace for political conflicts and difficult times.[8]

The Lament, then, is not the factual description of a state of things it purports to be – that is, "We used to have shame and now we don't" – but a highly normative political claim that functions to *constitute* the shameful and the proper, the private and the public, the decent and the uncivil.[9] It shares this feature with the actual space of the imperial pale. As one critic notes in her call to recover the aesthetic benefits of a lost "reticent sensibility," any discussion of shame is necessarily a discussion about the appropriate parameters of the naked body and what kinds of covering it needs to present itself before an audience of others. This is evident in the French *pudeur*, the Latin *pudenda*, and the German *Scham*.[10] To lament the death of shame is to suggest that bodies are now, routinely, undressed and uncovered in ways that have significant public consequences. The Lament thus operates as a regulative strategy that relies on a naturalized discourse of the naked body in need of the civilizational mark of clothing, the content and form of which The Lament and shame's enthusiastic defenders are all too eager to provide. The Lament emerges each time with fervent urgency: "Aha! Shame is officially dead (now)!" But The

[8] See Tarnopolsky, *Prudes, Perverts, and Tyrants*; Taylor, *Pride, Shame, and Guilt*. To a lesser extent this is also true in Nussbaum, *Hiding from Humanity*; Warner, *The Trouble with Normal*. For a discussion of shame of more aspirational, and less nostalgic variety, see Abdel-Nour, "National Responsibility"; Lebron, *The Color of Our Shame*; Manion, "The Moral Relevance of Shame"; Jacquet, *Is Shame Necessary?*.

[9] In the contemporary landscape, Jean Bethke Elshtain defends shame as a way of protecting the public from the performances of "drag queen[s] and sado-masochist[s], [whose] variations are nigh endless"; Thomas Nagel's concealment is intended to silence a general feminist tendency to publicize (through potentially humiliating indictments) prominent men's sexual behavior, which Nagel believes should remain private; and while Christopher Hitchens begins his polemic criticizing the public vulgarity of the hardly disenfranchised Howard Stern, his lament scandalizes not Stern per se but also the proliferation of sexual diversity (read as deviance) in the West. On this point, see Lauren Berlant and Michael Warner, "Sex in Public," *Critical Inquiry* 24, no. 2 (1998): 547–566.

[10] Rochelle Gurstein, *The Repeal of Reticence: America's Cultural and Legal Struggles over Free Speech, Obscenity, Sexual Liberation, and Modern Art* (New York: Hill and Wang, 1999), 11.

Lament and its iterations are not new. To the contrary, they appear again and again in Western political history in response to critiques of artificial hierarchy and a defense of the authentic ideal of each person's right to determine the social, economic, personal, *and political* regimes under which she or he lives. *Democracy and the Death of Shame* uncovers these anxious reiterations and their democratic significance.

Aidōs, Hubris, Tragedy

As I have suggested, The Lament relies on a naïve and overly naturalized a priori conception of "public" and "private," "political" and "personal." It also presumes the clarity of the "we" who are easily able to identify shameless behavior. The particularity of the subjects who know what to properly hide in shame and what to reveal in public are clear. Jean Bethke Elshtain's defense of shame identifies the "gay liberationist" as the paradigmatic shameless subject. Thomas Nagel calls for more civility and reticence using the example of knowing what to say at an academic cocktail party or in the chambers of the US Senate. For him, the Senate Committee's questioning of Clarence Thomas about the prurient details of his relationship with Anita Hill is an example of uncivil behavior that takes the "personal is political" *too far*.[11] The public/private, exposure/concealment dichotomy in these cases does not appear to fall equally at all. Rather, an "identity politics" that serves the status quo among defenders of shame and civility raises suspicions about whether "everybody" does in fact *know* and share the same view of just what should be revealed and what should be concealed in order to protect individual dignity, common space, public life, democracy, and the many things their theories of concealment are said to protect and guarantee.[12]

But the questions posed by The Lament run deeper than Elshtain and Nagel's facile nostalgia – beyond the familiar concerns about protecting public and private spheres or filtering out personal information that clouds citizens' commonalities. The Lament and its fears also raise legitimate questions about the ways in which people, often under the guise of political action or the quest for freedom, idealistically "speak (personal) truth to power" and empty their more intimate life stories into the public and undress their bodies before potentially hostile audiences in order to make political demands – demands that they then hope the public will affirm and recognize.[13] Often this affirmation or recognition is disciplinary in character or scathing in its judgment of the particular confessing or testifying citizen. The Lament and its underlying distrust of the

[11] Elshtain, *Democracy on Trial*, 52–53; Nagel, "Concealment and Exposure," 12, 26.

[12] I discuss this at length in Jill Locke, "Hiding for Whom? Obscurity, Dignity, and the Politics of Truth," *Theory & Event* 3, no. 3 (1999), https://muse.jhu.edu/journals/theory_and_event/v003/3.3locke.html.

[13] Brown, *Edgework*. On this point, see especially "Freedom's Silences."

politics of the "natural" and "authentic" therefore speak to the desirability and nature of the progress that is gained by hewing too closely to the belief that speaking one's inner truth will set you free. And finally, to the extent that The Lament juxtaposes shame as a restraint against an unfettered commitment to the ideal of authenticity, it draws attention to the well-catalogued limitations and violence of the project of authentic existences and construction of a life that is "true" and "natural."[14]

With these concerns in mind, I want to consider a body of work that shares The Lament's central fears about confessional politics, the desire to escape shame, and the general entanglement of democratic political equality and a therapeutic politics of self-fashioning and authenticity. I call this work "tragic" in character, as it reads the desire to escape the wound of shame and other "negative emotions" as a dangerous and misguided desire to overcome essential elements of human experience. Tragic political theory considers the ways in which practices of confession, testimony, and demands for civil recognition of the shamed or wounded self do not always deliver the healing and reparation the shamed subject seeks. To the contrary, the tragic critique shows how a politics of recognition that turns on a discourse of authenticity and the seeing the "true self" for who she "really is" can legitimize state control over already-vulnerable people.[15] In other words, the tragic perspective – going back to the pull of *aidōs* – suggests that shame is not necessarily something to be lifted or overcome. There is a danger involved in waging battle against *aidōs*; as students of tragedy know, acts of hubris backfire in unexpected ways.

There are good reasons to wonder whether, in fact, the dream of an authentic life *free of shame*, in particular, is legitimate or desirable political territory. Given that social exclusions and inequalities are so often the source of one's shame, an authentic life free from shame is perhaps too much to demand of politics. How might a political order, after all, address social adjustment and one's sense of self-worth without becoming totalizing in its reach? The politicization of personalized, confessional stories about suffering and healing are not necessarily consistent with robust democratic political action and political freedom. These reservations speak to the work of theorists far afield from the sentimental and moralizing territory with which I began, to theorists informed by Arendtian, Foucauldian, and Nietzschean skepticism about the emancipatory power of confessing or testifying about one's injuries in the presence of a public that could liberate one's shame and stigma, recognize and heal her wounds, help her fit in (to social norms), and – once and for all – deem her "free." These criticisms highlight that however disciplinary The Lament may

[14] See Adorno, *Jargon of Authenticity*.

[15] On both the limits and dangers of a politics pursuing state recognition, see Patchen Markell, *Bound by Recognition* (Princeton, NJ: Princeton University Press, 2003); Elizabeth A. Povinelli, *The Cunning of Recognition: Indigenous Alterities and the Making of Australian Multiculturalism* (Durham, NC: Duke University Press, 2002).

be, confessions and testimonies and the "escape from shame" are not simply "free," but disciplinary in their own right, as well. The confessional subject who expects her injuries and trauma to be represented and articulated in the putatively liberatory potentialities of law, in particular, is ensnared in what Lauren Berlant describes as a "tangle of optimism that the seduction of the law to one's appeal will finally be achieved despite what is also clear, that one is defined as intelligible only by one's prior negation, which can be drowned out by other signs but never entirely erased as a condition of one's own intelligibility/possibility."[16] The law's response to claims of shame, humiliation, desperation, and injury grounds and fixes those harms and negations in ways that live on even as subject(s) reorient their politics and political demands.

These concerns relate to the general hazards political and critical theorists have identified in the antipolitical, quasitherapeutic dimensions of "confessional politics."[17] While The Lament indulges in the conventions of "public" and "private" and, accordingly, seeks to protect and preserve the public as a space that is "neutral" (cf. Nagel) or "political" in the sense of what is common (cf. Elshtain), concerns about "the therapeutic turn" and the public it generates can also be seen as a problem of power and freedom. Drawing primarily from Nietzsche and Foucault, Wendy Brown, for example, argues that the stakes of this public and its politics have little to do with aesthetics, boorishness, or civility, and much to do with the ways in which the desire for freedom manifests itself in a desire for speech and representation, specifically in the law, so much that these institutions are underscrutinized among progressives and Left intellectuals in feminist, lesbian, gay, bisexual, and transgender (LGBT), and civil rights struggles.[18] The litany of confessions about "coming out" and representing injuries in language and the law in order to seek remedies for them have

[16] Lauren Berlant, "Trauma and Ineloquence," *Cultural Values* 5, no. 1 (2001) 41–58: 50–51; See also Lauren Berlant, *Cruel Optimism* (Durham, NC: Duke University Press, 2011).

[17] Much of this work originates with Philip Rieff. See Philip Rieff, *The Triumph of the Therapeutic: Uses of Faith after Freud* (New York: Harper & Row, 1966). See also Nikolas S. Rose, *Governing the Soul: The Shaping of the Private Self* (London; New York: Routledge, 1990).

[18] Wendy Brown has spent much of the past twenty-five years challenging some of the central assumptions of feminist, lesbian, and gay politics, specifically with respect to the need to identify one's injury and "come out" through a therapeutic gesture that promises to substitute pride for shame, and she develops more fully Elshtain's point about the odd paradox of identity-based grievance politics whereby people, as members of particular groups simultaneously insist upon their weak and injured status and then ask the dominant majority (which has afflicted much of the harm against them) for recognition as weak and injured. First in her *States of Injury* (1995) and a decade later in *Edgework* (2005), Brown cautioned against the move toward a politics that is primarily oriented toward healing particular wounds that individuals and groups have suffered, and especially toward seeing speech about one's injuries or the desire to represent their "truth" in language, as the path to that healing. Brown, *States of Injury*, 30–76; See also Wendy Brown, *Politics Out of History* (Princeton, NJ: Princeton University Press, 2001), 18–61. For a more sympathetic overview of the "therapeutic turn" in politics, see Arlene Stein, "The Forum: Therapeutic Politics – An Oxymoron?," *Sociological Forum* 26, no. 1 (March 1, 2011): 187–193.

made "a fetish of breaking silence," Brown notes, and need to be reevaluated and rethought.[19]

Brown's critique illuminates how the questions posed by confessional politics are not chiefly related to those who must *witness* these speech acts – The Lament's primary concerns, as is evident in the reiteration of tropes of *invasion* of public space – but what happens to wounded subjects and the "public's" relationship to them when they engage in public confession, even of a politically savvy and self-conscious variety. These hesitations about a therapeutic or confessional politics involve a sympathetic awareness of the fact that the subject decried as shameless is often someone who is already socially and politically marginalized – cast out "beyond the pale," which is precisely why she or he is drawn to strategies of self-narration as a means to self-actualization and freedom. For example, Brown's concerns, like those of other feminist and cultural critics who interrogate a "therapeutic politics," are quite different in their character from the liberal concerns with keeping the public "neutral" or communitarian preoccupations with a thick conception of public good and common civic identity. Rather, they take as their starting point the fact that the subject who wants to tell her story – her "truth" in order to cultivate "pride" or, at least, to make her story visible and recognized by others – is unjustly shamed and stigmatized. But her confessional strategy may not be advisable, because even as it was "intended as a practice of freedom (premised on the modernist conceit that the truth makes us free)," it "may have the capacity not only to chain us to our injurious histories as well as the stations of our small lives, [and] ... to instigate the further regulation of those lives while depoliticizing their conditions."[20] In other words, Brown's critique expresses the legitimate fear that good-intentioned strategies of self-exposure may not increase political power, affinity with others, or democratic understanding. Instead they leave the intimate matters of already vulnerable subjects naked and exposed to the scrutiny and judgment of other citizens and the state, who may respond with cruelty and punishment. There are dangers in well-intentioned idealistic politics, a category in which we can include the politics of authenticity and confession: "A decent [civil] society, alert to the tragic dynamic," notes Steven Johnston, "seeks to redress the wounds it inflicts. [Yet] the effort to correct one evil frequently ... produces others."[21] It is understandable, to follow this line of reasoning, that people, alone and together, have dreamed of a life free from shame and other self-negating emotions, but the political or state-sanctioned effort to cure shame's pain may open the door to new harms in its place.

Other work in political theory has also illuminated some of the tragic dangers in the modern dream of a natural and authentic self who is not constrained by

[19] Brown, *Edgework*, 84.

[20] Ibid., 85.

[21] Steven Johnston, *Encountering Tragedy: Rousseau and the Project of Democratic Order* (Ithaca: Cornell University Press, 1999), 6.

the past. Less concerned with confessional declarations of shame and humiliation, these theorists note the hazards of assimilation. For example, Peter Euben analyzes the character of Coleman Silk, the protagonist in Philip Roth's novel about an African American man who reinvents himself as a "white" Jew in an American college town and severs all ties to his past as a way of escaping the racism that would frame his life as a Black man.[22] Rather than live in shame as Black, Silk decides not to "allow [his] prospects to be unjustly limited by so arbitrary a designation as race."[23] Reading Roth's novel as a tragedy, Euben draws attention to the ways in which the quest to master one's fate and indulge in the hubris of self-invention generates losses that come back to haunt us. For Silk, it is being charged with racism when he "wonders out loud whether the two missing students in his class are 'spooks' and they turn out to be African American women."[24] Exemplifying the hubris Euben (like Roth) wants to criticize, Silk invokes the classic language of authenticity – championing the "'I' against the despotism of the 'we'."[25] In denying the "facts" of his identity and the social rules of the "we," Silk denies himself some of the resources of living in the world as a sentient being. In seeking a harmonious identity, free of pain and shame, he takes on profound loss.[26] By repudiating the shame of blackness as only negative, Silk does not in fact escape it, but becomes further ensnared in the very toxicity he seeks to avoid. The tragic lesson is that there are some aspects of our lives that are unpleasant reminders of our flaws and mortality, which are aspects of life we share with others and grounds for intersubjective relations; trying to escape them only brings them back to haunt us even further. We cannot control the conditions and persons who trigger our shame. Shame marks our vulnerability before others.[27] Here the desire to escape shame is not through confession, but through adopting a false persona. Both cases distance the self from the shameful identity to be more true to who one "really is" on the inside. Assimilation is thus an attempt to escape shaming and stigmatizing that in the end concedes power to the despotism of the "we."

Thus shame may *intensify* through repeated efforts to erase it, whether by self-exposure or assimilation, especially when done with the hopes of achieving freedom from one's wounded or shamed identity.[28] The concern need not

[22] Bernard Williams would describe part of what Silk loses as a "necessary identity," which structures how an individual experiences shame in specific ways relevant to his identity, but also give him a richer perspective and a way to make ethical decisions and act politically in the world. Williams, *Shame and Necessity*; see chapter 5.

[23] J. Peter Euben, *Platonic Noise* (Princeton, NJ: Princeton University Press, 2003), 3.

[24] Ibid., 1.

[25] Roth, *The Human Stain*, cited in ibid., 3.

[26] Ibid., 5.

[27] Cairns, *Aidōs*, 105.

[28] Hannah Arendt's work on Rahel Varnhagen's Romantic belief that self-disclosure would assuage her shame of being Jewish makes this point explicitly; there is an unstated affinity between the tragic critique and Arendt's skepticism toward confession as a mode of freedom or action. Hannah Arendt, *Rahel Varnhagen: The Life of a Jewess*, ed. Liliane Weissberg, trans. Richard

be an aesthetic objection to seeing indecorous things in the public sphere, the need to maintain a "thin" or content-neutral public; or that commonality must be maintained in political life as is present in some of the more conventional communitarian and liberal accounts of The Lament. Rather, a tragic perspective raises questions about the extent to which a conception of the public that involves therapeutic confessions in the name of the pursuit of authentic selves or therapeutic motivations to escape shamed identities deliver harm, discipline, and normalization rather than freedom to those at the margins of public life, that is, the people who by most accounts are extraordinarily *un*free. That marginalized people and groups often take up and embrace such strategies does not make them less problematic. Quite the opposite: by this account, confessional politics of injury looking for public recognition or healing from a hostile audience can reflect a perverse *desire*, as Brown notes, to "restage the scene ... of [bodily violation or] invasion."[29] Highly publicized disclosures of suffering involve seeking recognition and affirmation from the institutions and audiences that have historically devalued the humanity of the sufferer. Brown fears, for example, that a confessional politics cannot deliver alchemical healing to African American women in the context of a racialized and sexualized public that disparages and regularly commits violence against them. This comes alive in her critique of Patricia Williams's quasiconfessional jurisprudence.

To take the Foucauldian critique seriously, the incitement to discourse and self-invention cannot be equated with an act of political freedom.[30] "Coming out" – so often framed as an act of negating or overcoming the power of shame in one's life – is not in fact an act of unfettered freedom; its very process is constructed by a belief that same-sex love and friendship are scandalous.[31] Telling the "truth" can play into mainstream fantasies about the "exotic" and "oppressed" rather than unsettle them. Skeptics reverse the therapeutic logic: confession and rights claiming and achievement potentially foster, rather than alleviate, self-negation and poor self-esteem for the already marginalized and dispossessed.[32] And finally, a therapeutic orientation may evacuate

Winston and Clare Winston (Baltimore: Johns Hopkins University Press, 1997); I discuss this in detail in Jill Locke, "Shame and the Future of Feminism," *Hypatia* 22, no. 4 (2007): 146–162.

[29] Brown, *States of Injury*, 125–126. This passage refers to Patricia Williams's self-disclosures. See Patricia J. Williams, *Alchemy of Race and Rights: Diary of a Law Professor* (Cambridge, MA: Harvard University Press, 1992). Although not preoccupied with the psychological dimensions of recognition politics, Patchen Markell's astute analysis of their pitfalls and tendency to backfire as the recognizing state gains sovereignty over newly recognized citizens and their bodies is also relevant for the critique I am describing as "tragic." See Markell, *Bound by Recognition*.

[30] Michel Foucault *The History of Sexuality* trans. Robert Hurley (New York: Pantheon Books, 1978).

[31] See Michael Warner, *The Trouble with Normal* (New York: Basic Books, 1999).

[32] For a terrific account of how rights claiming can avoid some of these concerns, see Karen Zivi, *Making Rights Claims: A Practice of Democratic Citizenship* (New York: Oxford University Press, 2011).

our capacity for a richer, more genuine democratic politics.[33] "Our challenge," Brown writes, "would be to configure a radically democratic political culture that can sustain [the project of releasing our pain and having it heard] ... without being overtaken by it, a challenge that includes guarding against abetting the steady slide of political into therapeutic discourse, even as we acknowledge the elements of suffering and healing we might be negotiating."[34] More sympathetic to the sufferer than The Lament that inveighs against the "sado-masochist or cross-dresser" *invading* and *threatening* the public sphere, Brown's concerns nonetheless replay The Lament's central tropes of excess and containment, suggesting that democratic politics must be managed through a balancing act of constraint and release.[35]

Whether invested in keeping politics antitherapeutic for the sake of civility, privacy, aesthetics, morality, or the preservation of politics and freedom, the work rehearsed up to this point shares a sense that political claims that invoke "therapeutic" language of "authenticity" and "pride" about the "true self" against artificial hierarchies and conventions and the shame that secures them mistakenly meld the "political" with the "personal," the "therapeutic" and the "social."

Identity, Recognition, Authenticity: A (More) Political Reappraisal

Signaling the theory and practice of "unashamed citizenship" that I develop throughout this book, and in particular in Part II (Chapters 2 and 3), I pause in the face of these lamentations about the evisceration of borders and boundaries, the "therapeutic turn," hubristic self-fashioning, and so on. To do so I want to revisit some of the work on identity and recognition politics, especially with respect to the ideal of authenticity. Within this tradition, politics is not about only constitutions, mores, and habits – as democratic theorists so often suggest, but also about the ways in which constitutes, mores, and habits often make people – especially people in particular social classes and locations – *feel badly*.

For multicultural, feminist, LGBT, critical race, Marxian, and some liberal theorists, there is a general sense of shame as a toxic and self-negating sensation that is best countered with a combination of pride, self-esteem, social equality, and self-determination. That is to say, shame is far from generic in its prescriptions and requirements; it is what people feel when the social order locates them in relatively lesser or marginalized positions, perhaps *includes* but also *dominates*. Here shame and low self-esteem or sense of self-worth

33 See also Shoshana Felman and Dori Laub, *Testimony: Crises of Witnessing in Literature, Psychoanalysis and History* (New York: Routledge, 1991).

34 Brown, *States of Injury*, 75. This theme is also central to Brown's critique of the confessional mode in "Freedom's Silences" (*Edgework*). See also *Politics Out of History*, where she calls for "radical democratic politics released from conviction." Brown, *Politics Out of History*, 94.

35 Elshtain, *Democracy on Trial*, 55.

are structural, and greater equality within the social order would alleviate the chronic experience of shame some people feel and live as ongoing realities.[36] Hence part of the political project of reorganizing the social world involves the psychological project of overcoming shame and prioritizing self-care as a radically political act. Audre Lorde notes: "Caring for myself is not self-indulgence, it is self-preservation, and that is an act of political warfare."[37] That self-care is part and parcel of more expressly world-oriented "political warfare," the effects of which would, in turn, circle back and alleviate some of the shame and negative sense of self-worth brought on by hierarchies that moralize, shame, and blame. In these traditions, shame feeds on economies of white supremacy, empire, heteronormativity, capital, and misogyny to discipline particular subjects in their personal, social, and public embodiments. As the story of *aidōs* with which we began makes clear, shame presumes and secures difference and deference. The burdens of shame and the social order shame presumes refract through identity and difference and exist under the broader umbrella of deference to the gods and the city. Today, the difference and deference of *aidōs* lives on in social stigma and inequalities even as formal, political equality appears secure. Its persistence renders political equality anemic and empty.

It is no wonder that Martin Luther King, Jr., in his 1967 Southern Christian Leadership Conference (SCLC) Convention address, delivered *after* the gains of the Civil Rights and Voting Rights Acts of 1964 and 1965, asks and then answers the question of *where we go from here* by addressing the problem of shame's ugly frontier. "First, we must massively assert our dignity and worth. We must stand up amid a system that still oppresses us and develop an unassailable and majestic sense of values. *We must no longer be ashamed of being black*. The job of arousing manhood [pride] within a people that have been taught for so many centuries that they are nobody [shame] is not easy."[38] Going on to catalog how blackness has been and continues to be stigmatized and degraded, and the deep disparities in Black and white social and economic power in spite of the legislative and judicial victories of postwar Reconstruction and the civil rights movement, King reclaims self-worth and

[36] For an excellent account of how mental health professionals have responded to political inequalities, see Jerome Agel, *The Radical Therapist: the Radical Therapist Collective* (New York: Ballantine Books, 1971).

[37] Audre Lorde, *A Burst of Light: Essays* (Ithaca: Firebrand Books, 1988), 131. This theme also appears in bell hooks, *Sisters of the Yam: Black Women and Self-Recovery* (Cambridge, MA: South End Press, 1993); Gloria Anzaldúa, "*La Prieta*," in *The Gloria Anzaldúa Reader* (Durham, NC: Duke University Press, 2009), 198–209; Combahee River Collective, *Combahee River Collective Statement: Black Feminist Organizations in the 70s and 80s* (New York: Kitchen Table/Women of Color, 1986).

[38] Martin Luther King, Jr., "Where Do We Go from Here?," Delivered at the Eleventh Annual SCLC Convention, Atlanta, GA, August 16, 1967, http://mlk-kpp01.stanford.edu/index.php/encyclopedia/documentsentry/where_do_we_go_from_here_delivered_at_the_11th_annual_sclc_convention. Emphasis added.

pride against an economy of mental and physical violence.[39] Formal legal equality had been granted, but social inequalities and the shame they carried remained. Here self-esteem and living free from shame are not merely personal or therapeutic in an indulgent sense; they are deeply political, as the social and political structures that applaud and reward whiteness and colonial power in the most ordinary and extraordinary ways constitute white pride and nonwhite shame and low self-esteem. King stresses that one cannot live freely as who he is or wants to be while mired in the strictures of shame. Shame, by his account, obstructs an authentic life that is lived on one's own terms. It constrains one's ability to live as who one genuinely is or wants to be, free from the scripts and stereotypes of racist (or sexist and imperial) society.

King's work reveals the ways in which the raced and gendered (and classed, although this is less explicitly referenced in this particular speech) experiences of shame undercut individuals' abilities to become authentic selves comes to the fore in much of the work that is critical of shame, most specifically work on the politics of recognition, which reads recognition by others as a remedy to assuage the low sense of self brought on by one's discriminatory social environment. For example, the politics of recognition insists that psychological trauma related to membership in an oppressed identity group is deeply political. Until African American women, notes Melissa Harris-Perry in her articulation of recognition politics, are recognized for their humanity and uniqueness and allowed to be the authors of their own life stories, the reciprocity, community, and social conditions necessary for democracy are impossible.[40] Her work builds on Charles Taylor's insight that the harms of nonrecognition and misrecognition are political (and not only therapeutic) in character and on a par with the more expressly political harms of inequality, exploitation, and injustice.[41]

Harris-Perry's point about shame and other negative emotional evaluations of the self-structuring peoples' lives frames other phenomenological accounts of shame's all-suffusing power, as well. Sandra Bartky levels a feminist critique of moral philosophers and psychologists who celebrate shame as a moment of moral consciousness that reminds the self of the standards by which he or she has agreed to live and triggers and guides him or her into correct ethical action. This self who finds in shame an occasion for moral health

[39] Frantz Fanon makes a similar point about the psychological damage and shame of colonialism – shame that only sovereignty can assuage. Frantz Fanon, *The Wretched of the Earth* trans. Richard Philcox (New York: Grove Press, 2004).

[40] Harris-Perry writes that Black women's experiences are a democratic litmus test for the nation and that three shame-inducing stereotypes (Jezebel, Mammy, and Sapphire) create the conditions that harm African American women's sense of themselves. Melissa V. Harris-Perry, *Sister Citizen: Shame, Stereotypes, and Black Women in America* (New Haven: Yale University Press, 2011), 16, 36–37.

[41] Charles Taylor, "The Politics of Recognition," in *Multiculturalism: Examining the Politics of Recognition*, ed. Amy Gutmann (Princeton, NJ: Princeton University Press, 1994), 25–74: 64.

is an abstract "Everyman," and not a living, breathing, and gendered person.[42] Because of the embodied dimensions of shame and our experience of it, the experience of shame cannot be abstracted from specific subjectivities of the bodies being shamed. In reality, the conditions that shape our sensitivity to shame are quiet and ordinary, operating at the level of sensation rather than belief. "Shame," from this perspective, "is not so much a particular feeling or emotion ... as a pervasive affective attunement to the social environment" – moreover, women's shame, in particular, is not an "*effect* of subordination" but constitutive of feminine subjectivity. "Within the larger universe of patriarchal social relations, Bartky notes, "[shame is] a profound mode of disclosure both of self and situation."[43] As such, the experience of shame – a state of "psychic distress occasioned by a self or a state of the self-apprehended as inferior, defective, or in some way diminished" – does not vanish with contrary evidence or persuasion about the appropriate subjects of shame, as those more optimistic about shame's potential might insist.[44] Against those who see shame as an occasion for moral awakening, Bartky's feminist phenomenology of shame suggests that shame doesn't make us better, only "weaker, more timid, less confident, ... and hence more easily dominated."[45]

A feminist phenomenology of shame may be less prescriptive in its political solution than advocates of a politics of recognition (who argue for state- and social-recognition), yet its critique of the suffusing nature of the shame experience for people at the bottom of social hierarchies complements their warnings. The phenomenological account suggests that a positively freer life exists if one can manage, if not negate altogether, the power of shame. Paying attention to the lived experience of women as a social class, however constructed, should complicate any attempt to recuperate shame as a normative emotion to be cultivated to steer and salvage democratic life and democratic equality. By this account, shame – with its call to hide and conceal and constant assessment and surveillance of the self, her thoughts, and acts – further negates and marginalizes the already politically estranged subject. This context illuminates the *desire* to move "beyond shame," "come out" in pride, raise one's consciousness, emerge "up from invisibility," and speak one's truth without shame or self-doubt, all of which have been significant to the struggle for recognition and inclusion.[46]

[42] Bartky, *Femininity and Domination*, 97.

[43] Ibid., 85. Emphasis added. On this point, see also Beauvoir, *The Second Sex*, 283–382; Elspeth Probyn, *Blush: Faces of Shame* (Minneapolis: University of Minnesota Press, 2005); Sonia Kruks, *Retrieving Experience: Subjectivity and Recognition in Feminist Politics* (Ithaca: Cornell University Press, 2001), 52–79; Woodward, "Traumatic Shame."

[44] Bartky, *Femininity and Domination*, 85.

[45] Ibid., 97.

[46] Larry P. Gross, *Up from Invisibility: Lesbians, Gay Men, and the Media in America* (New York: Columbia University Press, 2001); Patrick Moore, *Beyond Shame: Reclaiming the Abandoned History of Radical Gay Sexuality* (Boston: Beacon Press, 2004); Gershon Kaufman and Lev Raphael, *Coming Out of Shame: Transforming Gay and Lesbian Lives*

Indeed, let us revisit the longstanding radical tradition of speaking the truth in the name of personal and political freedom. Shame is part of the "epistemology of the closet," to use Eve Sedgwick's phrase, whereby the gay or queer subject is shamed by the heteronormative structures of civil society and thus feels the subjective experience of shame.[47] The logic of "coming out" is consistent with a long feminist and antiracist tradition of "speaking out" to fight shame and stigma against sexual violence. Fannie Lou Hamer, for example, famously testified – refused to hide in shame – about the brutal sexual abuse and assaults she experienced at the hand of white police officers. "Like many of her foremothers," notes Danielle McGuire, "Hamer did not shy away from detailing the sexual aspects of her beating. She told her story on national television at the Democratic National Convention in 1964, and to congressmen investigating civil rights abuses in June 1964, and she continued to tell it 'until the day she died,' offering up her testimony as a form of resistance to the sexual and racial injustice of segregation."[48] Hamer's story and the theme of fighting shame and the structures that deliver it through testimonials about racialized sexual violence (and sexualized racial violence) were essential to the birth of the civil rights movement in the United States. The civil rights movement and its victories – however imperfect and incomplete – have resulted from African American women organizing speak outs against abuse as part of a longstanding "'radical black feminist tradition of resistance,' ... [of] testimony, ... [and] bear[ing] witness to one another's horror stories."[49]

The preponderance of feminist, gay liberationist, multicultural, and antiracist scholarship demonstrates that shame is alive and well in the "wrong" people and in the "wrong" ways. We have reason to be suspicious of hopes that the "right" people will be awakened from their moral slumber by shaming or making appeals to discourses of shame. This critical work suggests that the vulnerability and occasion for human connection engendered through the experience of shame and the fantasies of a robust ethic of shame that would transform political and social environments are misplaced, Rather, people marginalized on account of class, race, gender, and sexuality ought not to invest in a politics oriented around shame. Given the social and political context in which the experience of shame so often emerges and the trove of critical work

(New York: Main Street Books, 1996); Harriet Perl and Gay Abarbanell, *Guidelines to Feminist Consciousness Raising* (Los Angeles, CA: H.M. Perl, 1979).

47 Eve Kosofsky Sedgwick, *Epistemology of the Closet* (Berkeley: University of California Press, 2008).

48 Danielle L. McGuire, *At the Dark End of the Street: Black Women, Rape, and Resistance – A New History of the Civil Rights Movement from Rosa Parks to the Rise of Black Power* (New York: Alfred A. Knopf, 2011), 159. (Perhaps proving McGuire's point that the story of sexual violence is relatively unknown in the history of the civil rights movement, Harris-Perry's discussion of Hamer makes no mention of the sexual characteristics of Hamer's abuse and testimony. Harris-Perry, *Sister Citizen*, 296–298.)

49 Ibid., 65–66.

that points out its harms, it is not clear – tragic and other warnings notwithstanding – what of democratic value could possibly come from a nostalgic preoccupation with the loss of shame and other negative emotions and brakes on self-fashioning. Thus the criticisms of identity, recognition, and phenomenological politics may be theoretically persuasive, but they fall short on political grounds. They fail to engage the overlap between their concerns and liberal preoccupations with public/private, and a thick communitarian conception of the common good. Most damningly, they fail to theorize adequately the actual work of people – like King and Hamer – publicly struggling against shame and shaming.[50]

Moreover, let us not forget that disavowing shame and critiquing the ways in which it cements social inequalities is part of what democratic citizens *do*. Again and again, when confronted with the shaming and stigmatizing force of inequalities, people – in practices of unashamed citizenship – take to the street to demand a life free from shame, drawing attention to the gross disparities in regimes of political equality that countenance and even depend upon social relations and hierarchies that rank some citizens more worthy of regard than others. Unashamed citizens understand and politicize the fact that social inequalities and the negative feelings associated with them do not obviously square with a democratic commitment to political equality. Even if democratic polities always have constitutional or residual social inequalities embedded in them, democratic ideals – specifically political equality and self-representation – naturally facilitate citizens' desires to extend the political commitments of democratic equality into what get called economic, social, and private spheres. Hence I want to heed some of the critics' warnings and the broader concerns of The Lament, but also recuperate the salient democratic and political vision in the identity, recognition, and phenomenological accounts of shame. Doing so means moving beyond what I read as a very earnest and philosophical account of "therapeutic" politics that politicizes the experiences of shame and negative self-esteem.

[50] Patchen Markell and Elizabeth Povinelli's critical work on recognition and multicultural policies are important exceptions. Both use empirical cases to show how state policies function to discipline newly recognized subjects in ways that compromise and undo the desires that motivate citizens to make such claims in the first place. Unlike the struggles for recognition critiqued in these books, which I admire, I am not focused on state policy so much as the ways in which the tropes of the "authentic" are too quickly foreclosed and disqualified in much of contemporary political theory. Although practices of "unashamed citizenship" deploy some of the language and foci Markell and Povinelli identify as problematic in recognition politics, unashamed citizens are not struggling *for recognition*. In this sense they bear closer resemblance to Holloway Sparks's ideas about "dissident citizenship" and Karen Zivi's articulation of a politics of "claims making" than a politics of recognition per se. Markell, *Bound by Recognition*; Povinelli, *The Cunning of Recognition*; Holloway Sparks, "Dissident Citizenship: Democratic Theory, Political Courage, and Activist Women," *Hypatia* 12, no. 4 (1997): 74–110; Zivi, *Making Rights Claims*.

Unashamed Citizenship

My account of unashamed citizenship involves a more political and less philosophical reading of a politics of authenticity that is neither a politics of recognition nor necessarily constituted *against* shame as if to overcome it altogether. Rather, unashamed citizenship emerges from within the experience of shame, which it names and politicizes in order to activate a set of political demands and practices. I take seriously the ways in which the experience of shame can valuably alert one to unjust social relations that then trigger political action. At the same time, I seek to reclaim an enduring democratic dimensions of the ideal of authenticity and the social critique of rank and hierarchy it involves. My reading acknowledges that authenticity – often manifest in the language of "pride" or "being true to oneself" – as an ideal can be constraining as well as emancipating, just as shame can trigger action or cause one to recoil and retreat from the world. Neither has a secure ontology that gives us a perfect politics. But the dream of an "authentic life" that is free from shame crafts a critical political subjectivity in the context of social hierarchies that shame and stigmatize. Specifically, the egalitarian commitments built into the ideal of authenticity, so forcefully elaborated by Taylor, and the insight (of recognition politics) that negative self-assessments connect to identity and status demand a political response invite further scholarly reflection.[51] There are legitimate fears about the violence done in the name of the "authentic" and the "natural," and well-intentioned strategies of assimilation and self-reinvention can backfire. But the political problems emerging in any given context are not best expressed as problems of shamelessness or an authentic ideal being taken *too far*. Hence, in the end, calls to address and repair political problems through the language for more restraint, civility, and shame are both politically problematic and theoretically insufficient.

Being attentive to the *political* context in which claims about shame and authenticity circulate means asking a set of questions largely missing from most contemporary discourse about shame and shamelessness: Who is attempting to shame whom and why? What political demands are being made in the name of shame? What does a citizen mean when she asks to be free from shame? *And who wants to shut her down*? These questions and context matter for assessing both the call for more shame and the dream of being free from it. Much of the work on Gay Shame is exemplary in this regard, as it shifts the question away from whether or not shame should be embraced or repudiated and toward the matters of public and personal investments in others' shame, as well as what we do with our shame, given that we all – as sexual beings who are prone to fail to live up to our own and others' expectations of us – have some degree of it. The Lament deflects one's own shame by focusing on the shamelessness of

[51] Taylor, *A Secular Age*, 473–504.

another member of the body politic. Warner describes this, aptly, as "pin[ning our shame] on someone else."[52]

An alternative to pinning one's shame on someone else is listening to the ethics of shame and what it tells you about the world you share with others. That is, shame ought to inspire you to "put on a wig before you judge" – to orient your politics toward those who are least advantaged and most often fall under the shadow of shame.[53] In queer spaces, Warner elaborates, "shame is bedrock" and "the rule is: Get over yourself.... You stand to learn the most from the people you think are beneath you. At its best, this ethic cuts against every form of hierarchy you could bring into the room."[54] The goal is not to get rid of shame or act as if it does not exist, but to claim an ethical tradition found in places most philosophers fear. The image on the poster for the Gay Shame conference and the cover of the book that grew out of it (*Trojan Whore* – a tattooed, muscular, masculine body in heels and a dress with a strand of silver beads coming out of the anus) occupies, disrupts, and mocks the heroic iconography of Homeric shame and those who pine for its regulative work.[55] This is not a resuscitation of some lost form of *aidōs*. "In these [unrespectable] scenes," Warner explains, "people try to imagine living without the sacrifices that dignity by 'community standards' commonly entails."[56] The ethics of Gay Shame build solidarity among those who live in the shadow of shame. One's own experience of shame signals the precarity of people at the margins, and demands an ethical orientation toward others. And finally, being attuned to the

[52] Warner, *The Trouble with Normal*, 3. Warner argues that something like The Lament operates in the politics of respectability in LGBT politics, most specifically in Andrew Sullivan's jeremiad against queer disrespectability. Sullivan argues that queers are overly invested in the dirty and shameful aspects of lesbian and gay existence. Warner quotes him as follows: "To respond to the taunt of 'queer' by simply embracing it" is mere relativism, or "a facile celebration of our woundedness" (137). According to Sullivan, embracing the *respectable* and *decent* dimensions of lesbian and gay life – like the desire to serve one's nation in the military, one's church in the pulpit, or civil society in the form of monogamous marriage – is a way of redeeming and correcting the views of homosexuality as shameful and belonging in the closet. It *is* shameful to be polygamous or polyamorous, Sullivan suggests. And the respectability and reputation of "good" lesbians and gays suffer at the hands of visibly indecent queers. Sullivan wants to come out and assimilate rather than revel in abjection, and to do so he differentiates respectable and decent lesbians and gays from their brothers and sisters in the queer underworld. Hence in Warner's reading, Sullivan's politics of respectability is deeply implicated in the politics of shame. Andrew Sullivan, *Virtually Normal: An Argument about Homosexuality* (New York: Vintage Books, 1996).

[53] Warner, like Rawls, focuses on the ethical perspective of the "least advantaged." Warner does not invoke a veil of ignorance that hides the so-called ascriptive features of our personality, and the "least advantaged" are identified in terms of sexual taste and behavior, not just economic status, but he shares Rawls's belief that the lens of normalcy necessarily skews our ability to derive principles of justice. John Rawls, *A Theory of Justice* (Cambridge, MA: Belknap Press of Harvard University Press, 1971).

[54] Warner, *The Trouble with Normal*, 35.

[55] David Halperin and Valerie Traub, eds. *Gay Shame* (Chicago: University of Chicago Press, 2009).

[56] Warner, *The Trouble with Normal*, 34.

relationship between one's experiences of shame and the social and political structures in which one lives calls for radically reorganizing social space as a piece of democratic politics.

Politicizing the experience of shame and other negative emotions in a way that asks for a life free of pain and a life that "feels true" need not entail an earnest and righteous project of ridding the self of bad feelings, emotional harms, psychological injuries, and so on. As Berlant notes in an interview about queer shame, the politics of "de-shaming queerness" involves more than a simple politics of "pride."[57] Moving beyond debates about identity and recognition, pride and shame, political theorists ought to consider on-the-ground political activity to imagine affect and the emotions in ways that neither romanticize them nor lapse into naïve rationalism as the ground for social and political life. A life *without* the vulnerabilities that develop through negative emotions would be bereft of human connection. These vulnerabilities animate friendships, commitments, and politics and ought not to be ignored or willed away. Yet at the same time, to romanticize the experience of negative emotions like shame to the point of ignoring the debilitating effects they often bring is also problematic. Political and critical theorists must attend to the debilitating power of negative emotions on political subjectivity in ways that do not envision a political life purged of affect and feeling. We need a political critique of the experience of shame and an understanding of how critiques of shame and the negative self-assessment it involves have operated in emancipatory political moments and movements. More specifically, we need to think about how the "therapeutic turn," so often read as a trend toward "truth" claims about injury that are not up for debate or argument, might be understood as compatible with political argumentation, persuasion, and disagreement. Neither the experience of shame nor the dream of an authentic life has any automatic political prescriptions, nor are these experiences felt uniformly among shamed and marginalized subjects.

The examples I highlight throughout this book suggest that practices of unashamed citizenship that involve a political language of authenticity and public disavowals of the requirements of shame draw attention to injustice.[58] The historical examples suggest that demands to "see me as I (really) am" function as more than naïve confessions or longings for recognition and affirmation. They testify to injustice by making political demands that emerge in the context of political and social inequality and realizations that promises of democracy have been more open to some than others. In this revised and more

[57] Lauren Berlant, Sina Najafi, and David Serlin, "The Broken Circuit: An interview with Lauren Berlant," *Cabinet* no. 31 (2008). http://www.cabinetmagazine.org/issues/31/najafi_serlin.php.

[58] The winning argument in the antisodomy case *Lawrence v. Texas* explicitly embraced language consistent with "unashamed citizenship," emphasizing the positive elements of sexual intimacy for all persons. See Dale Carpenter, *Flagrant Conduct: The Story of Lawrence V. Texas: How a Bedroom Arrest Decriminalized Gay Americans* (New York: W. W. Norton, 2012).

political view, the language and ideal of authenticity provide a way of speaking that does not require an earnest, willful desire to know one's true self and make it known to the world. These gestures function as political critique. Confessions that traffic in the discourses of therapy and authenticity can operate as *political* interventions. They disrupt, puncture, and interrogate the confident borders between public and private, political and therapeutic, in ways that highlight the normative investments these boundaries advance and conceal.

The interpretations of authenticity as an earnest dream that the demanding subject actually expects to be realized miss the strategic and critical qualities of its politics. Speaking out about who one *really is* and asking others to hear these stories may be less an opening of the heart to the public and more of a disruption of the dominant picture and representation of oneself and others who share your subject position. That is to say, attacks on dominant representations (and misrepresentations) are not simply desires to have the self recognized, affirmed, made part of the curriculum, and so on. Quite the opposite, they craft a public persona – enter the public domain and criticize the exclusionary institutions that preside there. This project is radical, as Anthony Appiah clarifies: "The search for authenticity is demonstrated at least as much in opposition to the demands of social life as it is in the recognition of one's real self."[59] Reading authenticity as a political enterprise and critique of social conditions that shame and stigmatize illuminates how situations that give rise to demands in the name of a "true" self are laden with politics and power. These demands must be seen in context.

Finally, I read these unashamed interventions and proclamations as acts of citizenship rather than individual truth-telling because they emerge in two contexts that I read, following Arendt, as essential to political action. While much of this book emphasizes Arendt's own participation in The Lament, my complaints with Arendt have to do with the ways in which her nostalgic anxieties about ruptures of the borders marking the political blind her – and some of her disciples – to political action that is often consistent with her account of political struggle. The first concept I take from Arendt as essential to the political life of the pariah is that of a peer group "whose destiny [one] share[s]."[60] As much as The Lament disciplines and pathologizes unashamed citizens in ways that present them as isolated actors who have no peer group, the people I describe as unashamed citizens (and the acts that constitute practices of unashamed citizenship) are part of a vibrant, intersubjective peer group that is in dialogue about the meaning of public – political – equality and its proper reach. The second concept I take from Arendt is the commitment to "plurality," the "presence and acting of others" that is "*the* condition ... of all political

[59] K. Anthony Appiah, "Identity, Authenticity, Survival," in *Multiculturalism and the Politics of Recognition*, ed. Amy Guttman (Princeton, NJ: Princeton University Press, 1994), 149–164: 152–53.

[60] Arendt, *Rahel Varnhagen*, 251.

life."[61] The Lament positions unashamed citizens as one-dimensional and singularly focused; my re-reading corrects this view.

Missing from the existing literature, then, including the postfoundationalist, tragic, agonistic, and queer work that informs my own, are two things: A sophisticated account of the radical character of public demands for an authentic life free from shame *and*, relatedly, the sheer reiteration in the ways in which citizens appeal to a discourse of authenticity and see the psychological requirements of shame as hostile to, or at least in tension with, democratic political equality. In turn, these demands are repeatedly met with anxieties about civilizational decline, demands for containment of the democratic excess, and various iterations of The Lament That Shame Is Dead. Without some textured perspective on this long arc, any given group's demands to be free from shame and psychological injury can look misguided, dangerous to themselves, and dangerous to the public. But looking at how this story appears again and again as part of egalitarian moments and movements complicates The Lament as well as the more widespread and convincing critique of authenticity and recognition politics, which presumes that an apparently therapeutic political discourse is fundamentally at odds with a more tragic and agonistic perspective. A genealogical account illustrates this sense of repetition and reiteration.

And so I take seriously the tragic insights and warnings – the critique of "wounded attachments" and the potential *value* of "negative emotions" like shame for a political vision that is sensitive to human limits – and turn to the normative and democratic questions in play. Berlant has illuminated the psychoanalytic and what we might call psychosocial reasons why the testimonial genre continues to appeal to the "socially minor" who fashion their tune for the "socially major," with the hopes that the "law might include [them] in the Musak of its promise of clarity."[62] But we can push this line of questioning in a different direction, focusing on the *political* (rather than psychological or psychoanalytic) desire of people who experience the world as political outsiders to constitute a democratic public and demand a life free from shame and other "bad feelings" about themselves. Moreover, we can illuminate how these citizens or would-be citizens organize on-the-ground political activity around stories about shame and humiliation, and whether there is a better way to theorize the desire to make one's psychological injuries public without fetishizing psychological injury as the ground of politics.[63] The desire for freedom

[61] Hannah Arendt, *The Human Condition* (Chicago: University of Chicago Press, 1958), 237, 7.

[62] Berlant, "Trauma and Ineloquence," 51.

[63] Katie Wright sums up the general concern as follows:

> [S]ocial-theoretical literature of the past half-century provides wide-ranging analyses of major dimensions of the therapeutic turn. What distinguishes these varying interpretations from those emanating from within the therapeutic itself – exemplified by the promise of the human potential movement and the industry of self-help that it spawned – is a broad consensus that the therapeutic is inimical to sociopolitical, cultural and personal life. That this dominant narrative is shared by vastly divergent intellectual traditions – from the conservatism of Rieffian cultural

manifests itself in strategies of self-narration and self-publicization, relying on a seemingly straightforward and earnest discourse of authenticity, again and again. Answers to these questions about the desire to live a life free of shame illuminate some of the paradoxes at the heart of democratic life, most specifically the often fragile and tense relationship between egalitarian commitments and preoccupations with what the political and politics are and should be. The need to delimit and constrain the properly political, the presumed value of negative emotions, and the fear that shame is in jeopardy or altogether dead at any particular historical juncture demand further exploration.

My broader motivation for writing this book pertains to political theorists' investments in policing the political, which risks debarring and disqualifying a range of portals through which ordinary people access, challenge, and disrupt the political world. Accordingly, this book rereads and reengages political-therapeutic entanglements that open up the political world, invite social disturbance and reorganization, and yet are lamented and disciplined for lacking in civility, manners, reticence, and shame. These cases show that policing the divide between the political and therapeutic, in particular, falls into a version of the problem of reading identity and subjectivity as something that must be secured prior to action, the critique most often leveled against identity and recognition politics themselves. That is to say, if we debar whatever we might call "the therapeutic" as a potential site of politics and publicity, we say to the "confessing" (or "testifying") subject, whose personal and social concerns leak into the properly public realm, something like the following: Go back home, sort out your problems, heal, and then get ready to speak and act in public. Second-wave feminist organizations agonized, debated, broke up, reunited, and dissolved again over these very difficult issues, arguing about whether a particular group was primarily "therapeutic" or "political."[64] It is one thing for people – alone and together – to navigate the tensions between political and therapeutic work and claims-making. These are legitimate debates and questions. But it is quite another thing, from the vantage of democratic theory and especially feminist theory, to discipline and delimit the scope and content of political-therapeutic entanglements. Fears about a politics of authenticity and the dream of a life free of shame are on point, but there are also legitimate fears to be had about efforts to disqualify the means by which people orient themselves, organize, and claim space in public. Doing so disqualifies

sociology to radical feminism, the materialism of neo-Marxism and Foucauldian analyses of power – suggests that it is a compelling critique. Nevertheless, there remain important issues that have yet to be addressed.

Katie Wright, "Theorizing Therapeutic Culture: Past Influences, Future Directions," *Journal of Sociology* 44, no. 4 (December 1, 2008), 321–336: 326.

64 Combahee River Collective, *Combahee River Collective Statement*; Alice Echols, *Daring to Be Bad: Radical Feminism in America, 1967–1975* (Minneapolis: University of Minnesota Press, 1989); Christine A. Kelly, "Whatever Happened to Women's Liberation? Feminist Legacies of '68," *New Political Science* 22, no. 2 (2000): 161–175.

many robust contemporary movements, which in turn disqualifies past movements and moments by deeming them improperly political because they were too confessional, therapeutic, or "shameless." *Democracy and the Death of Shame* reorients this pattern of critique and lamentation. It investigates the commingling of the democratic and therapeutic, the political and the social, the public and the private, to illuminate the conditions under which a radically democratic political culture can thrive.

PART TWO

UNASHAMED CITIZENS

2

"A Socrates Gone Mad"

Plato's Lament and the Threat of Cynic Shamelessness

> There are four reasons why the "Cynics" are so named. First because of the "indifference" of their way of life, for they make a cult of shamelessness and, like dogs, eat and make love in public, go barefoot, and sleep in tubs and at crossroads.... The second reason is that the dog is a shameless animal, and they make a cult of shamelessness, not as being beneath modesty, but as superior to it.... The third reason is that the dog is a good guard, and they guard the tenets of their philosophy.... The fourth reason is that the dog is a discriminating animal which can distinguish between its friends and enemies.... So do they recognize as friends those who are suited to philosophy, and receive them kindly, while those unfitted they drive away, like dogs, by barking at them.
>
> – Aristotle

> Diogenes' shamelessness knew no bounds, recognized no exceptions, and accepted no prohibitions, just as if he were an untrained street dog, because such a dog does whatever nature calls him to do, indifferent to the restrictions created by human customs and conventions. Indeed, could there have been for him a more visual and graphic way of demonstrating his desire to deface the 'currency' of his contemporaries than by acting out his defiance of society in public, in the marketplace, and wherever he was in the public light?
>
> – Cicero

Plato's Lament

Shifting out of the contemporary frame, I want to turn to the relationship between fears about shamelessness and the meaning of equality and democratic citizenship by looking at ancient Athens and the flamboyant, cosmopolitan character of Diogenes the Cynic (421–323 BCE).[1] Diogenes was the

[1] The dates of Diogenes' exile and arrival in Athens are contested. Donald Dudley approximates it at 340 BCE, which is consistent with Aristotle's account, but William Desmond's more recent

notoriously shameless exile from Sinope, who lived in Athens during the fourth-century BCE after Socrates' execution and during the period in which the democracy shifted from a more direct form of rule to a more representative one, ending (in 322/321) when Macedonians captured Athens and imposed property qualifications that excluded ordinary Athenians from political participation (in the assemblies).[2] Diogenes is known for his outrageous and indecent self-exposure and his performances of disrespect for traditional authorities like Plato, Demosthenes, and Alexander, all of whom he mocked along with the crowds who came to hear him speak.

The details of Diogenes' life are murky, in terms of what he said on the street, what he wrote, and what he argued.[3] There is no clear arc of development marking Diogenes' theory or practice; "he is presented to us as a constant factor in the society of his day, criticizing conventional values, exposing shams, unimpressed by reputation of any kind."[4] Most treatments of Cynicism and Diogenes, in particular, begin with the account given by Diogenes Laertius, the third-century CE Roman historian who synthesized Diogenes' anecdotes in his opus, *Lives of the Eminent Philosophers*. Laertius wrote roughly 600 years after we assume Diogenes to have lived, the veracity of his account is not fully known, and his sympathetic account is inflected with his own investments. But we can confidently take from Laertius a story of Diogenes as a philosopher whose fundamental mission was to critique and transform Athenians' standard values. The story of values-changing is built into his biography, which provides a narrative of his life in Athens and its mission.[5]

As Laertius tells the story, Diogenes' father, who ran the Sinopean mint, put Diogenes in charge of managing the mint's workers. They allegedly told him to strike the faces off a number of coins so they would be taken out of circulation. Diogenes went to the Oracle (at Delphi or Delos) and asked Apollo what to do. "When the god gave him permission to alter the *political* currency,

work suggests that the dates are unclear, as are the reasons for his exile. Desmond writes: "Diogenes *might* have gone into exile in the 330s, 340s, 350s, or even before 380....The possibilities are literally endless, and there seems little point in speculating." William D. Desmond, *The Greek Praise of Poverty: Origins of Ancient Cynicism* (Notre Dame, IN: University of Notre Dame Press, 2006), 7.

[2] Mogens Herman Hansen, *The Athenian Democracy in the Age of Demosthenes: Structure, Principles, and Ideology* (Norman: University of Oklahoma Press, 1999), 161, 303–304.

[3] Diogenes Laertius identifies twenty-one works (fourteen dialogues and seven tragedies); Donald Dudley insists that only the *Republic*, the *Tragedies*, and four dialogues (*Cephalion*, *Pordalus*, *Aristarchus*, and *Eroticus*) can be confirmed as his. Donald R. Dudley, *A History of Cynicism – From Diogenes to the 6th Century A.D.* (London: Methuen & Company, 1937), 27; William Desmond, *Cynics* (Berkeley: University of California Press, 2008), 22.

[4] Dudley, *A History of Cynicism*, 27.

[5] It is because of the neat symmetry between changing the value of the money and changing the value of the polis that some scholars have suspected Diogenes invented the story of his exile. Dudley makes a case that given that the Sinopean currency was actually adulterated during the relevant period, it is likely true. See ibid. 23.

not understanding what this meant, [Diogenes] adulterated the state coinage." He left once his crime was discovered – some say by banishment, others by self-imposed exile.[6] Extending Socrates' critique of Athenian values, anticipating Rousseau's eighteenth-century critique of modernity, and gesturing to Nietzsche's nineteenth-century call for a genealogy of morals, Diogenes argued that the "standard of values [in Athens] was completely distorted."[7] Changing the city's values thus became his life project. "Very valuable things," he explained, "were bartered for things of no value, and *vice versa*.... A statue fetches three thousand drachmae, while a quart of barley-flour is sold for two copper coins."[8] Diogenes and his followers took up the mantra "Remint the coinage" as part of their belief that everything needed to be reworked from the ground up.[9] Before Athens could build correct values, it needed to destroy the old ones, and Cynic shamelessness became associated with this kind of destruction. French revolutionaries' rewriting of the calendar to break with aristocratic conventions reflects this Cynical impulse, just as the nostalgic lamentations about the loss of traditional France mirror the criticisms made by Diogenes' Athenian peers and some of his twentieth- and twenty-first-century readers, as well.

Diogenes' philosophy brought together both humor and moral seriousness. He offered bawdy and comic critiques of Athenian shame and manners, which he read as threats to an authentic and unshamed existence and dangerous for the political community, as well. One of the better-known stories about Diogenes relates to when Alexander, who had praised Diogenes by saying that if he could not be Alexander he would like to be Diogenes, asked the sun-bathing Diogenes what he could do as a favor to him. Diogenes answered, "Stand out of my light," indicating his lack of respect for Alexander's authority and his refusal to flatter it.[10] Here Diogenes rejects the difference and deference of *aidōs* and speaks the wrong things at the wrong times and in the wrong places. He also exposes his body in the agora, masturbates and urinates in public, and spits in people's faces as he flippantly claims that a tyrant's face functions nicely as a spittoon. He occupied the agora to speak out about poverty and the hungry, needy body. He built his life story by insulting the values of shame and reverence (*aidōs*). Shamelessness, for Diogenes, was a way of life. He embodied and enacted the incivility decried by those who lament that shame is dead.

Political theorists' views of Diogenes have been shaped by Plato, who famously described him as "a Socrates gone mad" for having taken the Socratic critique

[6] Diogenes Laertius, *Lives of Eminent Philosophers, Volume II, Books 6–10*, trans. R. D. Hicks (Cambridge, MA: Loeb Classical Library, 1925), 23; Desmond, *Cynics*, 20. Emphasis added.

[7] Dudley, *A History of Cynicism*, 28. This recalls Rousseau's critique of Paris in his *Letter to M. D'Alembert on the Theater*, where he criticizes the ways in which the theater enacts a transvaluation of values.

[8] Laertius, *Lives of Eminent Philosophers*, 37.

[9] Kristen Kennedy, "Cynic Rhetoric: The Ethics and Tactics of Resistance," *Rhetoric Review* 18, no. 1 (October 1, 1999), 26–45: 32, 28.

[10] Laertius, *Lives of Eminent Philosophers*, 41.

of Athenian mores and conventions *too far.*[11] Plato's battle with Diogenes was clearly personal, as they were in an ongoing struggle over who was the proper heir to Socrates, with Plato seeking to extend and systematize the teaching of virtue and Diogenes embracing Socrates' irreverent philosophy in the street. Plato was not a clear defender of shame – he emphasized the need for the best people to be unencumbered by the gaze and judgment of others, yet he understood political and social conventions like shame to be useful for actually existing political life.[12] During Plato's encounters with Diogenes, he would speak authoritatively about something like human nature, and Diogenes would deconstruct and destroy his account. In another often-repeated anecdote, Diogenes mocked Plato's lecture about the nature of man, whom Plato described as "an animal, biped and featherless" – a definition that his students rewarded with great applause. In response to Plato's definition, "Diogenes plucked a fowl and brought it into the lecture-room with the words, 'Here is Plato's man.... having broad nails.' "[13] Illustrating Diogenes' combative and comic style, this particular barb criticized the content of Platonic philosophy – Diogenes was known to laugh at the idea of Plato's Forms – and also challenged the space in which philosophy occurred. (Diogenes made his point about "Plato's man" as he barged into Plato's classroom.)[14] Diogenes called the traditional philosopher a "pretender of wisdom"; his own philosophy was embodied, performative, kinesthetic, and in the streets rather than the school.[15] Plato thus names Diogenes the dog (*Kyon*) as an epithet to draw attention to his crass and immodest lifestyle as well as the unbridled and shameless ferocity with which he attacked his enemies.

But Diogenes, unashamed, embraced the dog identity as a site of pride, and his followers became the Cynics (Kynics). If the "citizen" is corrupt and artificial, the dog is natural and instinctively righteous. Diogenes could not have picked a better metaphor to capture his moral and political critique of Athenian men. The Cynics thus became known "for their way of living in public like dogs, 'shamelessly indifferent' to the most entrenched social norms. Their deliberate rejection of shame ... authorized them to engage in modes of life that scandalized their society but that they regarded as 'natural.' "[16]

[11] Ibid., 55.

[12] See Tarnopolsky, *Prudes, Perverts, and Tyrants.*

[13] Laertius, *Lives of Eminent Philosophers*, 43. David Mazella elaborates this plucked fowl scene as an example of Diogenes "*moralizing* the gap between his own ethically driven *parrhêsia* and Plato's institutionalized version of philosophy, a philosophy of the lecture room but not a way of life" that does not in fact produce "men" at all. "From Diogenes's point of view," Mazella continues, "the institutionalization of philosophy represents ... a thoroughgoing perversion of its characteristic 'style of existence,' its program of self-testing." Mazella, *The Making of Modern Cynicism*, 39–41.

[14] Laertius, *Lives of Eminent Philosophers*, 55.

[15] Ibid., 65, 67.

[16] "Introduction," in R. Bracht Branham and Marie-Odile Goulet-Cazé, *The Cynics: The Cynic Movement in Antiquity and Its Legacy* (Berkeley: University of California Press, 2000), 4–5.

Political theorists have been held captive by Plato's lament about the ways in which Diogenes bastardized Socratic politics and philosophy.[17] Indeed, the force of Plato's aristocratic critique of Diogenes has blinded our ability to take seriously the radically democratic character of ancient Cynicism and the ways in which it speaks to contemporary debates about the social disturbance essential to meaningful political equality. Cynicism highlights how noncitizens or nascent citizens necessarily puncture the norms of shame and civility as they appear on the political scene. The limits of contemporary engagements with Diogenes and the Cynics are significant for two reasons. First, from a scholarly perspective, they neglect the political richness of Cynicism. They ignore several generations of work in Classics and more recent works in Rhetoric that highlight the political and egalitarian claims and practices that constitute Cynicism, most specifically the Cynics' piercing critiques of economic inequality and Athenian xenophobia. Second, and perhaps of greater significance, by taking the "truth" of Diogenes and the Cynics' shamelessness as evidence of their antipolitics and the need for democracy to cultivate and preserve shame and civility, they disqualify generations of latter-day Cynics who have resisted the requirements of shame and politicize sedimented social inequalities in order to disturb the social order. Anyone disavowing shame or criticizing its "artificial" requirements can therefore be read as outside of the bounds of legitimate democratic politics, tethered to a dangerous, apolitical ideal of "nature" and the "authentic" – categories political theorists claim to have settled. The force of Plato's lament thus robs us of an opportunity to retrieve a historical example of an egalitarian critique of shame that resonates with many dilemmas framing democratic theory and politics today.

Plato's Lament and Its Residue

There are three primary ways in which contemporary political theorists and philosophers have read the ancient Cynics, all of which are hamstrung by the force of The Lament That Shame Is Dead. This is true of (1) cosmopolitans who seek to resurrect the moral force of Cynicism while ignoring or bracketing its indecorous elements, the social disorder they involve, and the agonizing and political dimensions of Cynic politics; (2) Socratic democrats' reading of Cynic shamelessness as borderless and boorish and therefore antipolitical and antidemocratic, in contrast with the appropriately dialectical work of Socratic dialogue that they burnish and update for contemporary politics; and (3) postmodern Kynics who resuscitate ancient Cynicism in order to unsettle and dislodge postmodern false consciousness, positioning Kynic politics as salvational cure for postmodern malaise. In each case, the authors accept and perpetuate

[17] Important exceptions include William Chaloupka, *Everybody Knows: Cynicism in America* (Minneapolis: University of Minnesota Press, 2001); Stanley, *The French Enlightenment and the Emergence of Modern Cynicism.*

a portrait of ancient Cynicism and Diogenes, in particular, as earnestly waging battle *against shame* and in favor of a morally righteous cosmopolis that rejects politics and the general work of governance as always corrupt and poisoned by "artifice." I want to offer a brief reading of the three approaches, turn to their limitations, and then move forward with my alternative account of the radically democratic character of Diogenes and the ancient Cynics' practices, which The Lament pathologizes and obscures.

Civilizing Cosmopolitanism: Moral Virtue versus Democratic Politics

Cosmopolitanism, the first interpretation of Cynicism I want to address, grows out of a reading of Diogenes as an engaged interlocutor in Athenian social life who was nonetheless a foreigner, an exile, a non-Athenian whose body was foreign to Athenian customs.[18] As an exile who nonetheless saw something of value in the vocabulary of the polis and citizenship in it, he claimed to be a "citizen of the world" – a member of the cosmo*polis* – who was loyal to the "true commonwealth" which was as "wide as the universe."[19] For the purposes of my argument about the Cynics' radically democratic character, cosmopolitans offer a key insight: The civic traditions and borders of the polis so often revered and celebrated by democratic theorists are also sites of inequality that serve elites rather than ordinary people. The Cynics are therefore skeptical about the geographical borders of the polis and the class and status borders within it because their philosophical orientation positions them to see how "accidents of birth," rather than natural virtue or goodness, ground the "artificial" borders of friend and enemy, powerful and powerless. On a more subjective level, we can see how Diogenes's critique of the polis grows out of his position as a socially inferior and abject foreigner in Athens who had been expelled from his home city to a life in exile.[20] Other Cynics, like Hipparchia, were exiles of a different sort – shut off from families who rejected them based upon their desire to practice philosophy rather than support and curry favor with the powerful or play conventional gender roles. Cynics thus performatively occupy the subject position of outsiders and live the tension between the "artificial" demands of the unequal social order and the dream of a life that is "true" and "authentic." In keeping with the awareness of being an outsider and exile and a skepticism toward social and political borders and boundaries,

[18] Cosmopolitanism is a diverse tradition and it is beyond the scope of this project to illuminate its nuances. I am focused on how ancient Cynicism is invoked as ground for some cosmopolitan politics. For a more complete treatment, see Bruce Robbins, "Cosmopolitanism: New and Newer," *Boundary* 2 34, no. 3 (September 21, 2007): 47–60.

[19] Laertius, *Lives of Eminent Philosophers*, 65, 75.

[20] On Diogenes' abjection, see Mazella, *The Making of Modern Cynicism*, 33. In Laertius's account, Diogenes was also captured by pirates and sent to Crete for sale into slavery, a story whose veracity is contested but nonetheless remains part of the folklore of Diogenes' abject body in Athens. Laertius, *Lives of Eminent Philosophers*, 77; On the mythology of the sale, see Page duBois, *Slaves and Other Objects* (Chicago: University of Chicago Press, 2008), 155.

contemporary cosmopolitanism raises critical questions about justice and responsibility toward others.[21]

The story of Hipparchia reflects this more universal view of citizenship that rejects the polis' borders and extends the false dichotomy of citizen/foreigner to the social hierarchies – specifically, gender difference and social class – within the polis. Hipparchia was born to an elite family who intended her to marry a man of similar wealth and high birth. But Hipparchia fell in love with the Cynic philosopher Crates and Cynic philosophy itself. She resisted her parents' efforts to sway her away from Crates and toward more appropriate suitors. Her parents managed to conscript Crates into their project of keeping her away from him.[22] As Laertius tells the story: "Crates was ... implored by her parents to dissuade the girl, and did all he could, and at last, failing to persuade her, got up, took off his clothes before her face and said, 'This is the bridegroom, here are his possessions; make your choice accordingly; for you will be no helpmeet of mine, unless you share my pursuits.' "[23] Hipparchia chose Crates and embraced the life of a Cynic philosopher, rejecting both the class and gender difference of her family of origin, adopting an ascetic lifestyle, and eschewing the norms of shame expected on account of her gender.

Hipparchia's story reflects the fiercely egalitarian commitments of Cynic cosmopolitanism that reads social inequalities as suspect, artificial conventions. Martha Nussbaum has developed a version of cosmopolitan feminism that extends the critique of artificial polis borders to the artifice of gender difference. Nussbaum's account of Hipparchia's decision to forsake her material wealth and status for the sake of love and philosophy highlights the cosmopolitan critique of *aidōs* and its requirements of difference and deference, and the appeal – especially for marginalized and oppressed groups – of an authentic life that is free from shame and other external standards. The cosmopolitan believes that racism, classicism, xenophobia, parochialism, and provincialism are easy; cosmopolitan justice is hard.[24] Cosmopolitan citizens see beyond the borders of their particular community and prioritize justice and the good above and beyond, in Nussbaum's words, "local origins and group memberships [that are] ... so central to the self-image of the conventional Greek male."[25] As with the "artificial" citizen/foreigner boundary, Cynicism critiqued

[21] See, for example, K. Anthony Appiah, "Global Citizenship," *Fordham Law Review* 75, no. 5 (2006): 2375–2391; K. Anthony Appiah, "Cosmopolitan Patriots," in *For Love of Country?*, ed. Martha Nussbaum and Joshua Cohen (Boston: Beacon Press, 1996) 21–29; K. Anthony Appiah, *Cosmopolitanism: Ethics in a World of Strangers* (New York: W. W. Norton, 2007).

[22] Laertius, *Lives of Eminent Philosophers*, 99, 101.

[23] Ibid., 101.

[24] Nussbaum elaborates: "Diogenes knew that the invitation to think as a world citizen was, in a sense, an invitation not to be an exile from the comfort of patriotism and its easy sentiments, to see our own ways of life from the point of view of justice and the good." Martha Nussbaum, "Patriotism and Cosmopolitanism," in *For Love of Country?*, eds. Joshua Cohen and Martha Nussbaum (Boston: Beacon Press, 2002), 3–20: 7.

[25] Ibid., 6–7.

Athenian gender norms and conventions as obstacles to women's (and men's) authentic self-expression. The separation between public and private, polis and oikôs, political and economic render Athenian women noncivic beings with limited duties beyond the home and family. By Nussbaum's account, the Cynics' unmasking of artificial distinctions and divisions exposes the existing social order as securing the privilege of the powerful. The Cynics' disturbance of particular cities' gender codes inaugurates a form of gender egalitarianism as part and parcel of the cosmopolitan ideal.

As the stories of Diogenes and Hipparchia make clear, most cosmopolitans invoke Cynicism's ideal of being a citizen of the world to call into question the assumption within democratic theory that democratic citizenship must be tethered to one place. This calling into question need not, however, call for a borderless world state or empire. This is evident in Anthony Appiah's reading of cosmopolitanism as more sentiment than blueprint or ideology.[26] Reading cosmopolitanism as a sentiment cultivated in the in-between space of multiple homes and travel in the world, Appiah develops the concept of "rooted cosmopolitanism" to express the ways in which rootedness and identity are complex and mobile. Diogenes has roots in Sinope; when exiled, he travels and finally puts roots down in Athens. He claims to be a citizen of the world because although he is never fully at home in one place, he invests in the place he inhabits by critiquing the local values. "Rooted cosmopolitanism" captures this space of in-between: "America is my country and Paris is my home town," Appiah quotes Gertrude Stein, approvingly.[27] Cosmopolitanism punctures the liberal container of the nation state as the appropriate site for equal rights and concern.

Relevant to my concerns about the disciplinary force of The Lament, Nussbaum and Appiah soften the radicalism of their liberal cosmopolitanism by acknowledging the value of the brake and moderating influence of shame. Recall that a central piece of The Lament is the fear of the untethered, autochthonous individual who is concerned only with him or herself and not the customs and traditions that bind people to each other and to place. As if to reassure their readers that they don't take their Cynicism too far, Nussbaum and Appiah appeal to ideals of bourgeois respectability, civility, and decency to moderate their otherwise forceful critiques of *aidōs* and the difference and deference it secures. Nussbaum embraces Hipparchia's gender radicalism and her performance of shamelessness (which manifests itself in public copulation) only to retreat from it, clarifying that she is "not exactly recommending Crates and Hipparchia as the marital ideal for students in [her] hypothetical cosmopolitan schools."[28] Nussbaum resists drawing out the implications of this relationship – foreclosing the sexual radicalism in favor of the (putatively nonsexual) anticonformist message, a point I will come back to with respect to the broader force of The Lament. And Appiah, so careful to differentiate his "rooted"

[26] Appiah, "Cosmopolitan Patriots," 23.
[27] Ibid., 22.
[28] Nussbaum, "Patriotism and Cosmopolitanism," 16–17.

cosmopolitanism from the "reckless," that is, shameless variety, emphasizes his own respectability by invoking the moral teachings of his nanny: "It is said that [Diogenes] did what my English nanny would have called 'his business' in public – and if you do not know what my English nanny would have called 'your business,' my nanny would not have wanted me to tell you."[29] His debt is not to the natural, ascetic, primitive Cynicism, but to a sophisticated version of cosmopolitanism that involves nannies and English respectability and knowing what material suits public discussion and what does not. It bears no resemblance to the coarse and indecorous spirit that runs through ancient Cynicism and grounds its scathing critiques of Athenian wealth disparities and the manners enforcing them. The Lament haunts cosmopolitanism, rooted in ancient Cynic ideals, prompting Nussbaum and Appiah to temper their cosmopolitan authenticity by acknowledging the need for some of the protections and checks that anti-Cynical conventions like shame and civility might guarantee.

Redeeming Socrates (against Diogenes)

I now turn to a second set of interpretations that shows how Plato's Lament in particular and The Lament That Shame Is Dead more generally frame contemporary conversations about Diogenes and the Cynics.[30] These texts read Socrates' admittedly shameless behavior and commitment to an authentic existence against Diogenes and the Cynics in order to redeem and contain Socrates' unruly and uncivil elements. They read the Cynics, specifically their hostility to shame and their commitment to the authentic life that shame obstructs, as antidemocratic and antipolitical.[31] This work acknowledges the moral critique in Cynicism that cosmopolitans leverage so well, but insists that its strong moral argument ignores the central role of shame and the local polis in cultivating democratic *politics* and the civility on which it rests. The Cynics are figured as precisely those untethered and autochthonous subjects who abjure the attachment and intersubjectivity flagged by The Lament. This work criticizes the Cynic insistence upon moral self-sufficiency and the shamelessness it

[29] Appiah, "Global Citizenship," 2375.

[30] Euben, *Platonic Noise*; J. Peter Euben, *Corrupting Youth* (Princeton, NJ: Princeton University Press, 1997); Raymond Geuss, *Public Goods, Private Goods* (Princeton, NJ: Princeton University Press, 2001).

[31] Raymond Geuss notes:

> To follow the Cynic path is to be deeply unpolitical in two senses. First, by aspiring to complete self-sufficiency one tries to remove oneself from the state of mutual dependence on other humans, which is one of the basic preconditions of politics. Second, to assume an attitude of complete indifference to others' opinions, and especially to behave in ways one knows others will find disgusting, is consciously to produce in others the experience of a barrier and tacitly to give them to understand that one expects to be able to do without their assistance, an assumption they might, justifiably or not, find insulting.... To erect such barriers consciously, systematically, and universally to all others in all circumstances is to try to position oneself outside the realm of politics.

Geuss, *Public Goods, Private Goods*, 28–29.

entails because it creates isolated individuals who are obsessed with their own sovereignty and fulfillment. Therefore, as Arendt argues, they are incapable of politics and the pursuit of political freedom.[32]

There are two aspects to this critique: First, the Cynics' rejection of the "walls of the city" as artificial and divisive ignores the moral quality of the polis.[33] The cosmopolitan's vantage point can provide a high ground that is useful for criticizing "slavery, ethnocentrism, and hierarchies of all kinds," but it leaves no structure of governance or political community to grapple with the tasks of reconstructing and repairing these inequalities.[34] Echoing The Lament's broader concerns about the evisceration of boundaries, Peter Euben warns that Cynic virtues entail an escape from the constraints of a democratic "citizenship of place" and "sharing of power with equals."[35] Second, Cynicism is both morally and aesthetically indecent in its carte blanche endorsement of "nature" and the "natural." Copulation, masturbation, defecation – all are natural and therefore, according to the Cynics, should not be hidden away in shame.[36] Raymond Geuss develops his critique of Diogenes and redemption of Socrates through the concept of "disattendability," his version of the brake of shame that inhibits and prohibits individuals from forcing themselves into others' space. Taken from the Stoic call to "live unnoticed," Geuss's disattendability directs us to "be unobtrusive," a command that Diogenes both refuses to obey and identifies as a site of inequality and injustice. Reiterating the central themes of The Lament, Geuss complains that Diogenes, who is "systematically obtrusive," invades others' space and disrespects his fellow citizens' sense of disgust."[37] Geuss reads shame as a necessary restraint against a culture of self-obsession and self-exposure that tells the individual she or he can be completely self-sufficient from others and not respect others' desires to be left alone.

This interpretation of the Cynics nicely sets up a redemptive reading of the more grandfatherly, proud Athenian that is Socrates, as it cautions against romanticizing the natural and authentic because of a suspicion of conventions like shame and decency. Juxtaposing Diogenes and Socrates, Euben and Geuss offer up Socrates' political dialectic as the proper substitute for Diogenes' shameless invective. Socrates is "the true patriot and true Athenian," in this account.[38] But this reading of Socrates, whose own political and democratic status is not self-evident, comes at the cost of caricaturing Diogenes and the Cynics. That is to say, because of the close sympathies between Diogenes and Socrates, and their shared suspicion of shame and Athenian conventions,

[32] Hannah Arendt, "What Is Freedom?," in *The Portable Hannah Arendt* (New York: Penguin Classics, 2000), 438–461.
[33] Euben, *Platonic Noise*, 121.
[34] Ibid., 129.
[35] Ibid., 121.
[36] Ibid.
[37] Geuss, *Public Goods, Private Goods*, 13–14, 20–21.
[38] Euben, *Corrupting Youth*, 33.

Socrates' contemporary admirers – like Plato – do not want him to be contaminated by association with the scandalous Diogenes.[39] In order to protect and redeem Socrates, they cast Diogenes in the starkest of terms – failing to acknowledge any political value in his iconoclasm. And so they give an account of Socrates as political and civic, and manage and control Socrates' potentially shameless moments by contrasting them with Cynicism, whose shamelessness presumably served no civic purpose. This forecloses a reading of Cynicism as politically subversive and democratic in spirit. Geuss and Euben thus echo Plato's initial redemption, which protected Socratic dialectics by describing Diogenes as a Socrates *out of his senses*.

Kynic Medicine

Let us turn to a third interpretation of Diogenes, a seemingly less earnest approach that reads Diogenes as offering a "gestural critique" that has the potential to unsettle some of the trappings of late modern power.[40] This third interpretation appears less beholden to the force of The Lament, as it reads shamelessness as a tactic of political resistance rather than a call to *live* with or without shame.[41] Whereas the first two reception traditions accept the limited nature of Diogenes' politics, and either applaud his borderless cosmopolitanism or lament the loss of the politics of place, Peter Sloterdijk recuperates Diogenes and the ancient Cynics, (whom he refers to as Kynics in order to differentiate them from modern cynics), precisely for their *political* salience. Affirming Donald Dudley's observation that Athens was "the most important scene for his life,"[42] Sloterdijk embraces a Diogenes whose cosmopolitanism squares with a commitment to a specific place; his engaged social criticism in fact works *to improve the polity* by holding it to high standards and providing appropriate moral vision.

For Sloterdijk, the problem of modernity is cynicism, the end stage of enlightenment critique.[43] Sloterdijk refers to modern cynicism as "enlightened false consciousness," the stage of knowing the extent of our alienation and yet

[39] Dana Villa's reading of "Socratic citizenship" does not contrast Socrates with Diogenes. Villa offers what I would describe as a nonredemptive engagement with Socrates. He reads Socrates as a "bad citizen" who was individualistic and not especially polis-centered in his life. In this sense, Villa's reading shares a surprising affinity with Arlene Saxonhouse's, which also reads Socrates as patently shameless and in part responsible for the destruction of the polis. Villa's Socrates is a closer cousin of Diogenes than Euben's or Geuss's. *Socratic Citizenship* (Princeton, NJ: Princeton University Press, 2001).

[40] Peter Sloterdijk, *Critique of Cynical Reason* (Minneapolis: University of Minnesota Press, 1988).

[41] David Mazella and Sharon Stanley also emphasize the Cynics' tactics, but they serve less salvational purposes in their accounts. See David Mazella, *The Making of Modern Cynicism*; Stanley, *The French Enlightenment and the Emergence of Modern Cynicism*.

[42] Dudley, *A History of Cynicism*, 25.

[43] Sloterdijk, *Critique of Cynical Reason*. Another account of modern cynicism can be found in Timothy Bewes, *Cynicism and Postmodernity* (New York: Verso Books, 1997).

being unable or unwilling to do anything about it.[44] For example, we might *know* that representative government is a sham, that multinational corporations are more influential than government officials, that Athenian government serves the tyrant and the oligarch but not the demos, and so on. We are cynics – especially about the ability of individual citizens or utopian visions to improve matters and make things more just. Moreover, we have cynically accepted this state of being as we pay lip service to democracy, shop to our heart's content, retreat into the private sphere, and concede power to elites. We see no way to break the lock of cynicism. As Slavoj Žižek explains it, "Cynical reason is no longer naïve, but it is a paradox of enlightened false consciousness: one knows the falsehood, ... but still one does not want to renounce it."[45] We know we are suffering and still cannot break out of it.

In this state of enlightened false consciousness, it is extraordinarily difficult to leverage critique, and we need a tack beyond rational argumentation to unsettle it. For Sloterdijk, Diogenes and the ancient Kynics provide such a model because the Kynic understands that cynicism is lodged in the unconscious and therefore proceeds with gestures that "show" rather than "argue." The Kynic is the "physical embodiment of critique" as she or he displays her life, not as a philosopher but as a performer, a gesturer who illuminates a way of life. To invoke the language of The Lament, Diogenes *puts his life on display* because he believes one cannot teach others to be moral if one presumes morality to be a private matter that is invisible from public view. The Kynic is cynical in the colloquial sense because she or he "resist[s] official ideologies" and is suspicious about official creeds and nostrums. Like Socrates, she or he retreats from formal politics in his time. But rather than beg off from public action and throw hands up in the air because nothing can be done and no one can be changed, she or he subjects these "official ideologies" to satire and irony. Kynics place their bodies in the public arena as visible challenge to "official culture."[46] Sloterdijk's Kynic taps into the Bakhtinian tradition of carnivalesque, which endows laughter with the power of infinite possibility (against seriousness, which is a mode of authoritarianism). He invokes the "kynical gaze" of Diogenes, which

> understands itself as looking through a laughable and hollow show.... Diogenes sees through the puffed up idealism and cultural arrogance of the Athenians.... He rivets his eyes on the naked facts of nature.... [T]he usual divisions are invalid; there is neither above nor below, neither dirty nor pure. This gaze is open, realistic, and generous, and it is not embarrassed to look at what is naked; it does not matter whether it is beautiful or ugly, as long as it is natural.

[44] Sloterdijk, *Critique of Cynical Reason*, 5.
[45] Slavoj Žižek, *The Sublime Object of Ideology* (New York: Verso Books, 1989), 29.
[46] Robert Halsall, "Sloterdijk's Theory of Cynicism, Ressentiment and Horizontal Communication," *International Journal of Media & Cultural Politics* 1, no. 2 (2005), 163–180: 169.

Contrast this with the "master cynic" whose world the Kynic unveils: "the gaze of the master cynic ... is unhappily broken, reflectively bent."[47] The Kynic therefore is less earnest than the cosmopolitan and Socratic interpretation of the Cynic because her or his performance is an ironic and playful dramatic comedy that has the possibility to dislodge modern cynicism. But its irony does not diminish its seriousness or Sloterdijk's belief in its transformative power. Kynicism is not "opposition for opposition's sake," but rather a "mockery of authority [that] was based on a strong, morally critical irritability" that has a "didactic moral and political intent."[48] In a similar vein, Kristen Kennedy invokes Diogenes and the Cynics as a model of feminist unmasking that reveals the degree to which the Kynics are at odds with the Aristotelian view, which is indebted to "order, civility, reason, decorum," and, I would add, shame.[49] The belief that politics must be orderly and reasonable will never address the problems of late-modernity, according to Sloterdijk, which is why he turns to Diogenes and Kynicism.

The desire to remedy late-modern problems through the cheeky critique of the Cynics is promising and inspiring in a climate of postmodern skepticism. In lionizing the position of mischievous gadflies who are not concerned with speaking in turn and honoring the rules of normal discursive exchange, Sloterdijk – as have others – persuasively suggests that Habermasian-styled rules of reasonable discourse are not the way to make change, nor are they available to all. Whenever a noncitizen speaks, it is potentially "shameless" and scandalous.

Yet ultimately, the Kynic – however comic and ironic he may be – falls prey to some of the same traps of the cosmopolitans and Socratic democrats. Sloterdijk does not frame the crisis of our time in terms of the death of shame per se, yet his critique of postmodern malaise and cynicism in which we have *lost* our capacity for genuine reflection and political action has similar characteristics. Recalling that Diogenes often asked of his interlocutors, "*Are you not ashamed*?" Sloterdijk's Kynic pines for a lost time when shame's message was clear and shaming was more salient.[50] Sloterdijk's Diogenes isn't shameless, incapable of having his conscience tugged, but *we* are. And even if his lost civilization is not the same as Homer's, his critique of postmodern malaise nonetheless operates as a narrative of The Fall with a jeremiadic quality. The Kynic is positioned as an agent of social change and political redemption who himself laments that a useful form of shame is dead. The fate of the future lies in him; he protects us from a sea of postmodern relativism; he can bring proper shame back. The stakes are high and the Kynic, following Diogenes' way of life, is offered up as our political salvation.

[47] Sloterdijk, *Critique of Cynical Reason*, 145.
[48] Halsall, "Sloterdijk's Theory of Cynicism, Ressentiment and Horizontal Communication," 170.
[49] Kennedy, "Cynic Rhetoric," 26.
[50] Laertius, *Lives of Eminent Philosophers*, 67. Emphasis added.

Each of the three dominant interpretations of Diogenes and the Cynics – those who celebrate their morality, excoriate their message and medium as antipolitical, or see them as equipped to solve the problems of immorality and malaise in postmodernity – are overly invested in reading Diogenes and his shamelessness as either the answer to politics or the key problem it must overcome. The above interpretations attribute tremendous agency to Diogenes and his shamelessness. Again and again, both critics and friends emphasize the transformative powers of Diogenes and his disciples, who are said either to save the polis (or politics) from itself or destroy its most hallowed attributes. By contrast, I want to shift the focus to the way Diogenes and the Cynics orient themselves in the world as citizens.

Equality, *Parrhesia*, and Comedy: The Politics of Cynic Critique

In the previous section, I noted that the philosophical and theoretical literature reviewed thus far generally fails to reckon with Cynicism's ambiguities. On the one hand, Diogenes and the Cynics articulate a generous dream of a universal bond among all people – a bond that transcends the particular location of city or place; the need to look upon the conventions of one's place with a fresh, skeptical, and foreign eye so as to evaluate their justice and injustice; and they reject artificial ranks of race, nation, class, and gender as anathema to our common humanity. On the other hand, they seem entirely content to live only with those who share their self-righteous moralism, refuse to acknowledge the social codes and manners that make life with others bearable, and appear unreasonably wedded to a view of politics and power as *always* serving one's own interests without regard for the genuine care of the commonwealth at all.

With few exceptions, this cut-and-dried reception of the Cynics stands in sharp contrast to the more nuanced and generous reception by Classics scholars.[51] Drawing upon the latter work, I read past the blinders imposed by Plato's lament and the broader Lament that Shame is Dead to reconsider the Cynics as democratic citizens whose disruption of social order provides a critical frame of reference for the politics and practices of newly enfranchised or newly visible citizens. Recall that the larger argument I am making pertains to how nascent citizens publicly disavow the requirements of shame in order to "get noticed" *and* to critique the naturalized, sedimented values and virtues that have contributed to their invisibility, exclusion, and domination.[52]

[51] Generally speaking, Classics scholars' accounts of the period lack the normative thrust of political theorists'. For example, Classicists tend not to speak of the "polis in decline" but rather chart the transformations of the polis, recognizing that while centers of power and governance shift, the concept of the polis persists. I am grateful to Eric Dugdale for drawing my attention to this contrast.

[52] Here, as throughout the book, I mean citizen in the nonlegal sense but in the sense of laying claim to the direction of the polity. The kinds of civic performances I describe can be taken up by – and often are, as Diogenes' case exemplifies – metics and resident "aliens."

They see this as a logical extension of democratic equality. Political theorists and philosophers' reaction to the Cynics as either salvational or antipolitical indicates a general failure to grapple with democratic action on the part of social outsiders who are committed to meaningful social and civic equality. As critics of existing – and hierarchical – norms and conventions that authorize exclusion, citizens who take up shameless strategies of exposure (and are disciplined for doing so) typically deploy claims of authenticity or "the natural" in order to claim space in public. The Cynics do precisely this, and they are chastised and lamented for it.

Three aspects of Cynic ideas and practice upend the portraits dominating political theory and philosophy – aspects we have been blinded to by the force of Plato's account of Diogenes and the power of The Lament in democratic theory. First, and most centrally, the Cynics are deeply committed to politicizing the chasms of wealth that dominate Athenian politics. Democratic theorists' failure to take the Cynics seriously reflects a larger failure or reluctance to politicize social and economic inequalities. Second, the Cynics' strong egalitarianism and practices of social disturbance and disruption should be understood as forms of political argument and not moralizing "truth" claims, as democratic theorists have argued. This is evident in their use of comedy and general awareness of the audience whom they are trying to persuade. Following from these two points is the third: The Cynics' practices – which I read as iterations of unashamed citizenship – belong in the tradition of agonistic democratic politics, as they take seriously the democratic goal of equality; deploy the quintessentially democratic practice of *parrhesia*; and do so within a vibrant peer group focused on plurality in an increasingly one-dimensional political and social landscape that is preoccupied with cultivating virtue at the expense of meaningful equality.

A sampling of Diogenes' *chreia* (anecdotes) that pertain to wealth and poverty reveals the centrality of social inequality as a problem for Cynic philosophy.[53] Diogenes proclaims that disability should refer to those without a wallet as well as those with physical disabilities like blindness;[54] he describes himself as a "spy upon … insatiable greed";[55] insists that the laziest of men are those who have servants;[56] calls the "love of money" the "mother-city of all evils";[57] and gives up his cup and drinks out of his hands when he sees a poor boy do the same.[58]

[53] *Chreia* are "the oldest stratum of the Cynic tradition, [which] represent [Diogenes] as the Dog in all his aspects of shamelessness (*anaideia*) and in his unrestrained freedom of speech (*parrhesia*)." Margarethe Billerbeck, "The Ideal Cynic from Epictetus to Julian," in Branham and Goulet-Cazé (eds.), *The Cynics*, 203–221: 205.

[54] Laertius, *Lives of Eminent Philosophers*, 35.

[55] Ibid., 45.

[56] Ibid., 47.

[57] Ibid., 53.

[58] Ibid., 39.

Even the notorious story of Diogenes' public masturbation highlights the absurdity and injustice of poverty amidst wealth and splendor.[59] His performance of what it means to be authentic and therefore shameless – to resist social conventions buttressed by shame – was directed at a highly specific social point about poverty. Eating in public reminded his audience that people need to eat and the city has an obligation to feed them or create conditions under which they can be fed. Foucault recounts the story here:

> Cynic[s] ... utilized the practice of bringing together two rules of behavior which seem contradictory and remote from one another. For example, regarding the problem of bodily needs. You eat. There is no scandal in eating, so you can eat in public (although, for the Greeks, this is not obvious and Diogenes was sometimes reproached for eating in the agora). Since Diogenes ate in the agora, he thought that there was no reason why he should not also masturbate in the agora; for in both cases he was satisfying a bodily need (adding that "he wished it were as easy to banish hunter by rubbing the belly"). Well, I will not try to conceal the shamelessness (*anaideia*) of the cynics as a scandalous practice or technique.[60]

Diogenes' shamelessness serves his soul but it also makes a political point about hunger and poverty. For Diogenes, the personal was always political, and the virtuous philosopher should model his ascetic politics in the way he lived his own life. The Cynics politicized the economic and class relations of Athenian society, "highlighting the exclusions of the *polis* and the rewards given the corrupt" as it advocated a philosophy that "helped to democratize education to all who were interested, men and women alike."[61] Thus in responding to the criticism of his public masturbation by pointing out how easy it should be to be to meet the basic need of hunger, Diogenes exposed the more significant crime of the Athenian state and the elites who ran it – allowing people to go hungry, something that a wealthy state could address and resolve as easily as sexual frustration.

The link between the subversion of sexual norms to critique the power of Athenian wealth also comes to the fore in Hipparchia's life story, as she embraces a shameless life to criticize the falseness of Athenians' love of wealth. Nussbaum reads Hipparchia as protofeminist, and rightly so, but her critique of wealth also reveals an understanding of how the difference and deference shame secures enforces interlocking social inequalities and identities. Hipparchia's story shows how class expectations shape her gendered experience of *aidōs*. She embraces a life of poverty to liberate her from an aristocratic gender code. Hipparchia chose Crates and the Cynic "way of life" against the wealthy suitors approved by her parents, a marriage to whom would have required a life of shame and artifice. Crates and Cynicism promised authenticity and freedom. When her parents tried to talk her out of marrying him,

[59] Ibid., 47.

[60] Michel Foucault, *Fearless Speech*, ed. Joseph Pearson (Los Angeles, CA: Semiotext(e), 2001), 122.

[61] Kennedy, "Cynic Rhetoric," 29.

she threatened to kill herself. When Crates stood before her and her parents, literally naked to signify both his shamelessness and his lack of material possessions, she chose naked shamelessness and all that it entailed.

Unashamed, Hipparchia rejected the difference and deference secured by *aidōs*, crafting a philosophical life for herself that shamelessly crosses borders by choosing the (masculine) realm of philosophy against the narrow borders of a feminine domestic life. She chose truth over status, speech over reticence, and membership in the whole universe rather than the narrow borders of the polis. Publicly embracing and performing shamelessness offered her a way out of the gender rules of *aidōs*, which, as Douglas Cairns notes, empowered men to see "that the women under their control remain faithful and sexually pure."[62] Her departures were all the more scandalous because of her class and gender. And she found strength to endure them through the concrete solidarity of the Cynic circle and the abstract idea of a cosmopolitan universe beyond the patriarchal, parochial, and money-loving borders of the polis.

This point about Cynic solidarity and the dynamics within the Cynic peer group speaks to the political dimensions of the Cynic life that are missed in readings of Cynics as morally righteous, apolitical individuals. Within the Cynic group, there was a context of a shared world that rooted their radical individualism. (This is in part Appiah's point with respect to "rooted cosmopolitanism," but the interpretation of Cynic politics I am offering here rejects the bourgeois respectability so present in his cosmopolitanism.) They were not individualistic and autochthonous, but part of a longstanding Greek tradition of ascetic skepticism about the compatibility of virtue and wealth.[63] And beyond the conversations within the Cynic group, Cynics were deeply attuned to the views of non-Cynics, whose opinions they sought to change. They understood their philosophy as "gestural" and performative, and they invoked the paradigmatically populist and democratic genre of comedy to get their antiaristocratic message across.

Their comic tactics indicate the extent to which the Cynics were attuned to the dramatic and democratic question of audience beyond their own peer group. They understood themselves as performing for others whom they were trying to convince to change their ways, if not to adopt the Cynic lifestyle whole cloth. Even Diogenes' less explicitly class-oriented *chreia* are shot through with antiaristocratic sentiment. A recent study by M.D. Usher compares Diogenes' *chreia* with Homer's verse to argue that Diogenes' shameless *parrhesia* self-consciously occupied and interpellated Homer, the "*prince* of poets."[64] Scholars have focused on the larger points of Diogenes's *chreia* but paid less attention to the specific literary references and tropes themselves.[65]

[62] Cairns, *Aidōs*, 120.

[63] Desmond, *The Greek Praise of Poverty*.

[64] M. D. Usher, "Diogenes' Doggerel: Chreia and Quotation in Cynic Performance," *The Classical Journal* 104, no. 3 (February 1, 2009), 207–223: 208. Emphasis added.

[65] Ibid., 209.

One of the examples given is Diogenes' "comic jab at a handsome young man ... lounging naked in a vulnerable position, ... presumably at the baths or palaestra." "'Watch out,' Diogenes warns the boy with a nod, 'lest someone stick his spear in your rear while you sleep.'" Usher makes a compelling case that the "template for [Diogenes'] line is from the *Iliad*, "where Diomedes warns Odysseus not to turn tail, but to stand and help defend Nestor." Another version appears later in the *Iliad* where Achilles and Hector are fighting and Hector says "he will fall with a spear not in his back but in his chest." With the Homeric precedent in mind, "Diogenes' remark seems to be directed less at loose boys in the palaestra than at sexual predation by older men."[66] The parallel grammatical structures between Homer and Diogenes suggest that Diogenes was speaking directly to his aristocratic audience and that even his less explicitly antiaristocratic arguments mocked aristocratic mythology and sensibility. Deploying Homeric verse, Diogenes relied on the speaker and hearer's common understanding: "For Diogenes and others in the Cynic tradition, Homer was a *langue* in which he and his audiences were competent, and thus an effective vehicle for communication and philosophical critique."[67] This invocation of Homer serves two purposes, then, to establish and play on what John Searle describes as "mutually shared background information" and, more significant for our purposes, simultaneously to occupy, critique, and mock aristocratic values and the patron saint who had given voice to them.[68] Occupying Homer was a way to live out the "Delphic injunction to 'deface the currency.'"[69]

To add to the antiaristocratic message of Diogenes' and the mockery of Homer, "prince of poets," the Cynics also self-consciously and strategically deployed *parrhesia*, the practice of frank, unashamed speech "irreducible to power or interest" and the consummate mark of Greek political discourse.[70] Diogenes described *parrhesia* as "the most beautiful thing in the world."[71] And it was the love of *parrhesia*, which he read as a foil for elite power, that brought Diogenes to mock ruthlessly Plato, Alexander, Demosthenes, and any other authority who got in his way.

The democratic significance of the Cynics' love for *parrhesia* and its beauty warrants some discussion of the fourth-century context in which the Cynics used it. Athens during the fourth century had shifted from its more radically democratic forms of rule by the popular Assembly, the sphere in which *parrhesia* reigned, to a more representative form. This move was justified based upon fears of democratic excess. Fears that the fifth century had taken democracy

[66] Ibid., 210–211.
[67] Ibid., 220.
[68] Ibid., 209.
[69] Ibid., 220.
[70] Nancy Luxon, *Crisis of Authority: Politics, Trust, and Truth-Telling in Freud and Foucault* (New York: Cambridge University Press, 2013), 133.
[71] Laertius, *Lives of Eminent Philosophers*, 71.

too far and needed aristocratic restraints echoed throughout the period. Moral teaching took on a new urgency based upon an emerging belief that the polis and its leaders needed a reinvigoration of aristocratic virtue. Prose writers took up their pens to educate elites about the virtues needed for political leadership.[72] The turn to written, rather than oral, teaching reflected the desire to prepare elites – the literate class – for political rule.[73] These writers emphasized justice, fairness, moderation, self-restraint, and the cultivation of *aidōs*.[74] *Parrhesia*, a vestige of a more radically democratic time was out of place and out of favor. Diogenes and the Cynics' strategies of *parrhesiastic* sparring and interruption hailed Athenian elites into the ordinary, dirty, and relatively impoverished scene of address on the street. Sloterdijk and Kennedy identify a democratic sensibility present in the Cynics' speech because of how Cynics used it to disrespect social rank and power. But there is a more important point here. The Cynics were not only disrespectful to elites in how they approached them: their choice of *parrhesia* as a mode of moral education was rooted in the more radically democratic period of Athenian democracy. In this climate of declining orality with respect to moral teaching, the Cynics politicized Athenians' unwillingness to extend social and political rights and privileges to the poor and unranked by using a populist and democratic form.[75]

This context of the shifting of power away from the demos and the egalitarian character of *parrhesia* that was opposed by aristocrats (both old and new), Diogenes' playful occupation and parodying of Homeric verse, and the Cynics' preoccupation with the "natural" injustice of wealth chasms indicate that the Cynic demand to live authentically in accordance with "nature" and reject "convention" has been misunderstood. It is certainly true that the Cynics eschewed convention (*nomos*) in favor of nature (*phusis*), "attempt[ing] to eat meat raw,"[76] walking barefoot in snow,[77] and so on in order to be as self-sufficient and "natural" as possible. But Diogenes' "natural" and authentic ascetic existence was also highly strategic and performative. A preponderance of evidence suggests that Diogenes intentionally played the role of the crazy Socrates – the polis was a stage, and he its prime actor.[78] Moreover, Diogenes' "natural" performances were, of course, acted out – they would not

[72] Frances Pownall, "From Orality to Literacy: The Moral Education of the Elite in Fourth-Century Athens," *Mnemosyne, Supplementum* 6, no. 280 (2007): 235–289.

[73] Ibid., 236.

[74] Ibid., 239, 241–243.

[75] Foucault notes that "[t]he Cynic parrhesiastic game is played at the very limits of the *parrhesiastic* contract. It borders on transgression because the parrhesiastes may have made too many insulting remarks." Foucault, *Fearless Speech*, 127.

[76] Laertius, *Lives of Eminent Philosophers*, 37.

[77] Ibid., 35.

[78] A.A. Long, "The Socratic Tradition: Diogenes, Crates, and Hellenistic Ethics," in *The Cynics*, ed. R. Bracht Branham and Marie-Odile Goulet-Cazé (Berkeley: University of California Press, 1996), 28–46: 33.

have worked without proper staging and props – the barrel, the knapsack, the walking stick, the beard.[79] Only the most earnest interpreter could read them as a naive call to return to nature and reject life in the world with others. Diogenes performatively represented himself as homeless exile without a city or country, but he was not antisocial or antipolitical in the strict sense. Anthony Long elaborates: "His way-out lifestyle had a philosophical purpose ... Although he attacked convention (*nomos*), his agenda was not the abandonment of all forms of social organization but a radical critique of the Greek polis."[80] The Cynics did not retreat from the world to nurture the purity of their souls. To the contrary, they lived in the streets, naked and unashamed, forcing themselves upon others, refusing to hide their unruly bodies and radical demands.

It warrants returning at this point to the status of shame (*aidōs*) in ancient Greece. *Aidōs* is a paradigmatically aristocratic virtue, taught through Homer and Hesiod, defended by tragedians against the relative leveling of social class under Pericles, and cultivated in the fourth century by Plato and the Academy and also prose poets writing for an elite audience.[81] The introduction to an edited volume on Cynicism emphasizes this point, noting that shame is "the cornerstone of [the] traditional Greek morality" that Cynics sought to dismantle and overcome.[82] Hesiod warns of a time when *aidōs*, the quality that separates humans from animals, disappears and justice gives way to naked violence.[83] Euripides' *Medea* warns that shamelessness (*anaidea*) "is the worst of all diseases."[84] Plato's dialogue the *Protagoras* includes the teaching that cities need shame (*aidōs*) and justice (*dike*) to survive and thrive.[85] "*Aidōs* was hallowed in tradition as a necessary mark of civilized life."[86] Political theorists and philosophers writing about shame tend to ignore this aspect of shame's social history.[87]

[79] Ineke Sluiter, "Communicating Cynicism: Diogenes' Gangsta Rap," in *Language and Learning* (Cambridge: Cambridge University Press, 2005), 139–163: 144.

[80] Long, "The Socratic Tradition: Diogenes, Crates, and Hellenistic Ethics," 40.

[81] I am grateful to Yurie Hong for helping me to understand the significance of this history. See also Cairns, *Aidōs*; Cynthia Farrar, *The Origins of Democratic Thinking: The Invention of Politics in Classical Athens* (New York: Cambridge University Press, 1988); Shirley Darcus Sullivan, *Psychological and Ethical Ideas: What Early Greeks Say* (Leiden: BRILL, 1995); Bonnie Honig, "Antigone's Laments, Creon's Grief: Mourning, Membership, and the Politics of Exception," *Political Theory* 37, no. 1 (February 1, 2009): 5–43; Pownall, "From Orality to Literacy: The Moral Education of the Elite in Fourth-Century Athens."

[82] Branham and Goulet-Cazé, "Introduction," *The Cynics*, 1–27: 4.

[83] Sullivan, *Psychological and Ethical Ideas*, 184, 189–193.

[84] Euripides, *Medea*, in Euripides, *Medea, Hippolytus, Heracles, Bacchae: Four Plays* (Hackett, 2012), 54, line 471. The chorus in *Medea* also sang, "Shame no longer resides in ancient Greece" (lines 440–441).

[85] Plato, *Protagoras*, trans. N. Denyer (Cambridge: Cambridge University Press, 2008), 322d.

[86] Long, "The Socratic Tradition: Diogenes, Crates, and Hellenistic Ethics," 35.

[87] Arlene Saxonhouse is an important exception: she argues that *aidōs* must be extended to the democratic era in order to protect it from its baser tendencies and the *parrhesia* that reigns there, but Saxonhouse's defense of *aidōs* does not dispute its aristocratic origins. To the contrary, her

Thus the Cynics were not democratic or political in the sense that they participated in rule-sharing and collective governance; their *parrhesia* was located in the social realm, politically inconsequential compared to *parrhesia* of the Athenian Assembly. But they politicized social inequality and preoccupied themselves with the "least advantaged" by publicly occupying the role of low social rank to direct attention to those citizens most often associated with a democratic polity. Like Socrates before them, the Cynics did not contain their *parrhesia* in the Assembly, but used the street, an essential venue of informal Athenian politicking. Given that the Cynics practiced a speech strategy "so thoroughly [associated with democracy] that opponents of democracy could only turn away from it in horror," any consideration of its political and democratic sensibility must consider both the political history of *parrhesia* and the workings of fourth-century social class and climate.[88] Opponents of democracy did not take up an aristocratic form of *parrhesia*; they rejected the ideal and practice of free speech entirely. Kurt Raaflaub elaborates: "[I]n the case of freedom of speech, no aristocratic counter-concept was ever developed.... [T]his was no accident – rather, throughout antiquity, freedom of speech was never a primary aristocratic concept"[89] This preoccupation with both the content (membership) and the Cynics' version of the tactic (*parrhesia*) of democracy triggers Plato's lament.

The political and public dimensions of Diogenes and the Cynics' critical lives is part of the messiness of cynic cosmopolitanism – a messiness that the contemporary cosmopolitan literature brackets and constrains. The Cynics, like Socrates, explicitly rejected the formal practices of politics. Yet they inhabited the city and needed to be in the city and before the audience of citizens they sought to doctor and heal.[90] Antisthenes, Socrates' friend who was at his side at death, and a link between Socrates and Diogenes, noted that the polis was like fire: "go too near and you burn; go too far away and you freeze."[91] The Cynics' radical individualism was framed in the context of a peer group whose practices and commitments were shared. "Cynic cosmopolitanism," John Moles writes, "has implications for the relations of the Cynic with his

concern reflects an impulse at the heart of The Lament, looking back to traditional virtues in order to steer and check an egalitarian ethos that suggests that anyone, without regard to social rank, can say and perform as she or he wishes. This is the paradox of democracy as Saxonhouse understands it: Democratic egalitarianism cannot thrive without *parrhesia* and the disregard for social rank that it involves; at the same time, without *aidōs* – some form of reverence and awe for something beyond "the people" – democracy cannot sustain itself. Saxonhouse, *Free Speech and Democracy in Ancient Athens*.

88 Kurt Raaflaub, "Aristocracy and Free Speech in the Greco-Roman World," in *Free Speech in Classical Antiquity*, eds. Ineke Suiter and Ralph Rosen (Leiden: Brill, 2004), 41–61: 41.

89 Ibid, 42.

90 John Moles, "Cynic Cosmopolitanism," in *The Cynics: The Cynic Movement in Antiquity and Its Legacy*, eds. R. Bracht Branham and Marie-Odile Goulet-Cazé (Berkeley: University of California Press, 2000), 105–120: 108.

91 Ibid., 108.

peers. The Cynics recognized the kinship or community of the wise."[92] A Cynic does not avoid a life in the world with others, but works to create it. Teaching, spying, inspection, mediation, reconciliation, and guardianship of the polis all focus on improving a world that others live in rather than (only) the ascetic self-care often associated with the self.[93]

Finally, to come back to the "stick a spear in your rear" anecdote and the ways in which Diogenes stretched and repurposed Homer's words, I want to consider the political and democratic significance of Diogenes and the Cynics' deployment of humor and what this means for how we understand them as antipolitical and overly preoccupied with self-sufficiency.[94] Diogenes describes himself as a character in Greek *tragedy* who arrives in Athens poor, naked, and unwelcome – an exile from his homeland who was expelled for heeding the Oracle.[95] Yet, as one scholar notes, "*[h]umor* is the chisel stamp of Cynic discourse."[96] Indeed, a comic "streak of buffoonery" runs throughout the Cynic tradition.[97]

The Cynic straddled the traditions of both tragedy and comedy, which suggests a deep awareness of the ways in which the self is always already embedded in relations with others. As the Cynic's Homeric invocations would have been pointless without an audience, so too does his or her dramatic comedy need others to laugh for it to serve its purpose. Ineke Sluiter sums this up nicely: "Cynic performance would be meaningless, ... without an audience, and consequently, the Cynic consciously chooses to be in the public arena; indeed, it would be hard to imagine a Cynic hermit.... [because] [t]he polis is the theater in which he performs."[98] Diogenes speaks the language of self-sufficiency and eschewing all conventions, yet his message and his humor require others' presence. Diogenes does not seek to escape his fate; he embraces it, fashioning a political mission to "remint the coinage" and "change the values" precisely in line with his origin story rather than as a rejection of it. Upon being called a "Socrates out of his senses," he adopts and performs that role, as well. It is precisely because of his awareness of himself as a tragic character who cannot deliver a utopian, morally perfect state, that he will never deliver the kind of perfectionist politics or Kynic enlightenment some of his contemporary

92 Ibid., 112.

93 Ibid., 116.

94 Peter Euben is much more sympathetic to Old Comedy than he is to ancient Cynicism. It bears asking how a more comedic interpretation of the Cynics would shape his criticism of them as antipolitical and polis-destroying. See Euben, *Platonic Noise*, Chapter 4, "Aristophanes in America."

95 R. Bracht Branham, "Defacing the Currency: Diogenes' Rhetoric and the Invention of Cynicism," in *The Cynics: The Cynic Movement in Antiquity and Its Legacy*, eds. R. Bracht Branham and Marie-Odile Goulet-Cazé (Berkeley: University of California Press, 2000), 81–104: 91.

96 Branham, "Defacing the Currency," 93, *Emphasis added.*

97 Sluiter, "Communicating Cynicism," 158.

98 Ibid., 162.

disciples desire. He takes tragedy as his starting point and comedy as his mode of delivery through the practice of *spoudogelois* – serious yet comedic critique that aims to unsettle received norms.[99]

These Cynic practices result in an engaged, intersubjective politics acutely aware of audience and the political message its practitioner wishes to communicate. This intersubjective project is not the earnest dialogue of deliberative democracy or normative political theory, and its presence does not address all of the concerns raised by scholars skeptical of Cynicism's civic value, but its political and public dimensions should not be dismissed.[100] It cannot destroy the polis nor deliver utopian redemption from the parochialism and xenophobia of local politics or the alleged malaise of late-modernity. It is a mode of civic practice directed toward inequality and the injustices secured by Greek norms of conduct.

Cynic Constitutions

Thus far I have argued for an interpretation of "nature" and "the authentic" in ancient Cynicism as a strategic deployment, a performative statement that gains its salience from its willingness to risk the foundationalist claim of nature and the authentic life that is removed from the social norms of the polis. The Cynics show the political *effort* involved in making a particular vision of "nature" materialize in the world and they direct their effort toward fiercely egalitarian claims that both extend from and complicate the democratic tradition in Athens. The Cynics invoked the "natural" to ground a particular vision that they believed preoccupations with conventions like shame obstructed and obscured. Diogenes' experience as a "cultivated philosopher" gave meaning to his "natural," dog-like performances. The traffic between nature and culture in his life's work was ongoing and symbiotic.[101] Moving back and forth between ideas about "nature" and "culture" or "*nomos*," the Cynics inaugurated a powerful critique of social inequality that Christian Lotz describes as "Greek critical theory."[102]

More importantly, the Cynics' critical practice involves tactics and strategies that democratic theorists typically celebrate – speech, persuasion, humor, and bodily performances that unsettle received norms and direct attention to new possibilities. The suspicion of *aidōs* was part and parcel of Athenian democracy. And the Cynics' preoccupations with "nature" against "shame" and

99 R. Bracht Branham, "Nietzsche's Cynicism: Uppercase or Lowercase," in *Nietzsche and Antiquity: His Reaction and Response to the Classical Tradition*, ed. Paul Bishop (Suffolk, UK: Camden House, 2004), 170–181: 176.

100 For a broader treatment of comedy's political and social significance, see Andrew Stott, *Comedy* (New York: Routledge, 2014).

101 Christian Lotz, "From Nature to Culture? Diogenes and Philosophical Anthropology," *Human Studies* 28, no. 1 (March 1, 2005), 41–56: 47.

102 Ibid., 53.

conventions of concealment and civility did not end in fourth-century Athens, but were self-consciously taken up by disciples in subsequent eras – "outsiders" and "misfits" questioning what shame and civility required of them. Again and again, those seeking to preserve and resurrect *aidōs* lament and decry the radical egalitarianism politicized through shameless critiques of the difference and deference *aidōs* secures.

Democratic theorists looking back to Athenian democracy typically focus on the periods preceding the Cynics. It is easy to write off the Cynics' era (even as contested as it is) as a period of nascent empire and therefore lacking in any meaningful practices of democratic citizenship. I have focused here for two reasons. First, to put it simply, political theorists have paid scant attention to the significance of shamelessness and the fears about lost traditional values in this time. This is related to our tendency to traffic in caricature when speaking and writing about Diogenes and the Cynics. Political theorists have given ample attention to Plato's ideas, Socrates' politics and dialogues, and the tragedians who have mourned the loss of aristocratic specificity that (Periclean) egalitarianism supplants.[103] Looking at the Cynics, by contrast, brings into relief some of the tensions inhabiting democratic theory, more broadly, especially the relationship between strong claims of equality and "civilizing" manners like shame and reverence, and the civic place of foreign, technical noncitizens in making political claims about the future of the city vis-à-vis the city's customs and traditions. Second, and more significant, Cynicism represents a strong egalitarian movement in its own right. It is not the formal egalitarianism of the constitution at that moment that is especially striking, but the radical rejection of inherited hierarchies in terms of gender and social rank both *within* the polis and also in terms of the polis' orientation toward foreigners. The Cynics problematize the constitutive xenophobia and "jingoistic 'blood and soil' doctrine," as Josiah Ober describes it, that marked the Athenian democratic order.[104] The very presence of Diogenes on the stage of the Athenian street as a foreign interlocutor with the arbiters of official power suggests a more robust scene of democratic politics than one might typically imagine. Thus the *constitution* of Athens during the early Cynic era may have been less directly democratic than in preceding eras, yet the Cynics – as much as if not more than the prized Athenian citizens of the Assembly – deliberately occupied and spoke for the lowest level of society.

In this sense, as technically foreign as Diogenes may have been, I read him and the Cynics as endogenous to a tradition of democratic politics in Athens.

[103] Honig, "Antigone's Laments, Creon's Grief: Mourning, Membership, and the Politics of Exception"; Villa, *Socratic Citizenship*; J. Peter Euben, *The Tragedy of Political Theory* (Princeton, NJ: Princeton University Press, 1990).

[104] Josiah Ober, *The Athenian Revolution* (Princeton, NJ: Princeton University Press, 1998), 20. On immigration practices and the status of metics in ancient Athens, see Demetra Kasimis, "The Tragedy of Blood-Based Membership: Secrecy and the Politics of Immigration in Euripides's *Ion*," *Political Theory* 41, no. 2 (April 1, 2013): 231–256.

Athenians' longstanding suspicion of wealth and the outright praise of asceticism and poverty had roots prior to the emergence of Cynicism. Moreover, as Ober argues, much of the power of Athenian democracy accrued outside of the bounds of the formal constitution.[105] Elites technically controlled formal power but the "mass" leveraged its own influence. In this view, "Athenian democracy [is] a submerged iceberg, only the top of which is visible from an institutional perspective."[106] This influence did not amount to formal equality – the preponderance of institutionalized social differences and inequalities makes it difficult to defend Athenian democracy as an egalitarian polity. But what it has to offer democratic theorists is "a genuine historical example of direct and relatively stable mass (versus elite) political power."[107] Diogenes and the Cynics emerged in the context of this history of nonelite power and politicking; they were both democratic citizens in the active sense and excluded from the formal seats of Athenian political power. This dynamic lies at the heart of actually existing democracies (and is arguably constitutive of them), just as it was present in the Athenian case from the start.

These rich, ambiguous, and paradoxical dimensions of early Cynicism and its relationship to Athenian democracy have been lost. Diogenes' name has become synonymous with both an asceticism and voluntary impoverishment that borders on pathological self-neglect as well as a narcissistic regard for one's own moral purity against the presumably heteronomous conventions of "society."[108] Yet Diogenes's life was political, even by the strictest of Aristotelian categories. He dedicated his life to the quest for a community whose egalitarian principles were not reserved for elites, but extended to all persons irrespective of their ethnicity, place of birth, or gender. In Diogenes's ideal community, individuals could live freely as themselves and could perform their search for their authentic selves even (or especially) when doing so offended community mores. He confused polis borders by politicizing economic inequality; he made the personal political; he taunted, shamed, and humiliated conventional authority; and upended the boundaries and principles that nurture it. To call this antipolitical, to call him an enemy of the polis when the polis was the space in which his critique emerged and the very condition under which he could speak, evades his context in ancient Athens and unfairly grounds arguments about the death of shame, the need for its revival, and the dangers of shamelessness and incivility today.

105 Ober's position contrasts with Mogens Herman Hansen's. Josiah Ober, *Mass and Elite in Democratic Athens: Rhetoric, Ideology, and the Power of the People* (Princeton, NJ: Princeton University Press, 1991); Ober, *The Athenian Revolution.* For an overview of Ober's dispute with Hansen, see *The Athenian Revolution*, Chapter 8, and Gottesman, *Politics and the Street in Democratic Athens*, 6–8.

106 Gottesman, *Politics and the Street in Democratic Athens*, 7.

107 Ober, *The Athenian Revolution*, 20.

108 Shabbir Amanullah, Sabu K. Oomman, and Soumitra Shankar Datta, "'Diogenes Syndrome' Revisited," *German Journal of Psychiatry* 12 (2009): 38–44.

The failure – and perhaps more pointedly, the inability – to comprehend or make sense of Diogenes without recourse to caricatures of him as a public masturbator or moral perfectionist says a great deal about the impoverished state of conversations about shame and its place in a democracy. By highlighting the context of Diogenes' life, emphasizing his place in the Cynic circle, and placing them in a spatial and temporal context, we can see that "death of shame" is not something that happened at a particular time. Myriad forms of shame live on. The Lament That Shame Is Dead is not an account of shame's *actual death*, but reflects an enduring anxiety about strongly egalitarian claims that exceed the bounds of what we consider "political" and extend in to the realms we have called "private" and "social." The Lament reaches a fevered pitch when subjects and new citizens engage in egalitarian, unashamed practices. When we mourn shame's death, or we mourn the death of the properly political, our lamentations constitute and secure a narrow vision of politics that disqualifies others and secures domination. Diogenes and the Cynics responded in kind by disavowing the terms on which elites had constituted the public and the political. Their disavowals, like those of other unashamed citizens, seek to constitute a new vision of the political itself.

3

Rousseau's Pariahs, Rousseau's Laments

Pudeur and the Authentic Ideal in Revolutionary France

> Rousseau is the Diogenes of our time.
>
> – Jean le Rond d'Alembert

> [I]nstinct impels them, and instinct stops them. What will be the substitute for this negative instinct when you have deprived women of modesty? To wait until they no longer care for men is equivalent to waiting until they are no longer good for anything.
>
> – Jean-Jacques Rousseau

Lamented, Lamenter

In this chapter, I turn to Rousseau and the peer group with whom he dwelled. I do so to investigate further the politics of The Lament That Shame Is Dead as an expression of anxiety about the ways in which the ideals of authenticity and self-fulfillment can disrupt the existing social order and unleash an untethered and autochthonous mass that lacks respect for the borders and boundaries the political community needs to survive. Rousseau is critical to this study precisely because he is a central theorist of the authentic ideal that criticizes "society" and Enlightenment civilization for its artificial constraints on man's essential character and ability to represent himself without shame or regret. His critics accuse him of fomenting civilizational decline because his radical egalitarianism calls for a total reworking of the social order. At the same time, unlike Diogenes, he offers up his own version of The Lament as he decries the loss of *pudeur* (feminine modesty) and the evisceration of the gender difference and deference *pudeur* guarantees. Unlike the relatively autonomous and self-sufficient Cynics, the fragile republican men in Rousseau's texts need constant affirmation and protection. Rousseau gives them this protection with *pudeur* and accuses the philosophes and literary men and women of destroying a more natural form of civilization, especially with respect to the gender roles Rousseau believes are essential to the social order.

Rousseau's politics and the paradoxes of transparency and concealment they engender therefore work both sides of the presumed opposition of shame and authenticity.[1] True to the paradoxes for which he is known, Rousseau is a lamenter in his own right whose life, ideals, and legacy are routinely lamented in both his time and ours. Each case – those who lament Rousseau's shameless destruction of the social order and status quo and those whose shamelessness Rousseau laments for their particular brand of destruction – traffics in the language of nostalgia and loss central to The Lament. This is significant because it indicates the degree to which "shame" – like its apparent opposites, "shamelessness," "authenticity," or "pride" – lacks an ontology that secures any particular normative politics. Rather, shame and its opposites are deployed as part of a signifying practice of braking and restraint that identifies the subject who disavows shame (or particular forms of shame) as unregulated and unchecked and assigns power – an "empire" – to those, especially women, who live with shame and modesty.[2] This chapter shows the ways in which preoccupations with brakes and restraint emerge when ideas of political equality extend to social outsiders and call into question hierarchical social orders based upon birth status, gender, and class.

I begin with a discussion of Rousseau's *Confessions* and the broader promise of what I call Rousseau's Romantic invitation and the authentic life it idealizes. From there, I place Rousseau's own shame and sense of himself as a pariah in the context of the shaming dynamics in play in the eighteenth-century "republic of letters." I then turn to Rousseau's implicit and explicit influence on (overlapping) prerevolutionary groups of agitators. I first consider the men of "Grub Street," who come alive in Robert Darnton's signature work about the literary side market comprised of men who strived to enter the "republic of letters" and were routinely denied entry for lack of aristocratic ties or status. I use Darnton's account of "Grub Street" lives and writings to get some purchase on how these writers performed the work of unashamed citizenship. I also turn to one of Darnton's critics, Darrin McMahon, to show how Rousseau's paeans to the "natural" life also authorized the work of counter-Enlightenment writers. And I close my discussion of Rousseau's readers with "disloyal daughters," women like Olympe de Gouges and Madame Roland, who found strength in Rousseau's ideas to challenge republican gender roles and were executed for both the impurity of their politics and the gender trouble they fomented in postrevolutionary France. Having established the unruly social

[1] On the paradoxes of transparency and concealment in Rousseau, see Jean Starobinski, *Jean-Jacques Rousseau: Transparency and Obstruction*, trans. Arthur Goldhammer (Chicago: University of Chicago Press, 1988); Elizabeth Rose Wingrove, *Rousseau's Republican Romance* (Princeton, NJ: Princeton University Press, 2000).

[2] Jean-Jacques Rousseau, *Emile: or, On Education*, trans. Allan Bloom (New York: Basic Books, 1979), 393.

and political cacophony that Rousseau's ideas authorize, I analyze the ways in which Rousseauean *pudeur* tempers and manages the social disruption authorized by Rousseau's critique of "society" and defense of the "natural" life. I close with some reflections on the ways in which on-the-ground social and political activity (evidenced in Rousseau's readers' politics) productively complicates theoretical and philosophical discussions of shame and authenticity.

Rousseau's Romantic Invitation

The theme of the person who is perennially misunderstood and expected to live by a life script so different from the one dictated by the heart undergirds Rousseau's works. One of Rousseau's central messages is that there is something unjust in having to live a "false" life in order to fit into the social world, and he underscores this injustice in his assaults on civility, politeness, fancy dress, theatricality, and other accoutrements of society. Rousseau's texts in general, and the *Confessions* and *Julie* (*La Nouvelle Héloïse*) in particular, reach out to his audience to forge an alliance between author and reader to make the readers feel his pain. In an introductory essay to the *Confessions*, J.M. Cohen notes, "One is readily drawn into [Rousseau's] dream world in which every man's hand is against him, and [watches] with horrified sympathy."[3] Tracy Strong argues that Rousseau shows how "the world in which we live makes it hard for us to act like ourselves."[4] This difficulty of living in the world as "true" selves underscores Rousseau's sense that genuine republican politics requires that citizens live authentic lives in which they feel free in their hearts and affirmed and loved by their fellow citizens, with whom they constitute the state.

I read Rousseau's oeuvre as seeking to establish a common human bond among men amidst a modern world that Rousseau believes has divided and isolated men from each other. That bond is forged through a common experience of shame that all men wish to overcome. The story of *Julie*, as Lori Marso explains, is the story of "a man at the margins of society, Saint-Preux" who is up against "a man already considered an upstanding citizen, ... Wolmar."[5] In a modern, bourgeois world, Rousseau asks: Who but a few of us feels like he fits in, comes from the right place, speaks the right way, and has the right knowledge? Who among us doesn't dream of being liberated from the self-doubt and self-negation brought on by social regimes of comparison and envy? His answer is no one. Everyone wants to live a life that feels authentic and true and relatively free from the constraints of artificial social expectations. Rousseau's

3 Jean-Jacques Rousseau, *The Confessions*, trans. J.M. Cohen (New York: Penguin Books, 1953), 12.

4 Tracy B. Strong, *Jean Jacques Rousseau: The Politics of the Ordinary* (Lanham, MD: Rowman & Littlefield, 2002), 31.

5 Lori Marso, *(Un)Manly Citizens: Jean-Jacques Rousseau's and Germaine de Staël's Subversive Women* (Baltimore: Johns Hopkins University Press, 1999), 56.

republicanism and his ideal of authenticity are therefore mutually reinforcing. As Charles Taylor notes in his work on the democratic and egalitarian character of the culture of authenticity, only imperious and imperial regimes require citizens to live as something other than who they are or believe themselves to be.[6] To modify Elizabeth Wingrove's apt phrase, Rousseau allows his readers to imagine a "romantic republic" in which citizens can feel the beat of each other's hearts and are, as Strong puts it, "able to live with others as what one is" – without shame or regret.[7] Rousseau therefore inserts an essential psychological and therapeutic requirement into prerevolutionary debates about what the nascent republican spirit must consider and how shame disables meaningful equality and civic engagement.

The *Confessions* was published posthumously, but Rousseau read the book aloud for public audiences during his lifetime.[8] These public readings would have only intensified the sense of identification between the audience and "Jean-Jacques," as he came to be known. Rousseau dramatized his life in terms of the outsider who did not fit into the social world. He projected his own experience as a pariah to launch a broader criticism of the literary world of *le monde* and the false virtues and values that reigned there. The work is generally understood to have inaugurated the modern confessional memoir as Rousseau inserted himself into a larger story governing his oeuvre – a story about man's natural goodness corrupted by an elite and effeminate literary world that valued social power and status over honesty and virtue. Rousseau's performance of his own unhappiness connected shame and misery to injustice and inequality as he told his own stories of shame and suffering at the hands of illegitimate authorities. Thus Rousseau sketches his "autonomy through self-subjection"; that is to say, it is only through a self-narration of injury and misery that Rousseau is able to represent himself as an autonomous subject.[9] He writes that for a long time he was a slave to the opinions of others, and easily made to feel ashamed or disgraced. In his words, "I was always extremely sensitive to disgrace" and "more upset at displeasing [others] ... than at being punished." Rousseau wanted his readers to believe and understand that his "strongest [and most plaguing] desire was to be loved by everyone who came near [him]."[10] He connected his misery to an unhealthy preoccupation with the impressions of others and the ease with which he could be made to feel ashamed. His narrative of self-loathing and longing to be free from the judgment of others who cast one as undesirable caught fire in Europe of the eighteenth century.

[6] Taylor, *A Secular Age*, 473–504.

[7] Wingrove, *Rousseau's Republican Romance*; Strong, *Jean Jacques Rousseau*, 149.

[8] Mary Seidman Trouille, *Sexual Politics in the Enlightenment: Women Writers Read Rousseau* (Albany: SUNY Press, 1997), 372 n32.

[9] Wingrove, *Rousseau's Republican Romance*, 132.

[10] Rousseau, *The Confessions*, 25.

Of particular relevance to the subtext of The Lament and its concerns, especially with respect to the contemporary critique(s) of the "therapeutic turn" in political discourse, the *Confessions* transformed imposed silence into a question of justice. The Lament seeks to conceal and suppress stories that are too personal or too therapeutic – too much of a display of private feeling and too intrusive on others. Rousseau performatively resisted this silencing. He regaled his readers with stories of public urination and masochism – "the ridiculous and the shameful," which are "hardest to confess." Like Diogenes, he promised to go on speaking frankly and coarsely – drawing upon the "courage" required in telling all and disregarding any social costs that will come from it.[11] He apologized for being so candid, but insisted that candor reveals the "truth."[12] This message from *The Confessions* reiterates a central lesson of *Emile* about the inherent goodness of the coarse and vulgar speech of country life compared to the evil and "polite" manners of "the rich," who teach their children "the words to use so that no one will dare to resist them."[13] Again and again, Rousseau told the story that nothing was worse than *imposed silence*; he would not "conceal[] the truth from the reader."[14] His readers (and listeners) got the message that their silence and fear about speaking the truth, even if it is unpopular, must also be overcome.

There is a double move at work in this aspect of the text as Rousseau describes both the pressure to be reticent as an author speaking to an audience in "society" and the pressure to be reticent he felt as a child living in the house of an "oafish, violent young man who managed in a very short time to quench all the fire of [his] childhood."[15] Rousseau's story of himself as a child who was afraid to speak engenders sympathy, naturalizing the link between reticence and injustice, which can then extend to his adult self who claims to stumble in speaking freely before his readers (or listeners) in the present moment. Like man in a more natural state, he writes, "I was used to … having no desires that I did not express.… Imagine my fate in a house where I dared not open my lips."[16] The house where the innocent child is too afraid to speak what he knows to be true tracks onto Rousseau's broader critique of society and the injustices of its conventions. Rousseau linked his representation of the house and his representation of eighteenth-century culture to underscore the injustice of life for the simple and sensitive man who could not dare to open his mouth and speak from the heart without inviting mockery and humiliation.

While much of this story was clearly an exaggerated performance, especially Rousseau's self-representation as a country boy who couldn't navigate Parisian

[11] Ibid., 28.
[12] Ibid., 65.
[13] Rousseau, *Emile*, 86.
[14] Rousseau, *The Confessions*, 170.
[15] Ibid., 39.
[16] Ibid., 40.

society, there is no question that Rousseau was mocked and humiliated by the arbiters of literary society who lamented his shameless sentimentality as an attack on civilization and its requirements. Similarly, there is also no question that Rousseau's message resonated with others who felt mocked and humiliated. Rousseau brings the *Confessions* to an end with an explanation of his falling out with Madame d'Epinay, Diderot, and Voltaire, the latter two of whom he charges with jealousy of his accomplishments. Eugene Stelzig, in his work on Romantic autobiography, puts it this way: "Clearly, Rousseau wanted to explain himself – to present his side of the story, his version of himself, which he thought had been willfully preempted by the false public image or maligned legend of 'Jean-Jacques' fabricated by his detractors and enemies, who after the traumatic shock of his flight from France began to loom large in his increasingly paranoid imagination."[17] Rousseau's *Confessions* were therefore not only a way to "identify, celebrate, and invoke as a standard the wholeness, integrity, and transparency progressively lost in, covered over, or corrupted by history," but also a chance for Rousseau to redeem his reputation and, perhaps more importantly, to disclose publicly and politicize openly the shame and suffering he experienced at the hands of "society." Stelzig elaborates: "The author's claims of full disclosure and of having the reader judge are really a strategy of disarming the reader's judgment. Rousseau's most compromising confessions are always self-exculpating – his intentions were always good, even if his misdeeds cannot be excused in terms of their putative consequences."[18] As the arbiters of French literary society worried about the social disorder Rousseau's Romantic naturalism would unleash, the *Confessions* modelled and promoted the undoing of received mores and manners and the tyranny on which they rested. Rousseau's autobiography presented an opportunity to indulge the democratic fantasy of a second birth – a reinvention of self – that could be possible once one is free from shame.

This fantasy of a new beginning was important for Rousseau and also inspired his many followers. By telling his version of his life story, Rousseau painted a sympathetic portrait of himself that offset the humiliating attacks by his contemporary interlocutors – "the carping Encyclopedist friends like Denis Diderot and Friedrich Melchior Grimm" who had mocked and lamented his unashamed "attempt to return to the standard of nature in modern society" and his literary-philosophical talent, more broadly.[19] Diderot called *Julie* "3 or 4 pages worth reading and 1,000 pages of 'moralizing speeches.' "[20] Grimm had referred to "priggish Julie and her pedantic tutor"; the antiphilosophe

[17] Eugene L. Stelzig, *The Romantic Subject in Autobiography: Rousseau and Goethe* (Charlottesville: University of Virginia Press, 2000), 29.

[18] Ibid., 38.

[19] Ibid., 19.

[20] Trouille, *Sexual Politics in the Enlightenment*, 105.

critic Élie Fréron called it fake, affected, artificial, and false wit.[21] Finally, and perhaps most scandalously, Madame d'Épinay, Rousseau's friend and literary rival, had written *Madame*, her own *Julie*, through which she explicitly hoped to attack and surpass Rousseau's reputation. "In my eyes, René [her name for Rousseau] is nothing but a moral dwarf perched on stilts," d'Épinay's protagonist proudly proclaims.[22]

Part of the power of the *Confessions* and its broader appeal was the way it communicated the idea that an individual *could* have the last word about the meaning of his own life. Social scripts written by others abound, yet Rousseau insisted that one could author his own life story, give it meaning, and die unashamed. Because Strong reads the *Confessions* as a "tracing" rather than an authored text, he insists that Rousseau avoids the transcendental position of the author.[23] Strong therefore prefers to see the *Confessions* as a book that is not about uncovering the "real" Rousseau per se, but telling the story of the human, whom only the citizen (and not the author) can know. The moral of the story is "by knowing me, you know yourself."[24] Yet the distinction is not so sharp. By getting in the last word against the slandering philosophes and the tales told about him, Rousseau may not in fact have redeemed his reputation or authorized the beginning of a new life story. But by speaking to and enacting this fantasy of second birth he reached out to the maligned heart and the sense of being misunderstood in everyone.

The *Confessions* therefore shores up an important Rousseauean message: the modern world is a particularly cruel place for those who dare to feel. Given that Rousseau claimed to see the greatest joys and pleasures of life as requiring this dare – and daring to enjoy the feeling of being open to each other, in particular – he thought it would be inhumane to ask men to steel themselves against the cruel world. Whereas contemporary discussions about the brutality of the world in the face of a politics of confession tend to ask the individual to be more reticent and to heed the impulses of shame, Rousseau's confessional politics are both individually therapeutic and politically necessary. Accordingly, he strives to craft a world in which his simple and sensitive men could speak and reveal their true selves without fear of shame or mockery. This involved changing the world from the ground up in order to protect men's fragility. I will return to this strategy of protection and its relationship to the gendered paradoxes of Rousseauean authenticity, in particular. But first I want to examine how many of Rousseau's readers took up his call for an authentic life and politicized shame as fundamentally antirepublican.

[21] Ibid.
[22] Ibid., 102.
[23] Strong, *Jean Jacques Rousseau*, 18.
[24] Ibid., 17.

Rousseau and the "Republic of Letters"

As many scholars have noted, a counterpublic with a republican spirit emerged in the waning years of the Ancien Régime. It was a site of intellectual and philosophical exchange among an emerging literary class, most of whom – like Marquis de Condorcet – had aristocratic provenance but embraced a republican spirit. (Some – like Denis Diderot – came from the nascent bourgeoisie, but the literary counterpublic was by and large comprised of elites.) People of the "republic of letters," as it came be known, attended the theater and salon gatherings, joined the various French national academies, and also penned epistolary exchanges that served to develop their philosophical and literary talent while advancing ideas they believed were for the good of France and humanity.[25] The philosophes, as leading men like d'Alembert, Diderot, and especially Voltaire were known, saw the republic of letters as what Darnton calls "the literary counterpart to the 'atomic' individualism of Physiocratic theory, a society of independent but fraternal individuals, in which the best men won but all derived dignity, as well as a living, from service to the common cause."[26] Yet the truth was much different from this alleged meritocracy of talent and effort. The "republic" existed quite comfortably in the shadow and protective cover of the Ancien Régime even as the philosophes saw their subculture as a relatively egalitarian literary community in which all voices were equally valued.

Part of the mythology of the "republican" part of the republic of letters was the fantasy that people from the provinces could migrate into Paris to join the literary world. Diderot had successfully navigated the provinces-to-Paris migration, becoming the exemplary philosophe who was once the "son of a cutler."[27] But the reality was much bleaker. The "republic of letters" operated like the rest of the Old Regime: "individuals got ahead as best they could

[25] Dena Goodman, *The Republic of Letters: A Cultural History of the French Enlightenment* (Ithaca: Cornell University Press, 1996); Steven Kale, "Women, Salons, and the State in the Aftermath of the French Revolution," *Journal of Women's History* 13, no. 4 (2002): 54–80; Steven Kale, *French Salons: High Society and Political Sociability from the Old Regime to the Revolution of 1848* (Baltimore: The Johns Hopkins University Press, 2005). There is some scholarly debate about the place of the salon in the "republic of letters." For a full treatment see Antoine Lilti, *The World of the Salons: Sociability and Worldliness in Eighteenth-Century Paris* (Oxford: Oxford University Press, 2015).

[26] Robert Darnton, "The High Enlightenment and the Low-Life of Literature in Pre-Revolutionary France," *Past & Present* no. 51 (May 1, 1971), 81–115: 99. Darnton's account is not universal, but it has become canonical. I am not taking sides in the "Darnton debates" but rather drawing from Darnton's accounts of the muckraking of "Grub Street"; the shame and humiliation felt among the "literary low-life"; and the extent to which the "republic of letters" lamented the arrival of men of low rank as legitimate participants in the conversation about the future of France. For the controversy, see Haydn Trevor Mason, *The Darnton Debate: Books and Revolution in the Eighteenth Century* (Voltaire Foundation, 1998).

[27] Peter France, *Politeness and Its Discontents: Problems in French Classical Culture* (New York: Cambridge University Press, 2006), 146.

in a labyrinth of baroque institutions ... [ruled by] privilege and protection, not ... demonstration of talent."[28] D'Alembert and others waxed poetic about a republic of letters that differed from the humiliating practices of patronage, yet as he stresses in the *Essai sur les gens de lettres et les grands* (1752), they believed that "society is and ought to be hierarchical and that the *grands* [literary elite] belonged on top."[29] Migration to Paris was significant, and the republic was small and exclusive. Diderot's exemplary case was not all that it appeared: His father was a tradesman and did not have a title (and hence was not in the First Estate), but his family were landowners and relatively wealthy compared to others forging their way in the Paris literary scene.[30]

Les Rousseaus du Ruisseau

As Darnton argues in his highly influential study, a resentful side economy and cultural scene emerged in "Grub Street," the space of the French prerevolutionary literary low-life. Publishing monopolies had prevented Grub Street books from reaching the formal market, which meant their writers had to write whatever would generate an income. They survived by "spying for the police and peddling pornography; and they filled their writings with imprecations against *le monde* that humiliated and corrupted them."[31] Because they existed outside of the literary elite, they could not be the authentic republican subject who wrote from the heart – they wrote whatever would garner payment. This precarious social status led them to become protorevolutionary pamphleteers, moralizing about the dangers and fraudulence of Court society. Their work was self-consciously libelous in spirit, as it attacked not only the ideas of the Ancien Régime but also the character of the people in it. Darnton notes: "The crude pamphleteering of Grub Street.... expressed the passion of men who hated the Old Regime in their guts, who ached with the hatred of it. It was from such visceral hatred, not from the refined abstractions of the contented cultural elite, that the extreme Jacobin revolution found its authentic voice."[32]

Adding to the humiliation of rejection was the extent to which Voltaire and the others characterized them as "poor hacks," "dregs of humanity," and

[28] Darnton, "The High Enlightenment and the Low-Life of Literature in Pre-Revolutionary France," 99.

[29] Ibid., 91.

[30] France, *Politeness and Its Discontents*, 146.

[31] Darnton, "The High Enlightenment and the Low-Life of Literature in Pre-Revolutionary France," 98.

[32] Ibid., 115. Scholars dispute the degree to which the men of Grub Street and the "psychological toll" of their humiliation drove the Revolution as much as Darnton suggests. There appears to be little dispute, however, about the exclusionary practices of the "republic of letters," its relationship to the Ancien Régime, and Darnton's general characterization of Grub Street life. See Darrin M. McMahon, "The Counter-Enlightenment and the Low-Life of Literature in Pre-Revolutionary France," *Past & Present* no. 159 (1998): 77–112. See also Mason, *The Darnton Debate*.

a "ragged rabble" that "crowded the bottom of the literary world."[33] Just as Voltaire and Diderot had lamented Rousseau's crass naturalism as a threat to eighteenth-century French civilization, so too did they read the "hacks" as threats to the legitimate, civil, and honest literary market. The "literary low-life" was characterized as "on a social level below prostitutes" because its writers were paid money rather than supported by the protective cover of elite patronage or the academies.[34] The philosophes pathologized them in all of the vocabulary of The Lament: They were uncivilized; they were immoral; they had come from the wrong place; they wrote and spoke in the wrong way; they did not heed the spatial divisions of the "republic of letters," and so on. They were (from) beyond the pale.

Most of the men of Grub Street's names are unrecognizable today.[35] A few stand out: One of its heroes was Jean-Paul Marat, the famous revolutionary pamphleteer and editor of the radical *L'Ami du Peuple* immortalized in *The Death of Marat* by Jacques-Louis David (1793).[36] Charles Thévenau de Morande, who referred to himself as "*le philosophe cynique*," was also a paradigmatic *libelliste*. His attack on Mme DuBarry, Louis XV's mistress, exemplified the Grub Street style: "passing directly from the brothel to the throne, toppling the most powerful and redoubtable minister, overthrowing the constitution of the monarchy, insulting the royal family, the presumptive heir to the throne, and his august consort by her incredible luxury, by her insolent talk, [and insulting] the entire nation, which is dying of hunger, by her vainglorious extravagance and by the well-known depredations of all the roués surrounding her, as she sees groveling at her feet not only the *grands* of the kingdom and the ministers, but the princes of the royal blood, foreign ambassadors, and the church itself, which canonizes her scandals and her debauchery."[37] This passage captures the *ressentiment* of the "psychological toll" of groveling for crumbs at the feet of *le monde,* being mocked for doing so, and realizing how indebted the literary republic was to the Ancien Régime.[38]

Rousseau was of course both part of *le monde* and thriving in it. He had won the Académie de Dijon prize for his *First Discourse*, and wrote and lived under the support of various patrons, most notably Madame d'Epinay, whose estate, l'Ermitage, was where he wrote most of *La Nouvelle Héloïse*. But after several fallings out with his friends, Rousseau took the occasion to attack Paris and the literary establishment explicitly. Rousseau tells his readers in his

[33] Darnton, "The High Enlightenment and the Low-Life of Literature in Pre-Revolutionary France," 94–95.

[34] Ibid., 95.

[35] Darnton notes that there were more than 600 men of Grub Street.

[36] Darnton, "The High Enlightenment and the Low-Life of Literature in Pre-Revolutionary France," 98. See also Ernest Belfort Bax, *Jean-Paul Marat: The People's Friend* (G. Richards, 1901).

[37] Darnton, "The High Enlightenment and the Low-Life of Literature in Pre-Revolutionary France," 110.

[38] Ibid., 104.

Confessions that as much as he found life in Paris quite pleasurable, he both needed and pined for the simplicity of Geneva to allow him to live as an ordinary man. That he spends most of his life outside of Geneva while writing as a "citizen" of it complicates the authenticity of Rousseau's own claims to the country, but it was certainly part of his strategy of representing himself as a social outsider who was never at home in the sophisticated and crowded city ruled by social elites.

Moreover, and central to Rousseau's concern about the simple man's shame and fledgling self-esteem, the Genevan patrician class's envious disposition toward Paris communicated the inadequacy and shamefulness of the artisanal culture with which Rousseau sought to identify. Some of this is complicated by the degree to which Encyclopedists saw their writing and contribution to knowledge as a craft – and a craft that was paid – but the division between the making of material objects associated with the countryside and the making of books for a newly Enlightened world was nonetheless significant. As Rousseau had written in the *Second Discourse*, he believed that men learned to be ashamed only when the world became big enough for them to compare themselves to others: "Everyone began to look at everyone else and to wish to be looked at himself, and public esteem acquired a value. The one who sang or danced best; the handsomest, the strongest, the most skillful, ... came to be the most highly regarded, and this was the first step at once toward inequality and vice: from these first preferences arose vanity and contempt on the one hand, shame and envy on the other; and the fermentation caused by these new leavens eventually produced compounds fatal to happiness and innocence."[39] The mere fact of Genevans' knowledge of opulent Paris, he worried, made it impossible for simple men *not* to be ashamed of who they were, and this shame made it impossible for them to cultivate the "life with others" (Strong) that was so central to Rousseau's idealized Genevan republicanism.[40] These concerns about the culture of seeing and being seen, of sizing each other up for marks of status and sophistication, are central to Rousseau's critique of d'Alembert's entry on Geneva and his insistence that the city was nothing without a theater.

[39] Jean-Jacques Rousseau, *First and Second Discourses, Together with Replies to the Critics and Essay on the Origin of Languages* (New York: Harper Collins, 1986), 175.

[40] In addition to making Genevan men ashamed of who they were and how they lived, there were express economic implications here, as well. The ascent of the patrician class and the banking industry with which it was associated would override the artisanal culture, destroying a simple, honest way of life and an endogenous economy, as well. When d'Alembert represents Geneva in terms of its failures to be Parisian enough, he taps into political divisions on the ground as well as Rousseau's fear that (Geneva's) Spartan virtues cannot in fact be reconciled with the urbanity of Athens, as d'Alembert promises. Rousseau's letter can be read as a eulogy for ordinary Geneva that is under assault on multiple fronts. D'Alembert's entry represents this broader assault; and in responding to d'Alembert, Rousseau writes back to Paris and those who would spread its values. See Helena Rosenblatt, *Rousseau and Geneva: From the First Discourse to the Social Contract, 1749–1762* (New York: Cambridge University Press, 1997).

Rousseau's *Letter to M. d'Alembert on the Theater* was undoubtedly also an occasion for a personal attack on d'Alembert and the philosophes who spent their days and nights at the salons, and one that would win him sympathy with literary outsiders. D'Alembert's relationship with Julie Lespinasse also provides some context for Rousseau's critique of the "womanish" salon men. D'Alembert had a long friendship with Lespinasse, the influential salonnière with whom he lived and collaborated on works that would attract the attention of other men of letters. In a typical collaboration, Lespinasse would dictate the letter to d'Alembert, whom she referred to as her "secretary"; she spoke, he transcribed. Susan Dalton elaborates:

> The very idea that Lespinasse is the creative force and d'Alembert is the scribe is in itself humorous, given that it is usually Lespinasse's job to promote, guide, and comment on the work of the philosophes. At the same time, the discipline to which Lespinasse subjects d'Alembert in forcing him into an inferior position in the letter-writing process satirizes the real power that she has to impose discipline in the salon. [In one letter] ... d'Alembert writes, in parentheses, that "the secretary [himself] would have liked to have offered his reflections on the matter, but he is forbidden to do so and it is the very least little sacrifice that he could make."[41]

Rousseau's depiction of the effeminate, unmanly men who are incapable of self-governance because they spend so much time in salons, "always constrained in these voluntary prisons, get[ing] up, sit[ting] down, ... turn[ing] and pirouette[ing] about the room, while the idol, stretched out motionlessly on her couch, has only her eyes and her tongue active," directly corresponds to d'Alembert's life and was surely a thinly veiled direct attack on him.[42]

That d'Alembert, Voltaire, and other philosophes analogized Rousseau to Diogenes, calling him the "Diogenes of our time," is quite telling on this question. The more refined Greek and Roman philosophers and orators (e.g., Aristotle, Cicero) and their contemporary heirs have lamented Diogenes and the Cynics' primitive, shameless, and uncivil disregard for the splendor of Athenian traditional morals, practices, and institutions. Similarly, the princes of France's literary establishment attacked Rousseau for his foolish naturalism and distrust of society, civilization, reason, and Enlightenment. Their critique resonates in Darnton's account of the men whose coarse and libelous writings brought down the Ancien Régime. By contrast, the philosophes are said to be engaged in philosophical and political exchanges of ideas; their attacks are generally understood as properly literary – respectful, civil, and decorous. The philosophes come from the right place; they speak and write in the right way. The hacks, perennial outsiders, are shameless, uncivil threats to nascent republican civilization based upon terms created in direct opposition to them.

For reasons that should be clear, the men of Grub Street identified directly with Rousseau. The story was that Rousseau had "risen from their ranks into

41 Susan Dalton, *Engendering the Republic of Letters: Reconnecting Public and Private Spheres in Eighteenth-Century Europe* (Montreal: McGill-Queen's University Press, 2003), 45.

42 Jean-Jacques Rousseau, *Politics and the Arts: Letter to M. D'Alembert on the Theater*, trans. Allan Bloom (Ithaca: Cornell University Press, 1968), 101–102.

le monde, seen it for what it was, exposed elitist culture itself as the very agent of social corruption, and returned with his semi-literate, working-class wife to a humble existence in the neighborhood of Grub Street, where he died pure and purged. The hacks respected him and despised Voltaire."[43] In their eyes, Rousseau understood their plight and the hypocrisy and faux-republican character of the Parisian literary scene. Aptly called the "Rousseaus du ruisseau" (Rousseaus of the gutter), they embraced the discourse of Rousseauean naturalism and authenticity to attack establishment and elitism in all of its forms.[44] As Darnton puts it, "their pornographic details got the point [that social rot was consuming French society] across to a public that could not assimilate the Social Contract."[45] They took Rousseauean disgust with elites and concern for the ordinary man and made it viscerally accessible to everyone. This democratization of Rousseau's message was seen as entirely consistent with Rousseau's republicanism as it provided a valuable political and social counterweight to the literary establishment that covered its power, privilege, and dependence upon the Court with the rhetoric of equality, reason, and civility.

Rousseauean Royalists

A follow-up study to Darnton's uncovers the extent to which many of the men of Grub Street sided with the traditionalism of the French Court and High Church, which they saw as natural (against the artificiality of reason). Their financial motives must also be considered, as they were also writing for money, and the traditionalists paid well. Exemplifying this group was Antoine Sabatier who had "come from Castres in *sabots*," as d'Alembert put it disparagingly.[46] Sabatier made a long journey into *le monde*, "mak[ing] a go of it in good hack fashion, seeing his first play ... through to production ... and supplementing his meager income with a variety of publications: epigrams, madrigals, epistles and licentious verse."[47] He was ultimately offered a small stipend, but Sabatier wanted more. "Not content with a mere pension," Darrin McMahon elaborates:

> [Sabatier] set about trying to take the literary *monde* by storm. He made the rounds of the salons. He sought out the eminent writers of the day. He published glowing panegyrics of Voltaire. But despite this determined effort, ... Sabatier was met with

[43] Darnton, "The High Enlightenment and the Low-Life of Literature in Pre-Revolutionary France," 111.

[44] "Rousseaus du ruisseau" was a term applied to Restif de la Bretonne in the eighteenth Century; it fits many of Restif's Grub Street comrades. Ibid., 110 n86.

[45] Ibid., 110.

[46] McMahon, "The Counter-Enlightenment and the Low-Life of Literature in Pre-Revolutionary France," 90. McMahon notes: "the word *sabot*, a play on Sabatier, refers to the wooden clogs worn by the *peuple*, and is thus a reference to [Sabatier's] less than genteel condition. Voltaire's letters are replete with other such damning portrayals of Sabatier, described as a *scélérat* (scoundrel) and a *petit monster* (little monster), whose writing is 'the worst' in the French language" (n43).

[47] Ibid., 89.

disappointment. His attempts to flatter the king of Ferney, and his overtures to the first minister of the intellectual world, d'Alembert, were bluntly refused. As d'Alembert later boasted in a letter to Voltaire, the perpetual secretary of the Academy had "chased" this "little vagabond" (*gueux*) ... out of his house "like a lackey."[48]

Frustrated and humiliated by these persistent attacks, Sabatier joined the antiphilosophes. He spent the rest of his literary life working on the *Tableau philosophique de l'esprit de M. de Voltaire*, a catalogue of Voltaire's "personal slurs, his *bons mots* and blows below the belt," which was designed to show the cruel alliance between Voltaire and the king of Ferney.[49] Critics described Sabatier's attacks on Voltaire as "character assassination, of the homeopathic variety," emphasizing the therapeutic release that came from being able to "write back" to the philosophes who had excluded, mocked, and humiliated them.[50]

For those struggling with the resentment they felt for being rejected by the literary republic, the fact that Rousseau had attacked salon culture and praised ancient, "natural" morals had great appeal. Sabatier had agreed with some of the attacks on Rousseau's work – the "Sorbonne's censure of *Emile* in 1762," for example – "[y]et he also defended Rousseau, describing him ... as the 'most manly, the most profound, the most sublime writer of the century,' despite his 'paradoxes' and 'errors.' On the whole, Sabatier was inclined to treat Rousseau as a case apart [from the rest of the literary establishment]."[51] Rousseau responded to the court loyalists sympathetically because of their common hostility to the *philosophe* and his world. What united the antiphilosophes was "bitter, cultural resentment: the conviction that France had been hoodwinked by charlatans and was much the worse for it."[52] Rousseau was sympathetic to this critique, and in the *Dialogues* Rousseau attacked the philosophes directly, writing in a voice sounding much like Sabatier.[53] Beyond the text, Rousseau the person came to the aid of people he saw as unjustly persecuted by the arbiters of the republic of letters.

One such person was the French writer Jean-Marie-Bernard Clément, whom Rousseau bailed out when he was thrown in jail for slandering the philosophe Jean François de Saint-Lambert. Clément had come to Paris from Dijon in order to join the republic of letters where he imagined a literary life alongside his heroes, most notably Voltaire but also Saint-Lambert himself. "At the tender age of eighteen, [Clément] wrote to Voltaire, beseeching guidance, describing himself as 'a young man who loves you because he loves your works, who owes you everything because your writings have taught him how to think.' "[54] But

[48] Ibid., 90.
[49] Ibid., 90–91.
[50] Ibid., 90.
[51] Ibid., 108.
[52] Ibid., 102.
[53] Ibid., 109.
[54] Ibid., 95.

Clément, like the others who came from the provinces in search of the company of philosophes and a life with them, was rebuffed and ultimately turned on the literary "republic" for its elitist hypocrisy.

Rousseau had written about the ways in which the city intensified the shame of rural poverty. To have been simply poor in the country was honorable, but to grovel for money in the city while living in poverty was humiliating.[55] Paid work of any kind, not only writing, was considered dishonorable by the arbiters of French society, and Rousseau provided a helpful frame for criticizing the paradox of being forced to work because of one's (low) social status and being pathologized for deigning to do so. Clément, like the others, found his way in the literary side market of the "low-life" or Grub Street, and never earned any recognition by Voltaire and the others. He became quickly disillusioned and began to embrace the traditionalist, counter-Enlightenment worldview. When given the chance to attack, he wrote a review that described Saint-Lambert's "*Les Saisons*" as an "eternally wearying monotony," indicative of the "devastating effects of *philosophie* on the century's taste."[56] This libel landed him in jail, arranged by Saint-Lambert, providing further evidence of the philosophes' cozy relationship with the Ancien Régime. Rousseau sympathized with Clément's critique and his predicament, and bailed him out. Rousseau was no doubt also happy to level his own blow at Saint-Lambert, who had been the lover of Sophie d'Houdetot, Rousseau's great love.[57]

Disloyal Daughters

For readers familiar with and sensitive to the patent misogyny in Rousseau's texts and the ways in which Rousseau figures Woman as a perennial threat to the sovereignty of republican man, it is initially surprising to learn the degree to which Rousseau befriended so many eighteenth-century women, who in turn drew strength from his friendship and ideas.[58] Women followed Rousseau for different reasons. Some women were, understandably, empowered by his domestic prescriptions that gave women a positive role in childrearing and home-making and criticized the familial distance of aristocratic institutions like convent schools for girls and wet nurses for infants. He had written *Emile*

[55] Rousseau, *The Confessions*, 55–57.

[56] McMahon, "The Counter-Enlightenment and the Low-Life of Literature in Pre-Revolutionary France," 96.

[57] Ibid., 96, 108. Rousseau recounts the triangulation among Saint-Lambert, Sophie, and himself in the *Confessions*. Rousseau, *The Confessions*, 445–456.

[58] An important exception within Rousseau scholarship in political theory is Lori Marso, *(Un)Manly Citizens*. Historians have generally been more conscious of the significance of Rousseau's women readers. See Mary Trouille, *Sexual Politics in the Enlightenment*; Jennifer J. Popiel, *Rousseau's Daughters: Domesticity, Education, and Autonomy in Modern France* (Lebanon: University of New Hampshire Press, 2008); and Annie Smart, *Citoyennes: Women and the Ideal of Citizenship in Eighteenth-Century France* (Lanham, MD: University of Delaware Press, 2011).

in order to "gratify a good mother who knows how to think"; there and elsewhere, Rousseau praised women's intelligence and thoughtfulness while criticizing the artificiality of a culture that limited their "natural" powers, most specifically the power to care for their children through breastfeeding.[59] Nothing epitomized Rousseau's understanding of women's natural, essential role in the republic and the degree to which the aristocracy squandered it than breastfeeding. So preoccupied with the practice, he wove sashes for his female friends as wedding presents, "to be worn on condition that they breastfeed their babies."[60] *Emile* did more than any public health campaign could have to increase breastfeeding in France.[61] Rousseau promised elite women real authority – authority over their home and families, authority to raise men and citizens.

Equally common was the case of women who found Rousseau's tributes to women's natural authority compelling and inspiring, but chose to exceed the roles that Rousseau had sought to prescribe so carefully. Madame Roland, who became a leader in Girondin circles, initially found Rousseau's cult of domesticity empowering.[62] *Julie* had resonated with her so much that she claimed to have read it for inspiration every year until her death.[63] Far and away the most popular novel in eighteenth-century France, *Julie* told a Romantic story of true love confounded by meaningless social customs that made people ashamed to follow their hearts. It drew thousands of women readers into Rousseau's fold.[64] Roland writes: "It seemed to me that [when I read *Julie*] I then found my true substance, that Rousseau became the interpreter of feelings and ideas I had had before him, but that he alone could explain to my satisfaction. He showed me the domestic happiness to which I had a right to aspire."[65] Roland said that her identification with Julie made it easier for her to endure the prison of her own marriage when her heart longed for another man (François Buzot), her own "worthy Saint-Preux."[66] Mary Trouille's account of Rousseau's influence

59 Rousseau, *Emile*, 33.

60 Trouille, *Sexual Politics in the Enlightenment*, 27.

61 Ibid., 26. Trouille elaborates: "Rousseau's breastfeeding campaign was addressed above all to aristocratic women ... the ideal of domesticity he was proposing was modeled after the lifestyle of the bourgeoisie – particularly the sober Genevan bourgeoisie of his youth recalled through the idealizing lens of memory and the unfulfilled longings of a motherless son."

62 Susan Dalton, "Gender and the Shifting Ground of Revolutionary Politics: The Case of Madame Roland," *Canadian Journal of History* 36, no. 2 (2001): 259–282.

63 Trouille, *Sexual Politics in the Enlightenment*, 166.

64 Eileen Hunt Botting, *Family Feuds: Wollstonecraft, Burke, and Rousseau on the Transformation of the Family* (Albany: SUNY Press, 2006), 39; Robert Darnton, *The Great Cat Massacre: And Other Episodes in French Cultural History* (Basic Books, 2009), 242; Jean-Jacques Rousseau, *La Nouvelle Héloïse: Julie, or the New Eloise: Letters of Two Lovers, Inhabitants of a Small Town at the Foot of the Alps*, trans. Judith H. McDowell (University Park: Pennsylvania State University Press, 1990), 1–2.

65 Trouille, *Sexual Politics in the Enlightenment*, 164.

66 Ibid., 177.

on literary and political women emphasizes that because Rousseau had lived in the company of women, listening to their stories and miseries as he wrote *Julie*, the book provided an especially salient representation of the misery of *la femme mal mariée*.[67]

It is unsurprising that *Julie* was especially influential among Rousseau's women readers. Rousseau writes in a feminine form expressly for literary women, and the themes of unhappy marriages that are dictated by social expectations resonated with women readers of a variety of social classes who identified with one aspect or another of the story line. There is a sense in the novel that the dangers of following one's heart and living a life that is true to it are worth the corresponding risks. At least one moral of *Julie* appears to be that sometimes the authentic life is an audacious life, and love, not marital contracts or social expectations, is the arbiter of the just. Julie and Saint-Preux are in search of love without shame. The public could not handle their love, and Julie achieves her goal only in death. *Julie* may have had a somber and sober ending, but even the tragedy could not contain the dramatic and romantic appeal of life and love unconstrained by convention.

Mme Roland, like so many women of the period, found in *Julie* a call to live a life as happy as possible. Empowered by this call, she felt authorized to pursue a vocation of formal politics, a path that Rousseau clearly denied women. Roland described herself as "seized by a feverish and continual preoccupation with public affairs," and she believed the right to happiness to mean the right to do as she pleased in public as well as private life.[68] Like many women of the time, she was devoted to Rousseau's educational prescriptions, as well. *Emile* was her parenting guide. But she explicitly ignored Book V and the treatment of Sophie in general and raised her daughter in keeping with the autonomy, natural education, and civic preparedness that Rousseau prescribed for Emile. Hence Roland was a committed Rousseauist in spite of his misogynies. It is one of many tragic ironies and paradoxes of the time that Roland, who so admired and defended Rousseau against criticism by women's rights advocates, was executed by masculinist Jacobins who saw her political authority as further evidence that the Girondins were not autonomous republican men, but puppets of an imperious woman.[69]

Also executed for "[forgetting] the virtues that belong to her sex," Marie-Olympe de Gouges, the protofeminist playwright, journalist, pamphleteer, and author of *The Declaration of the Rights of Woman and Citizen* claimed a direct debt to Rousseau.[70] In a sense, de Gouges *was* the autochthonous

[67] Ibid., 96.

[68] Ibid., 172.

[69] Ibid., 182–187.

[70] Joan W. Scott, *Only Paradoxes to Offer: French Feminists and the Rights of Man* (Cambridge, MA: Harvard University Press, 1997), 52. See also, John R. Cole, *Between the Queen and the Cabby: Olympe de Gouges's Rights of Woman* (Montréal: McGill-Queens University Press, 2011); Gregory S. Brown, "The Self-Fashionings of Olympe de Gouges, 1784–1789," *Eighteenth-Century Studies* 34, no. 3 (Spring 2001): 383–401.

threat pathologized in The Lament. "Her self originated with herself," notes Joan Scott.[71] She reinvented herself, starting with her name, to overcome the shame and stigma of her birth and craft the life she desired. In her words, she was drawn to Rousseau "as a *déclassée*."[72] "I am the product of Nature.... I owe nothing to book learning. I am my own creation," de Gouges wrote in the preface to *Le Philosophe Corrigé*.[73] Born as Marie Gouze in Montauban to working-class parents, she had no formal education, and moved to Paris and gave herself an aristocratic-sounding name, which bought her access to the city's literary world. She fabricated a story about her lineage, claiming to be the "illegitimate daughter of the marquis le Franc de Pompignan, a minor playwright [and a] ... member of the Académie Française."[74] Her "artificial" self-construction and the erasure of personal history it involved felt more authentic and natural than the identity and station she inherited. She was a courtesan, a playwright, and a prolific political writer. She also proposed a French national women's theater.

Even as de Gouges trampled on every requirement of Rousseau's gendered republic by participating in politics, theater, and art and pushing for the rights and privileges of more women to do so in the context of the emerging republican spirit of the literary world, she idolized Rousseau and saw him as "her literary father."[75] Like Mme Roland, who drew strength from Rousseau to support her political career, de Gouges invoked Rousseau's authority in order to defend herself against those who criticized her involvement in the women's theater proposal. "Proud and strong-willed like Jean-Jacques, I persisted in my ambitious plan nonetheless," she proclaimed.[76] For his women readers, the story of the ordinary person doing battle against the arbiters of society again and again trumped the relatively static gender conventions upon which it was grounded. In 1791, three years after Rousseau's death, de Gouges finished her tribute to him, *Les Rêveries de Jean-Jacques, le Mort de Rousseau à Ermenonville*.[77] "Like [Rousseau]," writes Trouille, "Gouges felt out of place in the petit bourgeois world of her childhood and ardently aspired to a place in the Republic of Letters."[78] Even with a fabricated self-representation, she saw her reconstructed life and work as part of a (more authentic) literary community and world.

[71] Ibid., 22.
[72] Trouille, *Sexual Politics in the Enlightenment*, 241.
[73] Ibid., 267.
[74] Ibid., 239.
[75] Trouille, *Sexual Politics in the Enlightenment*, 240. Many women opera composers were inspired by Rousseau's ideas and works, especially *Le Divan du Village*. They were self-taught, like Rousseau, and followed his operatic form as a "natural and 'democratic' art" that had "love as its center." Jacqueline Letzter and Robert Adelson, "French Women Opera Composers and the Aesthetics of Rousseau," *Feminist Studies* 26, no. 1 (April 1, 2000): 69–100: 76.
[76] Trouille, *Sexual Politics in the Enlightenment*, 240.
[77] Ibid., 241.
[78] Ibid.

A brief turn to some of Rousseau's prescriptions about *pudeur* and gender difference provide some context for the Jacobins' femicides. Whatever personal debt Roland and de Gouges had to Rousseau the man as well as Rousseauean ideas, their self-representations undercut the gendered essence of Rousseau's republicanism. Rousseau's own version of The Lament was a nostalgic story of an imagined past in which women's modesty both empowered them and protected men, children, and the city. This passage from the *Letter to d'Alembert on the Theater*, which was Rousseau's response to d'Alembert's "Geneva" entry in the *Encylopedia*, shows both the necessity of *pudeur* and Rousseau's lack of investment in "nature" per se. Rousseau strived for gendered social relations that would protect his fragile and simple men who were so quick to feel shame and doubt themselves:

> Even if it could be denied that a special sentiment of chasteness was natural to women, would it be any the less true that in society their lot ought to be a domestic and retired life, and that they ought to be raised in principles appropriate to it? *If the timidity, chasteness, and modesty which are proper to them are social inventions, it is in society's interest that women acquire these qualities; they must be cultivated in women, and any woman who disdains them offends good morals [manners].* Is there a sight in the world so touching, so respectable, as that of a mother surrounded by her children...? It is here that she shows herself in all the dignity of a decent woman; it is here that she really commands respect, and beauty shares with honor the homages rendered to virtue.... [W]hether this impression comes to us from nature or education, it is common to all the peoples of the world; everywhere, women are esteemed in proportion to their modesty.... Among all the ancient civilized peoples [women] led very retired lives: they appeared rarely in public; never with men, ... they did not *put themselves on display*.... If, on occasion, women stepped out of the bounds of this modesty, the public outcry showed that this was an exception.... *Everything is changed.*[79]

The concern and anxiety surrounding Rousseau's lamentations about *pudeur*'s waning influence and prevalence in the modern world reveal several of the paradoxes at the heart of Rousseau's work that are germane to this book and my larger argument about the political investments of nostalgic and naturalized appeals to shame. Note the extent to which Rousseau acknowledges that *pudeur's* natural status is in question; he is concerned with the social work it performs, irrespective of its origins. But even as he acknowledges the potentially conventional and contingent nature of *pudeur*, he nonetheless locates it on a temporal spectrum as more securely grounded in the past of antiquity than in the present of European modernity. *Pudeur*, rather than natural, is *necessary* in order to guarantee the admittedly fragile achievement of masculine authenticity. Man cannot be himself – live in a way that is true and natural, which is necessary for the general will to operate – if he lives in fear of being mocked and humiliated. And the primary reason men are mocked, according

[79] Rousseau, *Politics and the Arts*, 87–89. Emphasis added.

to Rousseau, is because of the presence and power of women who flaunt the requirements of *pudeur*. To put it simply, Rousseau's fears about honest men being humiliated and mocked in society have to do with the shameless audacity he fears might be authentic and delightful to women. And so women's audacity – even if authorized by his paeans to authenticity – must be managed and closed down. True to the tropes of The Lament, *pudeur* operates as a "brake" that protects civilization by limiting women (and some men) from taking the ideas of equality circulating in the eighteenth century *too far*.

As the extended passage shows, the gendered republicanism that hinges a dynamic of masculine authenticity to feminine *pudeur* is a product of painstaking instruction and care. We see it operating also in *Emile*. Emile is educated in strength and endurance – so as not to become "soft," he is neither swaddled nor coddled. He is taught the lessons of the school yard, made to sleep in an uncomfortable bed, and sent outside to play in winter wearing summer clothes.[80] His education is in fact designed to strengthen him against the feminizing, vexing forces of society, to escape the "stupidity" that comes from being "raised indoors."[81] Emile is not to be afraid of the dark because, the tutor tells him, it would be "womanish"; he learns tennis rather than shuttlecock, which is "a woman's game," and so on.[82] An acknowledgment of the "empire" of woman's power frames Rousseau's work, and its potential threat looms in the background of Emile's education. As feminist interpreters have long noted, Rousseauean manhood is not "natural," but an achievement.[83]

Critics thus figured Roland and de Gouges, like other women who took up the cause of politics and the public sphere rather than tend the hearth, as threats to the newly established republican order. Natural difference and deference could not be trusted to organize gender behavior. The guillotine was invoked as an enforcer. Immediately following de Gouges and Roland's executions (November 3 and 8, 1793, respectively), Jacobin authorities shut down women's political clubs and societies in explicitly Rousseauean language. They defended their actions, like the executions themselves, in the terms of The Lament: "Since when is it *decent* to see women abandoning the pious cares of their households, the cribs of their children, to come to public places, to harangues in the galleries, at the bar of the Senate? Is it to men that nature confided domestic cares? Has she given us breasts to feed our children?"[84] Jacobins characterized political women like Roland and de Gouges as emasculating, mannish monsters whose shameless disregard for "natural" gender conventions threatened to bring down the republic.[85] It is unsurprising that some women participated in their own version of The Lament, seeking to

[80] Rousseau, *Emile*, 125–140.
[81] Ibid., 124–125.
[82] Ibid., 134, 147.
[83] Lynda Lange, ed. *Feminist Interpretations of Jean-Jacques Rousseau* (University Park: Pennsylvania State University Press, 2002).
[84] Scott, *Only Paradoxes to Offer*, 48. Emphasis added.
[85] Ibid., 47–53.

quell the untethered and unchecked spirit of shameless Jacobinism.[86] Their crime was deigning to craft lives on their own terms without concern for the republican social order and its spheric divisions. They refused to play the role of good republican daughters to Rousseau, their philosophical father. Claiming their own lives, they displaced his, and were punished accordingly.

Fragility, Authenticity, and The Lament That Shame Is Dead

With these overlapping receptions of Rousseau in mind, let us return to the broader issues implicit in The Lament That Shame Is Dead and the anxieties about the loss of manners, civility, reticence, reverence, and shame therein. Rousseau, as I have argued, straddles both sides of The Lament. He authorizes and inaugurates a confessional mode of politics rooted in an earnest account of authenticity against the tyranny of shame. At the same time, he shuts down the reach of the confessional mode by instantiating and naturalizing the sensibility of *pudeur* as a brake that constrains the speech of women, their location in public, sexual behavior, and implicitly the lives of the men in their orbit. Rousseau's paradoxes are clearly alive and well in the work of his diverse readers. We see how they are inspired by his authentic ideal and frame the injustice of the world in terms of the ways in which the world casts some as pariahs for no fault of their own, thus dooming them to lives that are hidden in shame. In spite of their relatively consistent appeal to Rousseau's authentic ideal, his disciples' politics are at cross-purposes. They look to Rousseau as inspiration for everything from antiestablishment attacks, counter-Enlightenment ideologies, national women's theaters, and feminist self-representation. Who has the balance between shame and authenticity right? Is it the one who hews most closely to Rousseau's prescriptions? The one who departs from them to live life on her own terms?

Let us switch the question and frame it in another way, away from seeing the shaming of pariahs, the penned attacks against the elites, and the violence of the guillotine as problems of too much or too little of the ideal of authenticity and the braking emotion of *pudeur*. Rousseau sets us up to look at it in this way as does the broader logic of The Lament in the eighteenth century that laments the death of shame as a proxy for a more political analysis. Standard critiques of Jacobinism and the violence that followed invoke the language of The Lament. Jacobins invoked their own version of it to justify the death of de Gouges and others. But in so doing they ignore the social and political questions and contexts that put people in the position to dream of a life free from shame and to look to "nature" against "society" in the first place.

[86] See, for example, the most obvious case of Charlotte Corday, who murdered Jean-Paul Marat. For a fascinating account of the (mis)representations of Charlotte Corday, see Nina Rattner Gelbart, "The Blonding of Charlotte Corday," *Eighteenth-Century Studies* 38, no. 1 (2004): 201–221.

This switching of the question asks us to read Rousseau's readers outside of the frame of his paradoxical balancing act and toward the lens of democratic citizenship – unashamed citizenship, in particular. It reads them as more than "Rousseaus du ruisseau" or "disloyal daughters," who are loyal or disloyal to Rousseau's impossible juggling act of authenticity and *pudeur*. This frame resists the temptation to understand the fracturing and conflict of pre- and postrevolutionary French politics in terms of a loss of the difference and deference that appears so secure in the mythical *aidōs* of Homer or the Ancien Régime. Rather than looking in terms of regulation and containment with The Lament's tropes of "too much" and "too far," the citizenship frame reveals Marat, Clement, Sabatier, de Gouges, and others as democratic citizens doing the hard work of navigating, negotiating, transforming, and arguing about the scope of the increasingly egalitarian social and political ideas and institutions of pre- and postrevolutionary France. Moreover, this frame of citizenship alerts us to the degrees to which their demands, dreams, proposals, institutions, and works are cut off through proclamations that their very presence on the stage of French national politics and participation in broader conversations about Enlightenment and republicanism is itself evidence that shame is in jeopardy and that shamelessness must be quelled.

To restate a point from Chapter 1 and the discussion of the Cynics and foreshadow what is to come, this motley assortment of pariahs, outcasts, and misfits shows vividly how citizens acting in nascent democratic or republican contexts are drawn to the language of authenticity, self-representation, and self-fulfillment. They see the hypocrisies of the limited degrees of equality and the stratified tiers that exist in an ostensibly more equal arrangement. And because of this gap between the stated values that are emerging and increasingly appear to be held in common, they come to feel ashamed. They read this shame, their own negative self-assessment, and the way in which the social order casts them as pariahs for no official reason as a flag or warning sign that the social conditions under which they live are unjust. This sense of shame and the injustice therein necessarily directs them to politicize shame's terms. This often involves a turn toward a discourse of authenticity and self-fulfillment and a critique of the "artificial" hierarchies and customs that make them feel this way. This is not to say that each gesture toward the discourse of authenticity generated by the felt response of shame is inclusive or liberating. For example, the proto-Jacobin "hacks" of Grub Street were not interested in assuaging women's shame. Their visions are partial – beholden to their own experience, which linked up with others' stories but could never include or account for them. This turn to the language of the authentic and natural is part of the work of democratic politics and the ideal of equality on which it rests. Rousseau mobilized it to great effect. His readers ignored many of his careful prescriptions and did as they wished in its name.

Rousseau's wide appeal in this context raises a set of questions quite familiar to political theorists. Specifically, a politics whose only requirement is a "feeling" of psychological injury may be too expansive. People with tremendous power and social capital can feel disempowered. The link between the Rousseauean-inspired counter-Enlightenment and the French Right confirms the point that reactionaries often frame their political claims in terms of the shame and humiliation they feel amidst modernization and progress. Echoing broader concerns about a politics of authenticity and recognition, when inclusion and acknowledgment of suffering are all that citizens demand, their needs can be met by the most antirepublican and disempowering of regimes. Note the Jacobins' readiness to execute women whose bold assertions of their own republican rights trampled on men's fragile egos. A regime that responds to its citizens' injuries and makes citizens feel a sense of belonging need not be republican in nature. And finally, in authorizing and legitimating the dream of living a life that is true to oneself – the rest of the world and its rules be damned – Rousseau and Romanticism, more broadly, ostensibly narrow the political universe in a way that makes everything about whether or not a particular individual feels like she or he "fits in."

Rousseau, founder of the modern authentic ideal, certainly offers ample evidence for scholars worried about these dangers.[87] *The Confessions* are narcissistic; *The Social Contract* is coercive and totalizing; *The First and Second Discourses* indict "society" and its "artificial" influences; *The Letter to d'Alembert on the Theater* censors anything that might undermine an idealized view of "Genevan values" or humiliate its simple civic men; and *Julie* dramatizes the story of the modern, social world's cruelty.[88] Indeed, Rousseau's texts conjure and politicize a fragile, male pariah who is under siege by society and in need of protection. This pariah appears unable to live in the presence of any person or institution that does not affirm his goodness and legitimacy in the world. The Lament and broader attacks on the culture of self-esteem respond to the legacies of this Rousseauean image of citizens who are so fragile as to need constant affirmation and reinforcement.

It is clear that Rousseau does not trust his male citizens, much less their wives and daughters, to engage in the work of self-actualization themselves. He is to identify the sources of men's shame (sexual indiscretions, salonnières, actresses, fancy clothing, illegitimacy, philosophes, and so on) and protect them from these threats. Rousseauean men need protection because, apparently, they become entirely unraveled in the presence of anything that does not affirm their existence. Presumably the role of the coercive social contract that forces its citizens into freedom is to provide this protective cover, allowing citizens to enjoy the benefits of their fragility – to see their neighbors as themselves. By

[87] Taylor, *The Ethics of Authenticity*, 25–29.

[88] Rousseau, *The Confessions*; Rousseau, *Politics and the Arts*; Jean-Jacques Rousseau, *The Social Contract*, trans. Maurice Cranston (Penguin Classics, 1968); Jean-Jacques Rousseau, *The First and Second Discourses*, Rousseau, *La Nouvelle Héloise: Julie*.

this account, the goal of Rousseau's republican politics is not to escape this fragile state, but to live in a state that militates against the dangers of their fragility – remaining, as he puts it in the *Social Contract*, "as free as before."

Yet, as I have shown, Rousseau's Romantic invitation to lead a life that is free of shame and social injuries authorized a set of political practices that are far removed from the sober Genevan circles[89] he idealized, the community in which the "*I*" melds into the "common unity," and the totalizing and protective elements of Rousseau's social contract.[90] His contemporaries – the unashamed citizens I have outlined here – saw his sympathetic tribute to the pariah as inviting an unruly and indecorous politics, which involved high stakes political battles and the agonizing, writing, speaking, performing, risking, and judging that goes along with them. This is true even of the so-called traditionalist men of the counter-Enlightenment, whose invective was just as flamboyant in its antidemocratic animus as their proto-Jacobin counterparts'. To put it differently, as much as Rousseau may have seen himself as the universal confessor who told his story so others did not have to, he failed to execute this ideal. He modeled and romanticized the practice of self-representation and self-narration and could not contain where it would go. He spoke and others followed, refusing to remain silent – refusing to let the lawgiver decide what would go and what would remain. As befits people who are drawn to live a life that is "true," those who read and took up Rousseau's invitation to an authentic life were less concerned with being protected than being able to author and enact their own social and political lives. Left and right, they called out those institutions and the people at their helm that stood in their way. Their unruliness offered no safeguards against tyranny, but it contained far more potential for enacting the robust egalitarianism that is Rousseau's great contribution to radical democracy than either his own prescriptions or his critics' lamentations about a Romantic reliance on "nature" against "society" and the dangers of an overly psychologized public sphere.

These two elements of Rousseau's work – the commitment to authenticity and the belief in human fragility – strain against each other. Rousseau presents them as coherent, suggesting that if one wants a life that feels true, one will need a force larger than oneself to guarantee it. But as his own works show, once protection from psychological suffering is the thing that one desires most, the reach of his radical politics closes down. Thus there are two aspects to Rousseau's account of authenticity. The first is to want a life free of shame; the second is to expect it to be guaranteed. Once protection becomes the overriding

89 "Our *circles* still preserve some image of ancient morals [manners] among us. By themselves, the men, exempted from having to lower their ideas to the range of women and to clothe reason in gallantry, can devote themselves to grave and serious discourse without fear of ridicule. They dare to speak of country and virtue without passing for windbags; they even dare to be themselves without being enslaved to the maxims of a magpie." Rousseau, *Politics and the Arts*, 105.

90 Rousseau, *Emile*, 40.

quality, de Gouges and Roland, for example, can never strive for authenticity, because the mere presence of them living public lives on their own terms threatens Rousseau's fragile men. By repeatedly emphasizing men's fragility as well as their need for authenticity, Rousseau disables the most radical aspects of his Romantic invitations. Yet many of his readers ignored this disabling and did what they liked in his name.

Rousseau and his readers speak to the dichotomous relationship between shame and authenticity framing many contemporary political debates. As we hear Rousseau decry the death of modesty among modern women and in modern society, he appears to be a progenitor of lamentations about moral and social decline. And yet, if you listen to the lamenters' sirens wail about people doing whatever they please with no regard for manners and civility, they are, in a sense, attacking the legacy of Rousseau. By paying attention to the ways in which Rousseau both opens up the public through his Romantic invitations and closes them down through his more didactic and legislative prescriptions, we garner a broader perspective on the persistent allure of an authentic life free of shame and the equally persistent fears about what that actually means. These political battles are fought on the ground by citizens who are invested in them and they cannot be resolved through theoretical accounts of shame, authenticity, and their appropriate domains.

PART THREE

CONTAMINATION AND LAMENTATION

4

Furious Democracy

Nineteenth-Century "Slut Shaming," Indian Removal, and the Ascent of the "Ill-Bred" Man

> The modern mind teaches (in extremes) that the nation exists for the individual; for the guardianship and education of every man. The Reformation contained the new thought. The English Revolution is its expansion. The American Declaration of Independence is a formal announcement of it by a nation to nations, though a very limited expression.... The Vote, – universal suffrage – is another; the downfall of war, the attack upon slavery, are others. The furious democracy which in this country from the beginning of its history, has shown a wish ... to leave out men of mark and send illiterate and low persons as deputies, ... is only a perverse or as yet obstructed operation of the same instinct, – a stammering and stuttering out of impatience to articulate the awful words *I am*.
>
> – Ralph Waldo Emerson

> I readily concede that "shame" has few defenders as we near the end of the twentieth century in the West. But I hope you will hear me out. If, as I have argued, and many of my betters before me, notably Tocqueville, have insisted, democracy is about not only constitutions, rules, public accountability, and deliberation but also everyday life, habits, and dispositions, then it makes some sense to think about shame and shamelessness.
>
> – Jean Bethke Elshtain

Jacksonian Territories

In Parts I and II (Shame's Allure and Unashamed Citizens) I laid out the phenomenon I call The Lament That Shame Is Dead and argued that it both obscures and pathologizes radically democratic activity that pushes the borders of respectable politics, invokes the language of "nature" and "authenticity," and productively traffics in the "therapeutic turn" in order to disturb the social identities and hierarchies that The Lament so forcefully conjures and defends. To this end, I have told the story of the undertheorized and underappreciated ancient Cynics and the people who took up the dream of an unashamed life in pre- and postrevolutionary France. In each case, political claims about the value of a life free from shame based upon one's status as an outsider or pariah authorized a politics of critique, agitation, and transformation. Yet critics across the intellectual and political spectrum have struggled to see how these movements are democratically and politically legitimate because of their reliance upon a "therapeutic" language of "nature" and the "authentic" that often suffuses the "public" with "social" and "private" concerns and claims.

I now turn to Part III: Contamination and Lamentation (Chapters 4 and 5), where I dig more deeply into the logic of The Lament by further exploring its nostalgic and normative investments and how it operates as a shaming practice in its own right. As we began to see in Plato's lament as well as the philosophes' lament against the shameless *libellistes* of Grub Street and Rousseau's fantasy of *pudeur* and the gender order he believed it secured, The Lament seizes the moral high ground and goes on to humiliate, expose, and tarnish citizens it deems to be shameless threats to civilization. The moral high ground attained through the declaration that "shame is dead" and "civilization is in decline" thus authorizes behavior that might be considered shameless by the very standards of The Lament were it not to come from self-proclaimed moral authorities who abide *within* the pale. The sacred categories of The Lament – public/private, civility, difference, deference – all disappear as one positions oneself as a defender of *aidōs* or *pudeur* against the onslaught of the autochthonous mass. Defenders of shame against a newly empowered demos take their own "shameless" liberties with their political tactics, justifying them in the name of morals, manners, and civilization itself. This reveals again the degree to which "shame" has no salvational ontology; it is not a "thing" that will save our politics or our morality. To the contrary, shame is a trope of political discourse deployed to specific ends. Most often, those ends pathologize and marginalize persons with relatively limited formal social and political power, and efforts by dispossessed peoples to shame those who exploit them do not typically deliver the moral correction they desire.

With this in mind, this chapter investigates the Jacksonian era and the moral panic and preoccupations with shamelessness and civilizational decline that Andrew Jackson's ascent to political (as opposed to military) power triggered among the founding elite and those who identified with and idealized them.[1] Specifically, it shows how a moralistic and highly gendered, raced, and classed politics of shame and shaming circulated during Jackson's 1824

[1] For overviews of the Jacksonian era, see Robert V. Remini, *The Life of Andrew Jackson* (New York: Harper Perennial Modern Classics, 2010); Charles Sellers, *The Market Revolution: Jacksonian America, 1815–1846* (New York: Oxford University Press, 1992); Daniel Walker Howe, *What Hath God Wrought: The Transformation of America, 1815–1848* (Oxford: Oxford University Press, 2009); Sean Wilentz, *Andrew Jackson: The 7th President, 1829–1837* (New York: Macmillan, 2007).

and 1828 campaigns for president as well as the Eaton Affair that began with his inauguration. During the elections, John Quincy Adams and his supporters lamented that shame is – or would be – dead if Andrew and Rachel Jackson govern the nation as president and first lady. Emphasizing themes of being "unfit" and poorly "bred," Adamsites attacked Jackson's status as a common man and scandalized Jackson's marriage to Rachel Robards. Adamsites' cries of civilizational ruin underscore how the emergence of Andrew and Rachel Jackson as potential members of the US ruling class indicate, once again, how The Lament emerges as a response to increasingly egalitarian ideas and practices, especially as they transform the hierarchies of the social sphere and the codes of class, race, and gender. Of particular relevance to democratic theorists, I explore Tocqueville's identification with Adams and his hostility to Jackson as fundamental to his account of democracy and its dilemmas. Tocqueville's identification with Adams in turn has influenced democratic theorists' focus on the need to cultivate constraining virtues and mores to check the spirit of equality. That is, *Democracy in America* canonized Adams's lament. The theories of democracy that Tocqueville generated while traveling in America must be understood in the context of political and social struggles on the ground. Yet most democratic theorists indebted to Tocqueville's vision of democratic politics have neglected the details of this context and the struggle it involved.

Drawing on the work of Tocqueville scholars, nineteenth-century historians, and feminist historians' accounts of sex and gender in the republican mother and wife, I provide the context of the elections of 1824 and 1828 and two scandals framing Jackson's presidency in order to show how debates about democratic politics played out through discourses of shame and shamelessness, aristocracy and democracy, tradition and self-invention with respect to aristocratic fears about democratic men's unbridled sexual desire and failure to respect the dictates of *pudeur*, the republican sense of feminine shame theorized so forcefully by Rousseau (see Chapter 3). I highlight the elite's fears about the democratic woman's sexual immorality and the racialized nature of the aristocratic critique of democratic conceptions of economic equality and class, as well. I then examine Jackson's project of Indian Removal to raise the question of whether or not a robust form of "good" shame (and Jackson's lack of it) – as opposed to the "sexual shame" of *pudeur*, so clearly rejected by the Jacksons – can help to account for the massacre Anglo-Americans inflicted on indigenous peoples in the early republic. I show that the idea of "good" or moral shame is not as separate and distinct from the sexual shame of *pudeur* as one might imagine. To the contrary, Jackson deployed a discourse of *pudeur* and the gender difference it guaranteed to fuel the avarice and hubris of his plan for Indian Removal. The political struggles during the Jacksonian era demonstrate how democratic contestation over the meanings of the political equality enshrined in the nation's founding play out through debates about shame, civility, and civilization, and the ideals, values, and bodies believed to threaten them.

Andrew Jackson: "*Sans pudeur et sans frein*" (Tocqueville's Lament)

Tocqueville and his companion, Gustave de Beaumont, arrived in the United States in 1831, three years after Andrew Jackson won the presidency in a landslide election against John Quincy Adams and Jacksonian Democrats took control of both Houses of Congress. The founding political class was at this point largely devoid of official public power as states increasingly lifted their bans on property requirements for white men's voting. Critics read Jackson's victory as a Jacobinesque win for the common man and Europeans worried about his "Bonapartist potential."[2] Excessive liquor was served at the inaugural ball, the White House was ransacked by Jackson's guests, and "social equality" was declared to be on the rise. Tocqueville's account of the French Revolution may have been decidedly un-nostalgic for aristocratic France, but Jackson's victory over Adams would haunt Tocqueville's theory of America and its future. "Not until the era of Andrew Jackson ... did the Jacobin doctrine become the popular political creed of the American democracy," notes Walter Lippmann.[3] Indeed, Jackson's populism and antiaristocratic ideology and demeanor were both a source of power and an Achilles Heel, as he was now subject to scrutiny, specifically in the areas of sex, gender, and race that had largely eluded his elite predecessors.

Tocqueville wrote in his travel diary and in *Democracy* about the dangers of Jackson, whom he referred to as "General" rather than president: "Since I have been in America, I have almost got proof that all the enlightened classes are opposed to General Jackson, but the people holds to him and he has numbers in his favor."[4] This juxtaposition between the "enlightened classes" and "the people" circulated in political discussion in the early republic and has been enshrined as an essential tension in *Demo*cracy *in America* and much of Tocquevillean democratic theory.[5] The division between "enlightened classes" and "the people" was not abstract but lived out empirically in the bodies of Adams and Jackson as they struggled to both represent and lead "the people." "Democracy," once an epithet to be contrasted with the gentle virtue and civility of republicanism, had changed in status as the republic grew and expanded its citizenry.[6] Even John Quincy had to acknowledge the legitimacy of democratic ideas that would undo his claim to inherited power.

[2] Isaac Kramnick, "Introduction," in Alexis de Tocqueville, *Democracy in America*, ed. Isaac Kramnick, trans. Gerald Bevan (Penguin Classics, 2003), xxviii–xxix.

[3] Walter Lippmann, Clinton Rossiter, and James Lare, *The Essential Lippmann: A Political Philosophy for Liberal Democracy* eds (Cambridge, MA: Harvard University Press, 1982), 62.

[4] Alexis de Tocqueville, *Journey to America* (New Haven: Yale University Press, 1959), 156.

[5] Benjamin Barber both interrogates and reinforces this tension in his case for an "aristocracy" of "the people." See Benjamin Barber, *By Benjamin Barber Aristocracy of Everyone* (Ballantine Books, 1992).

[6] Alexander Hamilton, James Madison, and John Jay, *The Federalist Papers* (New York: Penguin Classics, 1987). On the dichotomy between the unruly "democracy" and the more refined representative republic, see especially *Federalist* 10, 14, 48.

Tocqueville's descriptions of Adams, in sharp contrast with his fears about "General Jackson," suggest that he saw Adams as personifying the aristocrat's proper role as servant to the public. Adams was a Tocquevillean dream, bringing aristocratic manners to bear on republican institutions. Heir to one of the most prominent political families in America, Adams understood his duty to lead in terms of an inherited, noble calling. He had trained to serve his country in elite European schools while accompanying his father, John Adams, on foreign missions, which prepared him for the career that preceded his presidency.[7] He assisted his father with French translation and cultivated in Europe a preoccupation with "browsing bookstores, buying what he thought valuable and interesting and sending them home to start his own private library."[8] During his presidency, John Quincy preoccupied himself with establishing the United States as a nation with international prominence; in a deeply Eurocentric world, this meant becoming a nation with a serious intellectual climate, in contrast to the paucity of intellectual activity Tocqueville is so distraught to find in America. In his travel notebooks, Tocqueville praised the "ease" and "elegance" of John Quincy's French and his upright moral character.[9] What Tocqueville found to criticize in America – the aggressive individualism, the tyranny of the majority, the anti-intellectual climate, the "industrial aristocracy" – are Jacksonian challenges to John Quincy's values. And what he praises – the religious sensibility, women's mores rooted in sexual chastity and marital fidelity, the endurance of the marriage tie – are vestiges of the waning republican aristocracy.[10] Abigail Adams *was* the "republican mother" par excellence, and Louisa Adams the "republican wife." When struggling to understand something in America and its "opinion[s], political practice[s], or remarks on manners," Tocqueville notes, "I sought to consult the most informed men."[11] Those men would be Adams and other members of the small but essential "civilized" class.

The first American newspaper Tocqueville claims to have read, which he excerpted in *Democracy in America* to show the power of the press to "modify customs as well as laws" and prevent evils, attacked the integrity of President Jackson by reference to a scandal that is especially relevant to the fears of

[7] Robert V. Remini, *John Quincy Adams* (New York: Times Books, 2002), 11. At the age of sixteen, John Quincy helped his father draft international treaties and cultivated a friendship with Thomas Jefferson, with whom he spent many days and evenings "talking about literature, science, the arts, history, and government" (16).

[8] Ibid., 12.

[9] Tocqueville, *Journey to America*, 60.

[10] Tocqueville's view dovetails with the "Whiggish" historiography on the Jacksonian era, which presumed that democracy always needed regulation in a way that differed from the regulative checks on aristocrats or monarchs. See Charles Grier Sellers, "Andrew Jackson versus the Historians," *The Mississippi Valley Historical Review* 44, no. 4 (1958): 615–634.

[11] Tocqueville, *Democracy in America*, 25.

Jackson as a shameless despot whose disavowal of republican gender roles would spell disaster for the nation.[12] It reads:

In this whole affair the language used by Jackson (the President) was that of a heartless despot, concerned only to preserve his own power. Ambition is his crime and it will be his punishment, too. Intrigue is his vocation ... He governs by corruption and his guilty maneuvers will result in his shame and confusion. He has acted in the political arena like a shameless and unbridled gambler [*sans pudeur et sans frein*]. He has had some success but the hour of his reckoning draws near. Soon he will have to return his winnings, throw his false dice away and end up in some backwater where he can freely curse his stupidity. For repentance [guilt, shame] is not a virtue with which his heart has ever been acquainted. (*Vincennes Gazette*).[13]

Tocqueville never referred to the specific details of "this whole affair," but the paper quite likely describes what became known as the "Eaton Affair," Jackson's decision to fire his entire cabinet in an explicit effort to control the political influence of his Cabinet members' wives. His mantra had become, "I did not come here to make a cabinet for the Ladies of this place." Recall that Tocqueville had parroted back to France the American version of the ideology of the "republican mother" that was revered in certain sectors of America. As Tocqueville told the story, Anglo-American women's morals secure America against the dangers of democratic leveling. Although gender was highly unstable during the first half of the nineteenth century as the republic emerged and expanded along axes of gender, race, and class, Tocqueville presented the idealized, chaste republican mother as empirical fact.[14] That is, Tocqueville laid the moral compass of the nation at the feet of Anglo-American women, who would be the guardian of the nation's morals – satellites of virtue that could funnel and restrain the baser elements of "democratic flux."[15] The 1831 scandal involved Jackson directly rejecting any political role for women and wives, declaring the public sphere as a realm for male leadership and women as objects of paternal protection. The details of how Jackson had been entangled with Washington "ladies," the appropriate place and role of republican wives and mothers in the early republic, and their desire to police the president's

[12] Ibid., 210.

[13] Ibid., 212.

[14] Kirsten E. Wood, "'One Woman so Dangerous to Public Morals': Gender and Power in the Eaton Affair," *Journal of the Early Republic* 17, no. 2 (1997), 237–275: 238; Much work has been done on the concept of "republican motherhood." Linda Kerber's work has been especially pathbreaking in this area. See Linda Kerber, "The Republican Mother: Women and the Enlightenment – An American Perspective," *American Quarterly* 28, no. 2 (1976): 187–205; Linda K. Kerber, "Separate Spheres, Female Worlds, Woman's Place: The Rhetoric of Women's History," *The Journal of American History* 75, no. 1 (1988): 9–39.

[15] On the gender politics of *Democracy in America* and women's roles in managing "democratic flux," see Laura Janara, *Democracy Growing Up: Authority, Autonomy, and Passion in Tocqueville's Democracy in America* (Albany: SUNY Press, 2002).

morals is both fascinating and overlooked in Tocqueville scholarship, feminist and otherwise.[16]

Tocqueville's account of American gender roles, born from the "truth" of the balance in America and its absence in France, has also been underscrutinized and undertheorized by democratic theorists who continue to accept as historical fact Tocqueville's focus on democratic checks, fetters, manners, religious sensibility, all of which he declares the province of women. Understanding Tocqueville's "truth" as influenced by his own investments coupled with his identification with Adams and the anti-Jackson elite complicates subsequent, often neo-Tocquevillean, lamentations and iterations of the "truth" that democracies must focus on cultivating civility and shame, maintained through gender difference, to ward off the dangers of an autochthonous mass.

The story leading up to Jackson's wholesale rejection of republican women's roles as virtuous satellites steering the nation's morals begins in 1824 with the presidential race between Secretary of State John Quincy Adams and Jackson, who was a recently-fêted war hero, credited with the saving of the young republic in the War of 1812 and the subsequent acquisition of a vast amount of territory.[17] Having played a critical role in establishing sovereignty for the United States, Jackson saw himself as free to establish his own sovereignty, untethered to the nation's past and the limitations on who counted as a legitimate male citizen and leader. His political ascent seemed to be the logical extension of the democratic-republic tradition in America, as he lacked familial ties to the ruling elite and had proven his loyalty to the nation in the generally universalizable tradition of the citizen-soldier.[18] Jackson constructed his presidential candidacy and his entire public persona in explicit opposition to the old, American aristocracy, which Adams personified.[19]

By 1824, Jackson threatened the New England elite because his war victories had made him extraordinarily popular – "the most popular man in the nation."[20] Many of Adams's diplomatic victories (as secretary of state under President James Monroe) were possible only because of Jackson's military prowess. Yet in spite of Jackson's popularity, Adams won the 1824 election. Jackson had a plurality of both popular and electoral votes, but he did not have a majority. The House of Representatives therefore had to make the final decision among the top three finishers, as per the Twelfth Amendment (1804).

[16] For two excellent historical accounts, see Wood, "One Woman so Dangerous to Public Morals"; Catherine Allgor, *Parlor Politics: In Which the Ladies of Washington Help Build a City and a Government* (Charlottesville: University of Virginia Press, 2000).

[17] Remini, *John Quincy Adams*, 64.

[18] On this tradition and its democratic significance, see Claire R. Snyder, *Citizen-Soldiers and Manly Warriors* (Lanham, MD: Rowman & Littlefield, 1999).

[19] Norma Basch, "Marriage, Morals, and Politics in the Election of 1828," *The Journal of American History* 80, no. 3 (1993): 890–918.

[20] Remini, *John Quincy Adams*, 64.

Henry Clay, speaker of the House, had placed fourth and was eliminated from the final slate of candidates, yet he would go on to influence the outcome. The third candidate, Crawford, had been debilitated by a stroke during the final days of the campaign, and the republicans simply kept his name on the ticket to preserve a party spot. As far as Clay was concerned, he was deciding between the first two finishers, Adams and Jackson. And this would not be a hard decision: Clay did not think that Jackson's key credential, "killing 2,500 Englishmen at N. Orleans qualifies for the various, difficult, and complicated duties of the Chief Magistracy"; furthermore, Adams had promised to serve Clay's "own future interests."[21] Clay's self-interest and opposition to Jackson proved alchemical, and he cast his vote for Adams, fueling the pro-Jackson forces, which could now position Jackson as the only democratic option against Adams's 1828 bid for reelection. They could highlight the cronyism of 1824 and cast it as an explicit opposition between democracy and aristocracy, amplifying Jackson's attacks on Adams's career in foreign service, his fluency in French, his connections abroad, and plan to develop a national university.[22] Tocqueville frequently noted the anti-intellectualism of Americans; this was clearly a reference to the Jacksonian democratic spirit rather than a limitation of the founding class.[23] Adams's love of billiards, for example, cultivated abroad and transplanted into the White House, became a symbolic lightening rod for the antiaristocratic sentiment flowing throughout the country.[24] Jackson deployed the now classic tropes of a populist campaign that sought to expose Adams as out of touch with ordinary Americans.

Also foreshadowing contemporary political debates, Adams was almost singularly focused on improving Americans' morals in a way that both revealed his antipopulist impulses and complicated his claim that Jackson was the candidate who was set on centralizing power and minimizing the voice of the people. Adams's plan for the country's future, "unveiled during his first annual message to Congress, projected a strong, unified nation-state, with a federal government active in physical and moral 'internal improvements.'"[25] Increasing divorce rates, the broadening frontier in young America, and the emergence of commercial and economic opportunities created opportunities for people to leave their spouses more easily.[26] Moralists like Adams tied these

[21] Ibid., 69.

[22] Ibid., 84–85.

[23] "Americans have, therefore, never felt the need to draw their philosophic method from books; they have discovered it within themselves." Tocqueville, *Democracy in America*, 495.

[24] Robert V. Remini, *Andrew Jackson: The Course of American Freedom, 1822–1832* (Baltimore: Johns Hopkins University Press, 1998), 130.

[25] Allgor, *Parlor Politics*, 191.

[26] Hendrik Hartog, *Man and Wife in America: A History* (Cambridge, MA: Harvard University Press, 2000), 1–33. The commonplace nature of divorce was the case only in established states. There were few divorces in unincorporated territories, such as Tennessee where the Jacksons lived. See Harriet Chappell Owsley, "The Marriages of Rachel Donelson," *Tennessee Historical Quarterly* 36, no. 4 (1977), 479–492: 487.

developments to democratic society and its allegedly more lax social values. His exhortations about how America had lost its moral way reflected the emergence of a nineteenth-century strand of moralism that linked the need for much stricter codes of virtue to the country's new democratic direction. With protofeminist preoccupations with the right to divorce on the rise, marital propriety became a quick and easy litmus test for a person's moral character, one that Adams exploited in the 1828 campaign.

Defending the morality they believed to be under attack from the democratic spirit of the times, Adamsites pathologized Jackson's marriage to Rachel Donelson Robards and Rachel herself. Rachel and Andrew had wed in 1791, when Rachel was still married to her first husband, Lewis Robards. Her legal bigamy was one of the many ways in which she did not live up to the standard of the *passionless* "republican wife" whose self-abnegation and lack of sexual desire was supposed to temper the passion of men.[27] John Quincy had fallen in love with a woman named Mary Frazier, but heeded his mother's advice and made the "prudent" choice of marrying Louise Johnson.[28] The Jacksons' entire marital script confounded the categories upon which discussion of republican husbands, wives, and marriages rested: There was no chaste virgin; there was no coquette. Rachel did not "seduce [Andrew] into virtue" and so she could never "preserve her husband in the exalted state to which her influence had raised him."[29] There was no traditional courtship period during which Rachel had the moral authority to influence Andrew. She was fleeing the misery of her first marriage, taking advantage of the expanse of the frontier and the ability of wives to desert their husbands if they felt it necessary for their safety or sanity. Regardless of the bigamy charge, the mere possibility of Rachel Jackson assuming the role of first lady gave the lie to republican fantasies about marriage and husbands' and wives' roles in them. She eschewed republican notions of femininity – she smoked a pipe, had no formal education, and refused to play the role of virtuous helpmeet to the abusive Lewis Robards. She was a woman escaping the clutches of a miserable marriage and was on the run.

The Jacksons' marriage was far outside of the script of republican virtue. Adamsites judged them accordingly and read them as immoral and lacking in character and regard for others by virtue of the legal ambiguities in their frontier marriage. Rather than reading Rachel as asserting the independence and the logical consequences of the ideal of "chosen" marriage reported by Tocqueville to be welcomed in America, Adamsites coded Rachel's tarnished virtue and Jackson's "theft" of another man's wife as evidence of Jackson's ill manners and lack of regard for feminine virtue, marital chastity, marital property, and morality at large. (The Jacksons insisted that the legal bigamy was a simple mistake – a claim

27 Nancy F. Cott, "Passionlessness: An Interpretation of Victorian Sexual Ideology, 1790–1850," *Signs* 4, no. 2 (1978): 219–236.

28 Remini, *John Quincy Adams*, 20–21.

29 Jan Lewis, "The Republican Wife: Virtue and Seduction in the Early Republic," *The William and Mary Quarterly*, 44, no. 4 (1987), 689–721: 701.

generally supported by historians' accounts of the incident.[30] Rachel thought the divorce had been finalized, but the Virginia legislature had merely granted Lewis permission to sue for divorce in civil court. He did not sue until 1793.[31] Once advised of the legal details, the Jacksons held a second marriage ceremony in 1794.) Decades after they had legally married, Adamsites used Rachel's unwitting bigamy to attack Jackson's character. Anxious to capitalize upon fears about his Tennessee, that is, "ill-bred" morals, Adams portrayed him as a reckless seducer and "wife stealer" who could malign the nation's fragile virtues just as he had maligned Rachel Robards's. Showing the incoherence of the republican attack, Rachel was simultaneously criticized for her "pipe smoking," called a "loose, impetuous, and immoral woman who willingly cast off her lawful husband for an arrogant and impassioned young suitor," and portrayed as a helpless victim of Jackson's guileful seductions.[32] Tocqueville would note that the "chastity of other men's wives must be preserved" as a "bulwark against democratic mayhem," affirming the claims made by Adams in his battle against Jackson for the White House in 1828.[33] Confirming his observation that male infidelity is acceptable in America so long as the woman in question is not honorable, that is, married, Adams's message was clear: "A vote for Jackson was a vote for sin."[34]

Adams analogized national unity and marriage on several levels.[35] First, a healthy nation required its citizens to be safely ensconced in the moral sobriety of monogamous marriages (like his own); and second, infidels and bigamists (like the Jacksons) would not only compromise their own marriages but the unity of the nation, as well.[36] Committed to their belief that Jackson would destroy the fragile republic, the Adams coalition pulled no punches. A column in the *Cincinnati Gazette* stated: "'In the summer of 1790,' ... 'Gen. Jackson prevailed upon the wife of Lewis Roberts [sic] of Mercer county, Kentucky, to desert her husband, and live with himself, in the character of a wife.'"[37] Another critic asked, "Ought a convicted adulteress and her *paramour* husband to be placed in the highest offices of this free and Christian Land?"[38] Adamsites saw no republican

[30] Nancy F. Cott, *Public Vows: A History of Marriage and the Nation* (Cambridge, MA: Harvard University Press, 2002); John F. Marszalek, *The Petticoat Affair: Manners, Mutiny, and Sex in Andrew Jackson's White House* (Baton Rouge: Louisiana State University Press, 2000); Basch, "Marriage, Morals, and Politics in the Election of 1828."

[31] Basch, "Marriage, Morals, and Politics in the Election of 1828," 890–891; Cott, *Public Vows*, 36.

[32] Basch, "Marriage, Morals, and Politics in the Election of 1828," 891.

[33] Janara, *Democracy Growing Up*, 180.

[34] Tocqueville, *Democracy in America*, 693; Basch, "Marriage, Morals, and Politics in the Election of 1828," 891.

[35] Note the link between Tocqueville and Rousseau's understanding of the marital tie; Tocqueville claims an explicit debt to Rousseau, and his chapters on women and marriage in America reflect principles similar to what Rousseau outlines in Book V of *Emile*.

[36] Allgor, *Parlor Politics*, 193–194; Basch, "Marriage, Morals, and Politics in the Election of 1828," 893.

[37] Remini, *Andrew Jackson*, 118–119.

[38] Basch, "Marriage, Morals, and Politics in the Election of 1828," 903.

controversy in conscripting the federal state to nationalize a particular code of morals.[39] Rather, monogamous marriage *was* republican character.[40] And the people deserved to know the facts behind this menacing man with such "callous disregard for the laws of marriage" if Jackson were to become president. Adams would insist that such disregard symbolized "the raw power of evil over institutional efforts to uphold virtue." The Adams camp attacked Rachel, as well: "[B]ecause the woman who was slated to share [the President's] bed at the White House was deemed unchaste," writes Norma Basch in her study of the 1828 election, "she [also] stood as a threat, albeit a lesser one, to the larger civic order."[41]

To invoke the imperial trope, Jackson was "beyond the pale" in terms of his origin and character and the Adams attacks show the ways in which origins, identity, character, and conduct become conflated in The Lament and more general anxieties about civilizational decline. Exemplifying this conflation, Adamsites ran simultaneous attacks against Jackson's lack of sexual morals, Tennessee provenance, and the integrity of his claims to "whiteness." The category of "whiteness" had expanded as men of relatively low status and wealth came into the fold as citizens following states' steady lifting of property requirements for white men.[42] Many white men benefited from this expansion as they inherited newly acquired "wages of whiteness."[43] At the same time, the founding elite whose reputation hung on a racialized, inborn right to rule, resisted. Adams's allies exploited this in "attack ads" that exemplified the racialized, gendered, and classed dimensions of the Adamsites' Lament: "'General Jackson's mother was a COMMON PROSTITUTE,' ... 'brought to this country by the British soldiers! She afterwards married a MULATTO MAN, with whom she had several children, of which number General JACKSON is one!!!'"[44] Another editorial claimed that Jackson's "older brother was sold as a slave in Carolina."[45] The political work of claims about whiteness and the Adams campaign's effort to question the racial origins and character for leadership were also on display in the specific claims about Rachel Robards, whom a Kentucky newspaper "likened ... to a 'dirty, black wench.'"[46] These claims

[39] Ibid., 895; Allgor, *Parlor Politics*, 191.

[40] Basch, "Marriage, Morals, and Politics in the Election of 1828," 895.

[41] Ibid., 894.

[42] Jacob Katz Cogan, "The Look Within: Property, Capacity, and Suffrage in Nineteenth-Century America," *The Yale Law Journal* 107, no. 2 (1997): 473–498; Alexander Saxton, *The Rise and Fall of the White Republic: Class Politics and Mass Culture in Nineteenth-Century America* (New York: Verso, 2003).

[43] David R. Roediger, *The Wages of Whiteness: Race and the Making of the American Working Class* (New York: Verso, 1999).

[44] Lynn Hudson Parsons, *The Birth of Modern Politics: Andrew Jackson, John Quincy Adams, and the Election of 1828* (New York: Oxford University Press, 2011), 143–144.

[45] David E. Johnson and Johnny Ray Johnson, *A Funny Thing Happened on the Way to the White House: Foolhardiness, Folly, and Fraud in Presidential Elections from Andrew Jackson to George W. Bush* (Lanham, MD: Taylor Trade, 2004), 16.

[46] Parsons, *The Birth of Modern Politics*, 144.

about legitimate whiteness went hand in hand with the attacks on Jackson's failure to respect another man's marital property – (wifely) property it had also deemed mannish and "spoilt" – and fears about Jackson's political leadership.

Adamsites thus characterized Jackson as shameless in every sense of the word. He was lacking brakes and restraint with respect to sexual modesty, property, political action, racial propriety, violence, and morality in general. He was from the wrong place and behaved in the wrong way. He was a military hero, not a political leader – a Guardian but not a Philosopher King. Adams's campaign's depiction of Jackson and the threat he posed to the republic exemplifies The Lament and its indictments: Jackson is shameless; Jackson is uncivil; his sexual indiscretions reveal that he cannot be trusted with the stewardship of the nation; he will go on to commit atrocious moral crimes; he has no manners; he has no debt to history; he has no religion other than himself; he is autochthonous, self-made, and dangerously preoccupied with living life on his own authentic and sovereign terms without regard to anyone else. Prefiguring the contemporary language of The Lament, Jackson's shameless, "loose morals" and "poor breeding" are constituted as an *intrusion* in the decent public sphere. This intrusion thus absolves Adams (and others who invoke The Lament) from having to abide by the norms of civility and shame they purport to defend. If Jackson is elected to the presidency, the Adams camp argued, shame will die and civilization will be destroyed.

Perhaps confirming elites' fear that certain forms of shame *were in fact dead*, voters overwhelmingly preferred Jackson. Still angry about 1824, they were drawn to Jackson's antiaristocratic message and the burgeoning notion of domestic privacy (in which certain aspects of our lives are not shameful but politically off-limits), which John Quincy's camp had so clearly violated.[47] Jackson had run on "spotless innocence in the face of the corruption that had infected politics," promised to "cleanse the fetid atmosphere of the nation's capital," and in the end, Adams's attacks appear to have backfired – at least in the short term.[48] Meanwhile, Jackson's supporters played up the common sense and common law spirit of their marriage. They refused to hide in shame because they saw nothing shameful about their marriage. Their public representation of their relationship was loud and proud, reflecting a nineteenth-century shift in marriage away from status and class and toward a relationship of unapologetic love. Even as Jackson had his own designs on centralized power, he successfully portrayed Adams as the meddling zealot who would leave nothing – even the most intimate matters – to the discretion and regulation of the people themselves.

The hypocrisy and paternalism of the patriarchal class and its anxieties about democratic peoples in need of regulation struck a chord. The Jackson campaign played up its own message about a moral war – one between those

[47] Basch, "Marriage, Morals, and Politics in the Election of 1828," 895.
[48] Parsons, *The Birth of Modern Politics*, 142.

who believed that public officials deserved the right to privacy – and those who insisted that "a candidate should regard the relentless scrutiny of his private life as a test of his republican principles," a test one happily takes when running for public office.[49] This is not to say the Jackson campaign was particularly scrupulous. Jackson insisted that he would "*never war against females* and it is only the base and cowardly that do," but his allies lobbed their share of attacks. One pamphlet noted that Adams was "a practicing pimp" who procured prostitutes for Czar Alexander.[50] Whether this (unfounded) rumor made citizens skeptical of the Adamses moral standards is hard to tell.[51] More clear is that as much as the Adams camp tried to make "the fundamental ground rules of marriage" synonymous with republicanism, Jackson's case for popular sovereignty in such matters – as opposed to obeisance to aristocratic conventions of modesty and shame – won over the voters, following the lead of Tennesseans who had never worried about the legal status of Jackson's marriage. The culture of Adams and its attendant values were rendered both antidemocratic and un-American, eclipsed by a surge of Jacksonian populism. That 1828 brought the victory of Jacksonians in both the House and Senate, with a large margin in the former, meant a mandate for the new populist agenda.[52] Jackson's anti-aristocratic critique of "sons of fortune ... nursed in the lap of luxury, who have never known ... adversity, [and] who have found ... every want supplied" took root.[53]

The attacks on Rachel Jackson's character during the 1828 campaign may not have cost Andrew Jackson the election, but Jackson and his friends blamed the stress it caused for Rachel's premature death.[54] She lived to see the campaign victory, but died of a heart attack just before the inauguration. Jackson thus entered his presidency as a widower, which again triggered concern in those who hewed to the republican belief that men need women to check their base tendencies. The company of a "pipe-smoking" bigamist was better than no marital company at all.[55]

Jackson against the "Ladies"

The context of Rachel Jackson's death, Jackson's widowed and unmarried status, and the general anxiety about Jackson's designs on centralized power laid

49 Basch, "Marriage, Morals, and Politics in the Election of 1828," 900–901.

50 Johnson and Johnson, *A Funny Thing Happened on the Way to the White House*, 14; Parsons, *The Birth of Modern Politics*, 144.

51 Parsons, *The Birth of Modern Politics*, 151–152.

52 Marszalak, *The Petticoat Affair*, 8; David S. Reynolds, *Waking Giant: America in the Age of Jackson* (New York: Harper Collins, 2008), 83.

53 Michael Paul Rogin, *Fathers and Children: Andrew Jackson and the Subjugation of the American Indian* (New Brunswick, NJ: Transaction, 1975), 49–50.

54 Allgor, *Parlor Politics*, 196–197.

55 Ibid., 225.

the groundwork for the scandal with which this chapter began. The event in question, during which the newspaper reported (which Tocqueville quotes as if to agree) that Jackson has "acted in the political arena like a shameless and unbridled gambler" who "will have to return his winnings, throw his false dice away and end up in some backwater where he can freely curse his stupidity," became known by various names: the "Eaton Affair," the "Petticoat War," and the "Eaton Malaria." Because the Eaton Affair, as I will refer to it, happened just months prior to Tocqueville and Beaumont's arrival and the aftershocks continued to reverberate throughout the nation while they were here, I read Tocqueville's general story of the necessary checks on democracy, the danger of majority tyranny, and his report of the success of republican virtue as a temper for avaricious social equality and the men it elevates as also a story about the Eaton Affair and the sex/gender, race, and class dynamics emerging out of the 1828 election and its aftermath.[56]

The Eaton Affair involved the marriage of John Eaton, Jackson's secretary of war, to Margaret "Peggy" (O'Neil) Timberlake, who had become involved with Eaton while her husband, John Timberlake, a Navy purser, was away at sea. "[W]hen [John Timberlake] died at sea in mysterious circumstances in 1828," notes Kirsten Wood in her study of the affair and its gender politics, "Washington gossips whispered … that he had killed himself upon learning of his wife's infidelity."[57] Whether by accident or suicide, his death made it possible for Margaret to marry John Eaton, which she did with Jackson's full blessing, just before the inauguration. Now a "Cabinet wife" and friend of the president, Margaret had access to the highest circles of Washington society – circles that had been poised against her for decades because of her reputation for promiscuity and her failure to adhere to republican gender rules. "To some Washingtonians," notes Wood, "Jackson's patronage of the Eatons seemed to be the second phase of his general attack on American morality. The first step had been [his] marriage to Rachel."[58]

When Margaret arrived at the inaugural ball, Floride Calhoun, wife of Vice President John C. Calhoun, launched her own attack. In the "first official shot in what came to be known as the 'Petticoat War,'" Floride Calhoun failed to acknowledge her.[59] The fallout was phenomenal, as Calhoun and the other "Cabinet wives" went on to refuse to attend any social gathering – dinner parties, balls, and so on – where Margaret Eaton would be present. In a political era where politics took place in social settings as much as if not more than

[56] For a full discussion of my interpretation of *Democracy in America* as constructed *against* Jackson, specifically Jackson's disregard for republican gender roles, see Jill Locke, "Aristocratic Mourning: Tocqueville, John Quincy Adams, and the Affairs of Andrew Jackson," in *Feminist Interpretations of Alexis de Tocqueville*, eds. Jill Locke and Eileen Hunt Botting (University Park: Pennsylvania State University Press, 2009), 125–150.

[57] Wood, "One Woman so Dangerous to Public Morals," 246.

[58] Ibid.

[59] Allgor, *Parlor Politics*, 202.

formal meetings, these refusals had the effect of stalling out the political work of Jackson's presidency and inciting his wrath against the "meddling" women of Washington who orchestrated this assault.[60] Their husbands, those with the official power of the Cabinet, became politically inert because of the pressure, politicking, and maneuvering of their wives' shaming campaign against Jackson and the Eatons.

What precisely *was* Margaret's crime that was so severe that her mere presence in Washington might be seen as an attack on American morals? Why did Jackson feel compelled to defend Margaret and the man he had urged to marry her? Much more than Rachel, Margaret had led a life that very publicly defied the mores and expectations of republican girls and wives. She had entered Washington society through the scandalous portal of the saloon, and she self-consciously delighted in shocking the mores of Washington's wives, daughters, and mothers of powerful men. Working as a barmaid at her father's bustling hotel and saloon placed her in close proximity to Washington's (male) power brokers – her father's patrons and boarders – and facilitated her relationships with Timberlake, Jackson, Eaton, and other men.[61] Margaret appeared to quite enjoy the sex and gender trouble she caused: "[She] seemed determined to fulfill the stereotype that any woman in such a setting must be sexually promiscuous. By the time she was sixteen, she had already tried to elope twice."[62] In her autobiography, she boasted, "While I was still in pantalets and rolling hoops with other girls I had the attentions of men, young and old, enough to turn a girl's head." According to Wood, "Some women may also have resented the time that their husbands or sons spent in the company of this woman 'of much beauty.' Most were simply disgusted by her unrestrained conversations with men and her refusal to seclude herself while her husband was away on his voyages."[63]

Yet here she was: married to the secretary of war and close friends with the recently widowed president, both of which rendered her especially threatening. Tocqueville's confident description of American wives' chastity that portrays the wife living "in her husband's home, ... in almost cloistered surroundings" clearly did not apply to Margaret.[64] Margaret did not concern herself with such matters and continued to tend bar long after her first marriage and well into her second. She was hardly alone in this violation; the anxious defense of republican femininity as an ideal likely arose from the extent to which, in the age of Andrew Jackson and an expanding, unsurveilled frontier, it was increasingly violated in practice. Margaret appears to have been precisely the kind of shameless woman whom Rousseau feared: "*having too much cause to*

[60] Wood, "One Woman so Dangerous to Public Morals," 248.
[61] Ibid., 244.
[62] Ibid., 244–245.
[63] Ibid., 245.
[64] Tocqueville, *Democracy in America*, 686.

blush ... she blushes no more."[65] As was the case with Rachel, who refused to perform shame about her unladylike manners (pipe-smoking) or the separation and ultimate divorce from Lewis Robards, Margaret lived life on her own terms, pursuing her own life in accordance with the terms she would set for herself rather than bowing to the customs enforced by Washington society. Although not as politically motivated as the shameless tactics of the Cynics or Rousseau's pariahs detailed in Chapters 2 and 3, Margaret seemed intent to expose the artificial and fraudulent virtues on which Washington appeared to rest. If Jackson's victory called into question the place of the republican mores of shame and *pudeur* in 1828, Margaret Eaton's ascent to Washington society appeared to be the final nail in their coffin. Washington women, conjuring their powers as virtuous satellites, publicly lamented this death of shame and fought back against its perpetrators – Jackson and the Eatons – triggering a government shutdown that culminated in the Eaton's relocation to Spain and the firing of the entire Cabinet.

From Jackson's perspective, both the moral police of the Adams campaign and the meddling cabinet wives (and the husbands who bowed to them) were evidence of excessive feminine power in the public sphere and aristocratic proclivities toward scandal and intrigue. They, too, proved another Rousseauean point about *pudeur* and the imperial-like power of women who are governed by (and promote) it: "The woman who is at once decent, lovable, and self-controlled, who forces those about her to respect her, who has reserve and modesty, ... sends her lovers with a nod to the end of the world, ... to anything she pleases. This seems to me a[n] ... empire ..."[66] Jackson was to be the sole emperor. Perhaps to avenge Rachel's death, perhaps to put Washington women in their place and send a message to their emasculated husbands, perhaps to assert his own authority, Jackson took up Margaret Eaton's defense as if it were his own. Jackson sought to unveil the social and political motivations behind the "ladies'" lament, arguing that they obscured and pathologized the legitimate work of governance he sought to do and the rearrangement of social mores so as not to scandalize girls and women as impure based upon the spaces and practices they inhabit and engage. Consistent with feminist and queer critiques of sexual virtue, Jackson's attack marked a shift away from republican considerations of virtuous restraints like *pudeur* as legitimate political territory and toward a more liberal critique of moralism that read preoccupations with sexual virtue as intrusions upon the ideal of a relatively neutral public sphere. Yet it was an odd sort of feminist "unashamed citizenship" that Jackson enacted on behalf of Rachel and Margaret, as it positioned Jackson as masculine protector and coded the "forces of slander" that took Rachel's life and ruined Margaret and John Eaton's in explicitly feminized terms. Jackson allegedly said to Margaret: "I tell you ..., I would rather have live vermin on

[65] Rousseau, *Politics and the Arts*, 91.
[66] Rousseau, *Emile*, 393. For Rousseau, modesty and shame were a means by which "nature armed the weak in order to enslave the strong" (358).

my back than the tongue of one of these Washington women on my reputation."[67] Jackson's "feminist" defense thus not only delegitimized republican mothers and wives' moral suasion in the public sphere, it delegitimized women's political voices of any kind. Rachel and Margaret did not speak; Jackson spoke for them.

Fighting back against the "ladies" consumed Jackson's entire first term – his response to the charges against Margaret "was longer than his inaugural address" and a full "ninety-three pages of [his] papers are devoted to refuting these charges."[68] He set out to prove the decency (or the irrelevance of her "indecency" by moralistic standards) of Margaret Eaton and the friend he had encouraged to marry her, and demanded that his cabinet members accept Margaret into their homes.[69] But the cabinet wives didn't balk, and their husbands appeared powerless in the face of their wives' demands. The "sharp-tongued Washington women," as Margaret once called them, may have provided moral education for America, but they were not Tocqueville's quiet and obedient republican brides.[70] The intransigence of both sides stalled out the day-to-day business of national politics. Jackson, determined not to be a puppet of his cabinet members' wives, was ready to be done with all of them. His closest cabinet ally, Secretary of State Van Buren, offered to step down with the hopes that others would follow. When they failed to do so, Jackson demanded the resignation of his cabinet and Vice President Calhoun. (Van Buren became vice president for the second term.) Evidencing a small victory for the Washington women, Margaret and John Eaton were banished from the country – reassigned to a post in Spain, where Jackson believed their scandalous history would be unremarkable.[71] Indeed, Jackson understood – perhaps better than Adams or Tocqueville (if not Rousseau, who theorized this imperial power and accordingly warned of Sophie's latent audacity) – the ways in which the ideal of the republican wife could ultimately run afoul of the doctrine of separate spheres as it supported women's education and (indirect) interest in public life. For the republican wives in Washington, the call to teach shame – to defend and enforce *pudeur* – was very much a call to action. It is significant that this civic work was far from feminist and involved a nineteenth-century version of what has come to be known as "slut-shaming" – hardly an ideal portal through which women could emerge as speakers, writers, organizers, and judges in the collective work of public life. *Pudeur*, like the shamelessness it was meant to regulate and check, was *implicated* in politics and politicking and not a fetter against it.

Like the Robards Affair, the Eaton Affair helps to explain Tocqueville's account of the period. Although some scholars have emphasized Tocqueville's

[67] Allgor, *Parlor Politics*, 201.
[68] Ibid., 203–204.
[69] Ibid., 200–203.
[70] Marszalek, *The Petticoat Affair*, vi.
[71] Allgor, *Parlor Politics*, 210, 235.

own ambivalence and sadness about the fate of women in democratic America, this context helps to illuminate the reasons why Tocqueville believed girls' sacrifices (and the marriages they produced) were "minor ills which must be braved for a greater good."[72] Tocqueville not only needed to criticize Jackson's wanton tendencies; he also needed to construct the democratic future against them. For Tocqueville, the threat of tyranny was far more dangerous than the demise of romance or the young girl's compromised liberty. The ways in which the feminine forces of public opinion with regard to sexual chastity challenge Jackson bring Tocqueville's willingness to accept the trade-off of cold and dispassionate women into sharp relief. The "ladies" in his midst proved most effective at stymieing Jackson's authoritarian efforts, and his belief that curtailed liberty for the "ladies" could potentially salvage (male) liberty rendered his approval for women's chastity a fairly uncomplicated calculation.

Following the Tocquevillean lens, it is worth emphasizing that the Jackson administration was often framed in explicitly European terms. Jackson represented Tocqueville's worries about the corrupting influences of absolute authority irrespective of the particular government form.[73] From a Tocquevillean perspective, it is entirely consistent that Jackson's inaugural festivities had been compared to the storming of the Bastille even as he was routinely caricatured as a despotic, European monarch. Commentators in the aftermath of the cabinet "disappearance" likened it to a scandal unbefitting America and of a European character.[74] Furthering this picture of Jackson, one 1832 portrait, "Born to Command: King Andrew the First," represents Jackson literally trampling on the constitution with a staff in one hand; and in the other, a document with "veto" written on it and a dead eagle dangling down below.[75] A recurrent theme in Tocqueville's work is how the absence of social striation renders the citizens vulnerable to (and eager for) the yoke of national administration. This point reflects Adams's fears as well, and the general panic about the loss of republican *pudeur* in a nation with him as commander. Hence the Eaton Affair confirmed one of the central tenets and fears of the ideal of the "republican wife": She can only provide virtuous tutelage to men who are open to being coaxed and taught. As Jan Lewis notes, "The Republican Wife represented ... a real and important role. Yet ... she was limited ..., for her capability always depended upon masculine susceptibility. She had no more power than man allowed ... [she] had no power over those who were not or did not want to be virtuous."[76] Jackson, as

[72] Tocqueville, *Democracy in America*, 686; Janara, *Democracy Growing Up*, 161, 163, 36. See also Eileen Hunt Botting, "Tocqueville's American Girl: A Pupil of Wollstonecraft," in *Feminist Interpretations of Alexis de Tocqueville*, eds. Jill Locke and Eileen Hunt Botting.

[73] Alexis de Tocqueville, *The Old Regime and the French Revolution*, trans. Stuart Gilbert (New York: Anchor, 1983), 60.

[74] Allgor, *Parlor Politics*, 192, 201.

[75] Ibid., 192. This cartoon refers to Jackson's 1832 veto of the rechartering of the Bank of the United States on the grounds that it advantages wealthy citizens and is unconstitutional.

[76] Lewis, "The Republican Wife," 720.

John Quincy and his campaigners feared, was not capable of being shamed by virtuous women; he was quite content to be in the company of "spoilt" women who deferred political authority to democratic men like himself. He married Rachel Robards; he befriended Margaret Eaton and encouraged his friend John Eaton to marry her; he delighted in her presence among the Cabinet wives; and he also gave her the kind of attention normally reserved for a first lady. Again, Jackson's ascent to power, crystallized here not in the election but in the inaugural moment, was read as evidence of the death of shame. He welcomed a woman of questionable repute into his inner circle and both refused and vilified the moral counsel of the Cabinet wives. Far from heeding their tutelage, Jackson coded the Cabinet wives who ostracized Margaret as illiberal moralists – "live vermin" whom he would go to great lengths to banish.[77] This context helps to explain why the stand-off between Jackson and the Washington "ladies" coincided with a shift away from the language of republican wife and toward the republican *mother*. "Thus the ideal of the wife would give way, by perhaps 1830," writes Lewis, "to that of the mother. Men might not be malleable, but children were."[78]

Massacre and the Case for "Good" Shame

These moralizing and gendered problems endemic to *pudeur* aside, perhaps Adams and Tocqueville (and later Arendt) have a legitimate point about the undifferentiated mass and the violent antipolitics associated with the emergence of men of "low mark" and the need for brakes and restraints. To the extent that we can read Jackson as an "unashamed citizen" who emerges to claim his own life in spite of the jeremiads about his uncivilized and shameless behavior, he is a complicated one. As president, Jackson does much more than marry a woman of dubious virtue, or "steal" another man's wife, as the Adams campaign puts it. He constructs the public sphere against women's voices. He owns and trades enslaved people. He engineers a policy of Indian Removal and executes it. Unlike the Cynics or the Enlightenment pariahs detailed in Chapters 2 and 3, he lacks the intersubjective ties of a peer group and tends to go at it alone, overly invested in his own sovereignty against the plurality and discord of the early republic's political landscape. We have seen how his unashamed critique of the moralists' nineteenth-century version of

77 While I hope I have made clear how *pudeur* becomes moralizing – especially when under siege by social and political forces that do not value it, Rousseau was emphatic that *pudeur* did not involve moralizing. Properly cultivated in girls from the beginning, it becomes an "inborn" moral habit and disposition that is reinforced socially and culturally and need not engage in moralizing. Rousseau appears to have understood the point Nietzsche would later make, that moralizing is the gasp of *ressentiment* – of being under siege. He writes: "The object is not to bore young girls with your long sermons or to recite your dry moralisms to them. Moralizing is, for both sexes, the death of all good education." Rousseau, *Emile*, 389–390.

78 Lewis, "The Republican Wife," 721.

"slut-shaming" also involved an attack on one of the few roles of any public consequence assigned to women. In these matters, perhaps Adams's lament and warning that shame is dead or dying so long as Jackson leads the nation is persuasive.

Jackson's recklessness and his occlusion of the voices of moral counsel that would counter his sovereignty provide a perfect occasion to investigate whether some forms of shame may be useful checks against morally egregious crimes. Following the typological accounts (discussed in Chapter 1), perhaps Jackson ought not to be ashamed of being from Tennessee, of the technical problems framing his wife's divorce, his "ill breeding," and so on. Adams deploys a "flattering" or "false" sense of shame in attacking Jackson on these grounds.[79] But the cases of slavery and Indian Removal suggest that Jackson also lacks a more essential form of shame. His failure to regard enslaved people and Native Americans as full persons and his willingness to traffic and exterminate them in the name of national sovereignty and legitimate state power is precisely the kind of behavior "respectful" or "true" shame is supposed to check and correct. This framework allows us to dispense with the kinds of shame we don't like and embrace and fortify what we do. It offers up the solace that with the right kinds of shame the world would be a more just and less violent place.

With these concerns in mind, I want to shift focus away from both Jackson's and Adams's violations of *pudeur* and republican virtue to the more invidious moral crimes done in the name of American democracy and sovereignty and the extent to which The Lament and a general concern about "shameless" behavior provides a useful way of explaining and criticizing Jackson's role in the case of Native Americans. The orchestration and execution of Jackson's campaign for Indian Removal in fact presents a hard case for my critique of lamentations about the death of shame, which I am arguing *do not* provide the moral compass or political solution their defenders believe them to guarantee. This position is controversial, as even fierce critics of *pudeur*, or the "politics of sexual shame," typically insist that "some shame may be well deserved."[80] Shame about massacres of Native Americans clearly falls into this category.

Following this line of reasoning, we might want to draw a line between the kinds of shameless behavior exhibited by Jackson. Surely there is a difference between violating *pudeur* and the general sensibilities of the American aristocracy's sexual mores and manners, and the extermination of Native Americans. When Tocqueville recounts the words of the American newspaper, following the narrative of John Quincy Adams, that Andrew Jackson is *sans pudeur* and *sans frein* (without shame or brake), we can read him to say that Jackson is accountable to no one and will destroy any shred of morals or civility that stands in his way. This means that he has no respect for *pudeur* (as Adams pointed out) and also that he disregards the civil traditions and community of

[79] Tarnopolsky, *Prudes, Perverts, and Tyrants*; Taylor, *Pride, Shame, and Guilt*.
[80] Warner, *The Trouble with Normal*, 5.

Native Americans that Tocqueville so clearly values. Hence even a critic who cared very little about Jackson's disregard for marriage laws or the need to respect the special moral counsel of republican women might still believe shame could have checked Jackson's actions against indigenous peoples. That is to say, one can denounce a politics of *pudeur* and still insist that a healthy democracy requires shame because it protects against serious moral crimes.[81] Jackson, true to the autochthonous portrait that circulated during the election, emerges in this story as indebted to no one and without any respect for intersubjective relations among people, connection to tradition, and reverence and awe for forces beyond himself. His lack of shame then helps to explain why he thought it acceptable and desirable to pursue both his own sovereignty and the sovereignty of the nation in a violent western expansion that involved destroying Native American people. Jackson represents the white masses' desire to live and do as they wish, eschewing the difference and deference and role specificity that *aidōs* and *pudeur* enshrine and guarantee. The presence of moral shame in Jackson and in the period, this line of reasoning suggests, might have saved Native Americans. Considering that John Quincy Adams, whose loss to Jackson can be read as the *death of shame* and decline of civilization as the Founders understood it, described the mass deaths as one of the "heinous sins of this nation" (June 30, 1841), we have good reason to presume that a political leader more attuned to the requirements of *aidōs* and *pudeur* would not have steered the nation in this direction.[82]

Let us look closely at Jackson's obsession with his own "natural" power and the need to be "authentic," self-made, and sovereign without respect for traditions, customs, and ultimately the *bodies* of others and whether a moral form of shame could protect against it. Jackson appears to lack the restraint and humanity that inherited forms of rule like aristocracy (formal or informal) claim to guarantee. His shamelessness is inhumane – totally lacking regard for the world he shares with others and the traditions and horizons that bound it. This is a version of Tocqueville's diagnosis of him and the period associated with his name. Tocqueville writes, as noted and popularized with the neo-Tocquevillean work on civil society, of the need for mores and local institutions and decentralized power to check avaricious democratic

[81] Speaking of French public opposition to the Vichy regime's anti-Semitism, Hannah Arendt writes that the French have shown sensitivity to shame and a desire to avoid the same fate as Germany, Poland, Romania, and Hungary. These feelings of shame and regard for France vis-à-vis Europe's moral crimes "are precisely the first signs of a reawakening national awareness," she writes. For Arendt, shame of "being human" and the atrocities committed in our name is "elemental, … what finally is left of our sense of international solidarity" and in need of "adequate political expression." Shame is still nonpolitical and "purely individual" according to Arendt, but as a moral sentiment it can provoke or inspire heroic political action. Hannah Arendt, *The Jewish Writings* (New York: Random House, 2008), 177. For a full discussion, see Manu Samnotra, "'Sensitive to Shame': Hannah Arendt on Becoming Worldly," *Constellations* 21, no. 3 (September 1, 2014): 338–350.

[82] Lynn Hudson Parsons, "'A Perpetual Harrow upon My Feelings': John Quincy Adams and the American Indian," *The New England Quarterly* 46, no. 3 (September 1, 1973): 339, 340.

men.[83] His low opinion of Jackson is clear throughout his writings, and he is aghast – freely using the term "evil" – with the young democracy's arrogant destruction of centuries-old traditions and customs. Describing the "evils of invasion" and the famine afflicting Native Americans after their buffalo were driven out by European settlers, Tocqueville writes:

> The fearful evils that attended these forced migrations are impossible to imagine. By the time the Indians leave their ancestral lands, they are already exhausted and worn down. The country they are about to settle is already occupied by tribes who view the incomers with jealousy. At their backs lies hunger, before them war and everywhere suffering. To avoid so many enemies, they divide up and each man in isolation furtively seeks the means of survival; he exists in the vast tracts of desert like some outcast in civilized society. The long-weakened social bonds then burst. Already their homeland has disappeared; soon they will have no people; families will scarcely survive; their common name is lost, their language is forgotten, and the traces of their origins vanish. The nation has ceased to exist. It hardly features in the memories of American antiquaries and is known only to a few European scholars.... I have witnessed evils I would find it impossible to relate.[84]

Several aspects of Tocqueville's argument complicate a straightforward defense of indigenous sovereignty, most specifically his tendency to fetishize "savage" primitivism and "savage women." Yet there is little doubt that he is morally outraged at the United States' arrogance on this question; that Jackson's Indian Removal project turned on contracts (treaties), swindling and coercing indigenous peoples under the auspices of liberal exchange, makes it all the more egregious from a Tocquevillean point of view.

Moreover, what is striking is that Tocqueville reads Native Americans as civilized, albeit in their own non-European way. The language of "forced migration" calls our attention to the loss of rootedness; and his reference to dividing up and becoming isolated signals some of his concerns about the dangers of democratic tyranny. More directly, he laments the destroying of "long-weakened social bonds" and the loss of the "people," language, name, traces of origins, and finally the "nation." His emphasis on "social bonds" mirrors what he admires in the Anglo-American civil society he spends most of time describing. In self-consciously using that language in his description of the devastation experienced by Native Americans, he signals the degree of the brutality and inhumanity of American policy. Given that he writes this after the Indian Removal Act (1830) but well before the "Trail of Tears" (1838–1839), we can only assume that Tocqueville's worries would have increased had he borne witness to the degree of Jackson's unfettered destruction of indigenous life.

[83] Robert D. Putnam, *Bowling Alone: The Collapse and Revival of American Community* (New York: Simon & Schuster, 2000).

[84] Tocqueville, *Democracy in America*, 378–380.

The Indian Removal campaign was Jackson's project, easily traced to him and his understanding of the ways in which this particular form of expansion was not a democratic exception or anomaly, but a democratic requirement. Jacksonian Indian policy brought together Jackson's obsessions with white supremacy and American expansion, as the move west allowed for the expansion of slavery, both of which were needed to grow the cotton industry by building plantations on indigenous peoples' land.[85] Military prowess and racial ideology became the foundation on which Jackson sought to stabilize the departure from inherited power that made his political power possible.

Civilizing Jackson

It is comforting to believe, with Tocqueville, that this "democratic man" would have been less dangerous had he internalized some of the civilizing features of shame and manners that characterized John Quincy and the generation of leaders he eclipsed. Yet this preoccupation with Indian Removal as strictly a problem of Jacksonian democracy and Jacksonian shamelessness is problematic. Adams's renunciation of Indian Removal comes late in his career. As one of his sympathetic biographers notes, for most of his professional life, Adams held the same view as Jackson with respect to Indians and the need to destroy them to make room for Anglo-American progress and expansion.[86] At the end of the War of 1812, Adams understood "extermination of all Indian rights a national duty"; as secretary of state, Adams defended Jackson's invasion of Florida (Spain) and the "execution of Indian prisoners without trial" as sound measures against the "barbarities of the Indians." His late-in-life change of heart notwithstanding, Adams remained committed to natural conquest, "white power," and the "inevitable expansion of Anglo-Saxon civilization."[87]

Moreover, Indian Removal, in particular, was not a by product of Jackson's coarse and indecorous manners or his obsession with "the authentic" and "nature" against the "artifice" of the founding aristocracy. It was effort to secure "civilization," which he accepted – following Adams and others – as needing gender roles as a regulative guide. Jackson and other supporters of Indian Removal deployed imperialistic discourses that juxtaposed properly civilized white Americans against uncivilized "savages" – and, more specifically, properly gendered whites against the disorderly gender economy of American Indians.

The place of an ethos of civility and *pudeur* in Jackson's campaign for Indian Removal comes alive in Michael Rogin's study of Jackson. As Rogin

[85] Reynolds, *Waking Giant*, 92–95.

[86] Parsons, "A Perpetual Harrow upon My Feelings," 340.

[87] Ibid., 340, 344.

demonstrates with archival documentation from the period, Jackson may not have wanted to legitimize his rule vis-à-vis an inheritance from the founding fathers, but neither did he want to squander their legacy. He was acutely aware of the extent to which people feared he would undo the virtues of the revolution. He knew that "[f]or Adams and his heirs, [he was] the symbol for the decline of the Republic of the Founding Fathers, the catalyst that precipitated the forces of demagoguery, hypocrisy, and greed [that became characteristic of] ... nineteenth-century America."[88]

To that end, even as he presented himself as a "self-made man" who was proud not to be one of the "sons of fortune ... nursed in the lap of luxury, who have never known ... adversity, [and] who have found ... every want supplied," he also insisted that he was not, in his own words, "of 'a degenerate race ... unworthy of the blessings which the blood of so many thousand heroes has purchased for them.' "[89] His autochthonous self-understanding meant he had to redeem the legitimacy of his leadership against his characterization as an uncivilized, "ill-bred," crass and unmannered Tennessean who was unfit to lead the young republic. Jackson's ascent signified a democratic "rupture with the order of [founding] kinship," yet Jackson could not sustain the democratic rule his election brought about.[90] Instead, he sought to secure the legitimacy of his own authority – invoking his military power to destroy others and destroying the chance that made his presidency possible. He compensated for his lack of historical credentials to rule with military power to destroy. In this sense, his strategies of legitimate self-representation fit into broader analyses of liberalism and empire, as war against indigenous persons, justified through a "*mission civilisatrice,*" compensates for and reinforces the strength of fledgling nations and their leaders. Across the nineteenth-century political spectrum, from John Quincy Adams to Jackson to the antislavery crusader Horace Greeley, Native Americans were routinely characterized as "children" – "slave[s] of appetite and sloth."[91] Jackson's anti-Indian sentiments were hardly his alone, and in fact he paradoxically saw himself as their caretaker.[92]

Just as children have been historically defined by their youth and relationship to parental authority and not by their gender, Anglo-Americans framed their view of Native Americans as child-like through their perceived absence of

[88] Ibid., 341.

[89] Rogin, *Fathers and Children*, 14, 49–50.

[90] Jacques Rancière, *Hatred of Democracy* (New York: Verso, 2007), 45.

[91] Rogin, *Fathers and Children*, 117.

[92] David Reynolds notes the extent to which Jackson believed he was "saving" the Indians and saw himself as their friend. He and Rachel had adopted a fourteen-year-old Indian boy who died only two years later. Jackson was not anti-Indian per se; he simply believed that Indians and whites could not live together – a view that was hardly only his. Reynolds, *Waking Giant*, 91, 103.

an indigenous view of gender difference. Rogin notes how Jackson and other supporters of Indian Removal believed that "savages" gained their "innocent bliss" of life in nature at the expense of Indian women, who were denied the special dignity of "women's natural role." Pro-Removal politicians blamed the lack of indigenous women's special moral voice for Native Americans' alleged proclivities for violence.[93] This lack of a special role – an indigenous equivalent of the republican mother – was apparently evident in the fact that "Indian men made their women work; white men did not." Driving home this point of Indian gender uniformity, Rogin notes that Indian languages contain only the masculine pronoun. In order for Indians to "grow up" and become civilized, they needed to learn the roles of male and female – the roles guaranteed by *pudeur*. One of the chief justifications for Indian Removal, which reflects other colonial discourses, is the extent to which Indians needed to "be civilized ... so they would learn to respect their women."[94] Both Jackson and Adams believed they respected women – one by protecting them from false and priggish moral codes, the other through a strict following of republican virtue. Jackson pursued Indian Removal as a way to speak in the language of the founding aristocracy. Through pathologizing the uncivilized characteristics of Native Americans, he occupies the ideology of the founding aristocrats' lament against him, the "ill-bred" man. In so doing, Jackson corrects the aristocrats' view that he was "as violent and barbaric as Indians."[95]

Indicting Jackson as unregulated, unchecked, and totally lacking in shame is an easy way to gloss over the competing aesthetic, political, and moral claims of the first half of the nineteenth century. Like all iterations of The Lament, it provides a straightforward, naturalized, and appealing indictment of what one doesn't like about Jackson's presidency: his lack of respect for the historic property of the White House, his centralization of power, unapologetic slaveholding and slave-trading, shunning of republican women and the sons they raised, opposition to women's suffrage, and crafting and executing of the slaughter of Native Americans. Each of these can be easily judged through the discourse of shame and shamelessness as they are held up as evidence that Jackson is shameless and so long as he is in power, shame is dead in America, as well. This simple accusation of Jackson and the people around him who carried out his political and moral vision for the country elevates the moral and political judgment of the founders without scrutinizing how anti-Indian attitudes and policy, opposition to women's suffrage, and the affirmation of slavery as consistent with republicanism, were far from inventions of the new, democratic "self-made" man. That is to say, to presume that a proper acquisition of shame could prevent the moral problems of the

93 Rogin, *Fathers and Children*, 119–120.
94 Ibid., 124.
95 Ibid., 120.

centralization of power under Jackson and the massacres growing out of it conceals the ways in which investments in shame's regulative and palliative properties transfer broader anxieties about democratic life onto ideas and practices of equality, authenticity, and self-invention. Scapegoating Jackson as the agent of Indian Removal is part of the broader "politics of deflection" present in The Lament: The aesthetic, political, and moral crimes of the moment are pinned on the "new arrival," the political parvenu enfranchised in the democratic moment rather than the legacy of the "civilized" and shame-defending past.[96]

Lamentations about the death of shame in the Jacksonian era and the broader demonization of Jackson are presented as concerns about how to save democracy, make it work, and redeem it, but they reveal underlying anxieties and ambivalences about what democracy entails. The Jackson story shows, yet again, the ways in which lamentations about the death of shame are typically uttered in the face of social equality, guided by the presumption that democracies and democratic constitutions have a special proclivity for excess and shamelessness. This was clearly Rousseau's fear, hence his insistence on such a robust theory of *pudeur* as a supplement for the gender disorder his radical republicanism of self-legislating citizens might permit. Certainly this is true in Tocqueville's work, as well: Under the conditions of a properly governed aristocracy, he suggests, gender disorder and extramarital affairs do not necessarily pose a threat. It is only in the context of his discussion of postrevolutionary France that Tocqueville raises concerns about the absence of fixed gender roles and sexual mores exacerbating the chaos of French politics. And here he echoes Rousseau's view that without the stabilizing effects of class difference, sexual mores guaranteed by *pudeur* assume new significance and need stricter enforcement.[97] Note the clear absence of lamentations or indictments of the founders, who fought a revolutionary war, declared independence, and constructed and ratified a republican constitution only to guarantee the perpetuation of slavery and the civic invisibility of Native Americans. In the popular memory, the colonists live on as gentle Pilgrims, in spite of the ways in which colonial "civility" established slavery and anti-Indian race wars.[98] The story of Indian Removal reveals that faith in sexually shaming *pudeur* is not as different from the faith in moral, "good" shame as it appears. Shame in each of

[96] I borrow the term "politics of deflection" from Jeanne Morefield. See Jeanne Morefield, *Empires without Imperialism: Anglo-American Decline and the Politics of Deflection* (New York: Oxford University Press, 2014).

[97] See Linda Zerilli, *Signifying Woman: Culture and Chaos in Rousseau, Burke, and Mill* (Ithaca: Cornell University Press, 1994); Wingrove, *Rousseau's Republican Romance.*

[98] Bernard Bailyn, *The Barbarous Years: The Peopling of British North America: The Conflict of Civilizations, 1600–1675* (New York: Alfred A. Knopf, 2012); Jorge Cañizares-Esguerra, *Puritan Conquistadors: Iberianizing the Atlantic, 1550–1700* (Palo Alto, CA: Stanford University Press, 2006).

its forms is a civilizing discourse that necessarily positions others as "beyond the pale."

Indeed, so familiar are exaltations of the founders and the republican virtue they leveraged to *build* American civilization that it seems strange to say that they were shameless *destroyers* of it. Even as we speak of their moral shortcomings, the founders' capacity for self-regulation is taken as given. As is now quite widely known, Thomas Jefferson carried on a thirty-eight-year relationship with Sally Hemings, an enslaved woman whom Jefferson owned as a result of his marriage to Martha Wayles.[99] Jefferson and Hemings had seven children together. His political enemies sought to shame and scandalize his relationship with Hemings and it was covered in newspapers across the country at the time. Yet the story remained buried until Annette Gordon-Reed's research and two books on the subject assembled a more complete picture.[100] "Virtually all late-nineteenth-century accounts focused on portraying Jefferson in harmony with the Victorian ideals of marriage and family," notes one study of the sex lives of the founding fathers.[101] Even through the late-twentieth century, the view of Jefferson as wholly devoted to his late wife, to whom he had promised he would not remarry, persisted.[102] The Jefferson-Hemings relationship breached the codes of republican virtue on several accounts. But Jefferson's reputation as a devoted widower who "trembled" in the face of a just God who would judge him and others about slavery (even as he did nothing to abet abolition) wholly lacked the significant details of his relationship with Hemings and the children they bore.

To place the erasure of Jefferson's relationship with Hemings in the framework of this book, there are two key (and inextricably linked) differences between Jefferson and Jackson's "illegitimate" relationships that lie outside the bounds of republican virtue. The first pertains to their class position; Jefferson obviously had a level of public esteem in the new republic that Jackson never came close to achieving. As author of the *Declaration of Independence*, Jefferson is in an important sense the original founding *father*. In good European fashion, precisely of the type praised by Tocqueville and Adams, he sought to build an intellectual and scholarly world for the American people. The Library of Congress *is* Jefferson and the wise men who inspired him. Jackson is a military

[99] Rumors also circulated about Jefferson's relationship with a woman named Betsey Walker, who was married to his friend and neighbor, John Walker, but this is not the legacy of Jefferson that survived. Jefferson's great-granddaughter's book, *The Domestic Life of Thomas Jefferson* (1871), greatly contributed to the view of Jefferson as a romantic who loved the "girls" in an entirely nonscandalous way. Thomas A Foster, *Sex and the Founding Fathers: The American Quest for a Relatable Past* (Philadelphia: Temple University, 2014) 47, 50–53.

[100] Annette Gordon-Reed, *Thomas Jefferson and Sally Hemings: An American Controversy* (Charlottesville: University of Virginia Press, 1997); Annette Gordon-Reed, *The Hemingses of Monticello: An American Family* (New York: W. W. Norton, 2009).

[101] Foster, *Sex and the Founding Fathers*, 54.

[102] Ibid., 56–57.

hero, not an Enlightenment son. The second reason, related to the first, is that as an arbiter of republican virtue, Jefferson never owned up to his relationship with Hemings. Hypocrisy, as the maxim goes, "is a tribute vice pays to virtue."[103] Jefferson knew that his relationship with Hemings was shame*ful* – against a largely agreed-upon code of mores of the time – and he did what any person feeling shame would do: he denied it to his death. In the hiding and the denial, Jefferson buttressed the republican virtues that turned on racial difference. Contrast this with Jackson, who denied the legitimacy of the virtues used to slander Rachel and himself. He asked for marital privacy but not out of shame. Jackson claimed pride against shame and natural love against artificial convention while Jefferson ceded to the power of social rules, accepting the judgment of disgrace, and hiding his relationship with Hemings in the cover of "protective" shame.[104]

The False Solace of Shame

What becomes clear in these stories about Jackson's rise to power and the division between the founding aristocracy and the new democratic class is the extent to which shame cannot be relied upon as a foundational concept to navigate difficult political times. It cannot and should not be expunged from political discourse and argument, but it has no stabilizing ontology. Rather, the idea of shame as a brake is part of a political discourse with a history that is routinely exploited for a false sense of solace and clarity in relatively egalitarian times. This is especially true with respect to the reformulation of social arrangements related to ascending ideas of democratic equality as is evident in the contest between Jackson and Adams. Jackson invoked the language of nature against artifice in his critique of Adams for moralizing from a position of aristocratic privilege and attacking the Jacksons' marital (moral) integrity. Adams shamed Jackson for running roughshod over the civilizing qualities of republican women and the marriage laws that are supposed to protect them. In both cases, this debate about the necessity of shame and what it regulates are clearly tied to debates about democracy and its requirements. Here we see how these debates constitute the struggle about the meaning and future of democratic life under increased equalities. The expansion of the demos gets coded as excessive; *pudeur* and the marital bonds protecting it are supposed to regulate and protect against democracy's dangers. Jackson's "authentic" democratic rule and Adams's appeals to civility and manners engage and seek to

[103] La Rochefoucauld, *Maxims* (New York: Penguin, 1981), Maxim 218.

[104] Alexander Hamilton's case is particularly germane to the questions I raise here. Hamilton had a highly publicized relationship with Maria Reynolds, which he never denied. He, like Jackson, came from the "wrong place" – he was born in Jamaica to unwed parents. Thomas Foster argues that Hamilton's failure to live on with the same status of Washington and Jefferson is related to both his lower-class birth and the affair he never denied. Foster, *Sex and the Founding Fathers*, 119–142.

regulate the political while appearing as clear trumps to the conflict and agony the political entails.

The extent to which shame cannot be relied upon as a foundational concept to regulate democracy becomes even clearer in Jackson's campaign for Indian Removal. While it appears that shame might provide a brake against egregious moral crimes, in fact it can also be used to abet them, as is evident in Jackson's deployment of *pudeur* and the gender difference it guarantees in his justifications for Indian Removal. This dynamic was in play in the Jacobin executions of public women who trampled on the virtues of their sex and saw themselves as citizens, rather than only mothers in the eyes of the republic. The horrors of the guillotine were done – at least in part – in the name of defending republican *pudeur*. Shame, regardless of who deploys it and toward whichever end does not appear capable of preventing the harms and dangers of Jacksonian America. It's not clear why we would want to lean on it for political and moral problems today.

There is another point to be made about the political power of shame as triggering a moral reckoning about what one is doing vis-à-vis the position she or he believes to be morally correct. This is the shame that Jefferson clearly feels with respect to slavery – the shame of the hypocrite who, as a republican committed to natural rights, knows that slavery is wrong, yet nonetheless has enslaved hundreds of people. Theorists of shame often identify how grappling with one's hypocrisy is a moment of moral reflection that can inspire just action. In some of the literature on shame and the Holocaust, shame of collaboration triggers resistance – the recognition, the feeling *on the skin* of being seen as a Nazi sympathizer or collaborator by the peers whom one admires.[105] Yet, needless to say, Jefferson's shame did not inspire just action in the form of freeing the people he had enslaved, and many who stood idly by as Nazism and the genocide it enacted moved forward may have felt shame and done nothing. To suggest that what we need is "more shame" in the face of moral crimes places far too much hope in its active power. Even if ashamed and self-consciously so, the shamed subject does not necessarily know how to act politically in the world. Much of the psychological literature, in fact, highlights how shame induces feelings of paralysis and moral grandiosity, that is, pride in knowing what is wrong even if one fails to act on it.[106]

Let us go back to Jackson with this framework in mind. One could say that Jackson felt great shame about his marriage to Rachel – not because of anything he believed to be intrinsically wrong with it, but because of how it was pathologized in the election against Adams. This social shame triggered his critique of Adams's moralizing and gave birth to a concept of privacy that has

105 See Ruth Leys, *From Guilt to Shame: Auschwitz and After* (Princeton, NJ: Princeton University Press, 2009).

106 I discuss the limitations of shame as a ground for action in Locke, "Shame and the Future of Feminism," 146–162. On this point, see Sara Ahmed, *The Cultural Politics of Emotion* (New York: Routledge, 2004), 101–121.

been an essential part of American political discourse, one that is unacknowledged in the Tocquevillean account of the period and evident in more contemporary iterations of The Lament. But one can also make the case that Jackson's shame of being cast as "ill-bred" and illegitimate – in both his marriage and his birth – fueled his desire to consolidate his identity as a legitimate and sovereign man, by enslaving and trading people expanding slavery, and "removing" Indians. This would affirm Michael Warner's point that the first thing people do with their shame is "pin it on someone else."[107] Jackson, committed to being his own "authentic" person who is not going to play by aristocratic, "artificial" rules, strives to enact and preserve his own sovereignty, which he wants because of the extent to which he feels ashamed. However much his political career was the result of "democratic chance" – a change in who could vote and run for office, he worked assiduously to close down that chance, invoking his own right to rule as a member of the planter class who had accumulated wealth and power as a slave-owner and slave-trader. Jackson's malice is easily diagnosed as evidence of his shamelessness. But to place the blame chiefly on his obsession with self-invention and his critique of the artificial mores of the aristocracy misses the point. Jackson's problem isn't that he lacked shame. For all we know he was wracked with it. The problem with Jackson was his total inability to share the world with others whose own visions of a "true" and "authentic" life threatened of his.

If one wants to insist that shame is a necessary brake that inhibits crimes against humanity – a check that was clearly absent in Indian Removal, it requires moving beyond the temporal frame that governs The Lament. This form of shame is not something that we have necessarily "lost" or has "died," and cultivating it needs something much more than lamentation. If what defenders of shame as precursor to ethical action want to defend is the ability of people to stand up and speak out against social, political, or moral harms, shame seems an odd place to turn in part because it is so focused on the subject's internal state and less attentive to the conditions in the world that make it possible to speak out, act up, revolt, and start anew. To paraphrase Hanna Pitkin, it's not clear what role shame plays in figuring out *why we act and don't act* in the world when it calls us.[108] The hard case of Jackson's massacre of Native Americans does not in fact provide a ringing endorsement of the need for democracies to cultivate and guarantee shame.

Democratic Theory and the Legacy of The Lament

I began this chapter with a question about whether the dangers of the Jacksonian era, especially the centralization of power, the expansion of slavery,

[107] Warner, The Trouble with Normal, 3.

[108] Hanna Pitkin, *The Attack of the Blob: Hannah Arendt's Concept of the Social* (Chicago: University of Chicago Press, 1998), 251–284.

and the project of Indian Removal can best be analyzed as problems of shamelessness. Commentators routinely describe the period and Jackson himself in terms of an unchecked, rampant individualism authorized in the name of authenticity that ran roughshod over civilizing influences like shame and civility. My answer is that the Jacksonian era reveals how discourses of shame and authenticity work both with and against each other to open up the political world of the new democracy and also to close it down. Neither can be relied upon to make democracy safe or guarantee specific outcomes, and treating either as the "thing" that will resolve political conflict threatens the vitality and unpredictability that is necessary for politics and political activity. In the name of both shame *and* authenticity, restraint and self-fashioning, Jackson and his enemies attempted to steer and intervene in the democratic zeitgeist of early nineteenth-century political culture in light of their own particular political imaginaries. A politics of "chance" had opened up several doors for new voices, new constitutions, new visions, and both Adams and Jackson sought to keep these doors open in their own ways. But in the end, neither the "aristocratic" founder nor the "democratic" natural man (and their allies) could live with the rupture in power that made their own leadership possible. They sought to discipline and contain it.

This broader anxiety about democratic equality persists in contemporary democratic theory, much of which has been influenced by Tocqueville and takes his obsession with cultivating and preserving democratic mores and manners as cardinal rule. Tocqueville tells us that this rule is established objectively, by witnessing actually existing politics in Jacksonian America and seeing how it worked, what regulated its democratic excesses, what prevented it from becoming a full-fledged instantiation of American Jacobinism. What I have shown in this chapter and is evident in historians' work on the nineteenth century is the degree to which Tocqueville's project – seeking a general theory of democracy rooted in the particular case of America – intentionally and inevitably must gloss over the conflict over the very morals and manners he presumes as essential and stabilizing. Shame and its cognates, as well as the impulses toward "authenticity" and self-invention, as was true in France in the eighteenth (and nineteenth) centuries, were not fixed and finished. Rather, they were tools of political discourse that emerged, as they had before, in struggles over the meaning of democratic equality. Most specifically, these struggles involved the extent to which democratic equality could be extended into the realm of a social order whose exclusions (of poor men, women of all races and classes, Native Americans, free and enslaved people, immigrants) provided the very groundwork for the robust conception of equality in the first place.

Thus one explanation for why political theorists have neglected the messy details of the Jacksonian era is the disproportionate influence of Tocqueville on our understanding of the period, specifically our understanding of it as excessive and in need of specific regulative forces and practices. In the standard reading of Tocqueville, democracy in the Jacksonian era and democracy in general are marked by relative social equality, by which he means that there is no clear link between one's social rank and one's public standing or political power. The emerging market economy and the extension of the revolution's ideals of natural rights have given American men (and women) access to social mobility and a vocabulary for calling into question inherited rights to rule. What impresses Tocqueville most about America is not the forms of democratic government, but the effects of democratic ideas on social life – everything from associations to religion and the family. When Tocqueville writes about democracy in America, notes Pitkin, he "mean[s] not so much a form of government as a 'social state, a great social revolution' that involved both an increasing 'equality of conditions' and a consuming passion for such equality."[109] To put it in Jacques Rancière's terms, the Jacksonian era symbolized the possibility of governance and politics dictated by *chance* rather than inheritance. Although not describing the Jacksonian era specifically, Rancière's point that "politics [democracy] effectively begins whenever the power of birth is undermined" captures the ideas of the period and Jackson's ascent to power.[110]

In the Tocquevillean narrative of both America and democracy, more generally, the opening up of politics and political rule to "chance" produces considerable anxiety. Hence Tocqueville's continued preoccupation with stabilizing institutions and social mores, and his reluctant and tentative acceptance of democracy as an inevitable and historically necessary form of rule, inherited from generations of aristocratic privilege and abuse. Tocqueville is uncertain about democracy in America; as a pragmatic reformer, he takes it seriously because he wants to believe democracy's shortcomings can be worked out, but his account is notoriously ambivalent. Madisonian preoccupations loom large, as he develops the concept of majority tyranny as both a cultural and constitutional threat, all the while struggling to identify actual examples of this presumably pervasive problem.[111] Tocqueville presents democratic ambivalence as a factual, incontrovertible observation about what democracy *is* – a condition that invites hesitation and reservation because of its tendency toward excess, which is built into the upending and leveling of the social order. When Tocqueville praises the democratic tendency to empower the people in active publics, he "surrounds his call for vigorous, widespread, assertive political contestation with a number of explicit restrictions and implicit limitations."[112] As Mark Reinhardt puts it, he is preoccupied with "mak[ing] safe his democratic activism."[113]

[109] Ibid., 116.
[110] Rancière, *Hatred of Democracy*, 44.
[111] Issac Kramnick, "Introduction," Tocqueville, *Democracy in America*, xxviii–xxix.
[112] Pitkin, *The Attack of the Blob*, 125.
[113] Ibid.

There are strong Tocquevillean undercurrents in Hannah Arendt's account of politics, as well. To this point I would add that her work, written over one hundred years later, is marked by a more intensive critique and more acute nostalgia than Tocqueville's with respect to democratic "men without mark" and the loss of the revolution's "treasure."[114] Consider Arendt's lament: "When, in America and elsewhere, the poor became wealthy, they did not become men of leisure whose actions were prompted by a desire to excel, but succumbed to the boredom of vacant time, and while they too developed a taste for 'consideration and congratulation,' they were content to get these 'goods' as cheaply as possible, that is, they eliminated the passion for distinction and excellence that can exert itself only in the broad daylight of the public. The end of government remained for them self-preservation."[115] And so the Tocquevillean account of general democratic excess, rooted in the empirical case of Jacksonian America, lives on in Arendt's work and Arendtian political theory that sees politics in the democratic age as perpetually in jeopardy and in danger of losing its specificity and plurality amidst the vast and uniform modern nation-state that reduces politics to little more than bureaucracy, social advancement, and "collective housekeeping." In the next chapter I consider more closely the specifics of Arendt's version of The Lament, specifically as it is tied to the "social," her anxieties about the social disturbance endemic to democratic politics, and her conception of proper political actors and the spheres in which they act.

[114] Ibid., 116–127.
[115] Hannah Arendt, *On Revolution* (New York: Penguin, 1990), 60.

5

Arendt's Lament

The Death of Shame and the Rise of Political Children

> A man should, whatever happens, keep to his own caste, race and breed. Let the White go to the White and the Black to the Black. Then, whatever trouble falls is in the ordinary course of things – neither sudden, alien, nor unexpected.
>
> This is the story of a man who wilfully stepped beyond the safe limits of decent every-day society, and paid for it heavily.
>
> – Opening lines of "Beyond the Pale" by Rudyard Kipling

> We do not believe any organized group of citizens would under any circumstances undertake to do violence to school children of any race.
>
> – Editorial Board Statement in *The Arkansas Gazette* prior to the Little Rock desegregation

In the months and years following *Brown v. Board of Education* (1954), the landmark US Supreme Court decision that deemed segregated schools unconstitutional, school districts throughout the South implemented gradual plans for racial integration. In the case of the all-white Central High School in Little Rock, Arkansas, the district decided in the spring of 1957 to enroll nine African American students. Students had volunteered by giving their name to their teachers that spring; if chosen, they were enrolled by the National Association for the Advancement of Colored People (NAACP) in the fall.[1] Absent the district's limit and insistence on gradual integration, more students would have participated. Everyone in Little Rock knew that Central was the region's best high school. It symbolized academic excellence and architectural beauty. When it opened in 1927, Central "was the most expensive schoolhouse ever constructed in the United States. The American Institute of Architects selected it as

[1] Ellen S. Levine, *Freedom's Children: Young Civil Rights Activists Tell Their Own Stories* (New York: Puffin, 2000), 42.

'the Most Beautiful High School in America.' "[2] Ernest Green, who enrolled as a senior, reflected in an oral history: "We all knew Central. And in many cases the course books that we used were hand-me-downs from Central.... You didn't have to be a rocket scientist to figure out that the building, the course curriculum, the laboratory facilities, all of that was significantly different from what we had at Horace Mann, the black high school."[3]

As has been recounted in the many histories of "The Battle at Little Rock," a mob of white youth and adults taunted, assaulted, threatened, and sought to humiliate the Little Rock Nine as they began their education at Central.[4] Only one student, Green, who had enrolled as a senior, graduated from there. Some opposition was expected, but the depths of it came as a surprise. Green recalls that the city of Little Rock understood itself as different from the Deep South on questions of race relations. In 1956, the city had integrated its public libraries and city buses without incident.[5] Yet Little Rock's identity as a moderate southern city, the imprimatur of the Supreme Court via *Brown v. Board*, and the Little Rock School Board's universal decision to integrate were not enough to protect the students from the vicious white crowd.

Elizabeth Eckford, one of the nine students, came to school on the first day alone; her particular assault was immortalized in the national and international media. At the last minute, the district superintendent had barred parents from accompanying their children to school. Owing to a miscommunication between Daisy Bates, the president of the Arkansas NAACP Conference, and Eckford's family, Elizabeth missed the announcement about where to meet before school and was unable to join the group who arrived with the benefit of a police and clergy escort that Bates had arranged.[6] Instead, Elizabeth faced down a mob of white students and adults alone. Nothing she could have done – presenting herself as deserving, bright, or respectable – would deter those who saw her as an eternal outsider to white Little Rock's social order. While the white mob raged on in Little Rock, much of the national and international media rallied support for Eckford and other African American youth desegregating schools, praising them as heroes of liberal democracy who were performing their rights

[2] Ernest Dumas, "A Perspective of Central High," in Ira Wilmer Counts ed. *A Life Is More Than a Moment: The Desegregation of Little Rock's Central High* (Bloomington, IN: Indiana University Press, 2007), 1–8: 1. I am grateful to Michaele Ferguson for drawing my attention to the particular elite character of Central High School.

[3] Levine, *Freedom's Children*, 42.

[4] Daisy Bates, *The Long Shadow of Little Rock: A Memoir* (Fayetteville: University of Arkansas Press, 2007); Carlotta Walls Lanier, Lisa Frazier Page, and Bill Clinton, *A Mighty Long Way: My Journey to Justice at Little Rock Central High School* (New York: Random House, 2010).

[5] Levine, *Freedom's Children*, 42.

[6] Daisy Bates, *The Long Shadow of Little Rock* (1962), cited in Danielle Allen, "Law's Necessary Forcefulness: Ralph Ellison vs. Hannah Arendt on the Battle of Little Rock," *Oklahoma City University Law Review* 26 (2001), 857–900: 865 n26.

to democratic citizenship against a reactionary Southern culture and antidemocratic sentiments, more broadly.[7]

The photos of Eckford and other students, especially girls, circulated to garner white sympathy both in the United States and abroad for the cause of school desegregation. But they did not persuade Hannah Arendt, who went on to write an essay that portrayed Eckford's solo march and the NAACP strategy of bringing civil rights to the schools as an example of the problem with politics and education in the "modern age," which have eroded the traditional boundaries governing human existence. Conjuring her characteristic tropes of lost traditions, borders, and sensibilities, Arendt lamented the extent to which "[t]he girl was, obviously, asked to be a hero."[8] As readers of Arendt know, heroism is part and parcel of her conception of civic life, and so heroic politics is not her objection. Rather, she fears both for "the girl" and the world if politics becomes the work of children.

In this final chapter, I draw primarily from Arendt's essays "Reflections on Little Rock" and "The Crisis in Education" to read her response to the crisis at Central High School and her broader critique of US education as an iteration of The Lament That Shame Is Dead. I argue that Arendt's critique of the equalizing and flattening of boundaries that separate adults and children, public and private, may have been offered with good intentions but could not protect youth or adult politics as she intended. The adult/child and public/private divisions in the United States that Arendt invoked to resolve the problems with a child-centered and antiauthority approach to politics and education were constituted through institutions and ideologies of white supremacy. These constitutive elements cannot be disentangled from the borders and boundaries Arendt praises for their protective capacities. Indeed, Arendt's anxieties about children entering into the fray of politics, the evisceration of public and private, the account of separate racial communities that flow naturally from racially segregated families, and the states' rights claims about the federal government not interfering in local and family matters map directly onto mid-century segregationist arguments. Rather than protect the children she fears the NAACP has dangerously politicized, the traditional boundaries of public and private in the United States have nurtured and facilitated the violence that makes Eckford's solo walk to school so heroic in the first place. That is to say, the public/private division in the United States and the boundaries of shame and modesty as checks against hubris and audacity naturalized a social order in favor of whites – one in which African American political action is *always already shameless*. That is, Black lives are rendered "social" and "apolitical" because of their location outside of these "traditional" boundaries. Because

[7] See Rebecca De Schweinitz, *If We Could Change the World: Young People and America's Long Struggle for Racial Equality* (Chapel Hill, NC: University of North Carolina Press, 2011), 103–120.

[8] Hannah Arendt, "Reflections on Little Rock and Reply to Critics," in *The Portable Hannah Arendt*, ed. Peter Baehr (New York: Penguin Classics, 2000), 231–246: 236.

African Americans were excised from the social and political order in 1957, any attempt to act publicly in the world – as Arendt understood it – constituted a rupture of the protective borders of shame that debar "private" or "social" questions from demanding the light of day. Invoking a mythical boundary of shame would not deliver the protection Arendt sought. To the contrary, preoccupations with child "protection" and a fear of children as citizens in a plural world was part of the ideology of the white mob who attacked Eckford and could not be summoned to protect her.

Arendt's Shame

Let me begin by emphasizing the egalitarian characteristics of the school desegregation movement, which pertain directly to Arendt's concerns and are germane to my argument about The Lament as a response to egalitarianism taken *too far*. First, and perhaps most obvious, the *Brown* case was decided on the basis of the equal protection clause of the Fourteenth Amendment. The plaintiffs' lawyers argued that separate schools based upon race were inherently unequal and thus children attending "colored" schools are being unjustly forced by the law into the status of second-class citizens, suffering indelible injuries brought on by inequality. School desegregation therefore promised to make good on unkept late-nineteenth century promises to treat all citizens equally without regard to race or creed. Second, *Brown* and the successes of the school desegregation movement expanded *who* counts as a US citizen. African American parents were recognized as adults with rights to make authoritative decisions about their children's education, rather than be subject to the supremacist paternalism that rendered them legal children. Not only racial, but age-related boundaries are also equalized as children became citizens in their own right – agents of social and political change and partners with adults in the quest for school equality. White children were, in turn, tasked with the job of welcoming Black children to their schools as equals – of forging egalitarian bonds in a civil society that had been defined by racial segregation, supremacy, and hierarchy. Third, school desegregation involved the spatial expansion of the political realm to include schools, whose place in civil society had generally insulated them from racial equality. Experiments with integrated education occurred during Reconstruction, yet they were short-lived and never granted Fourteenth-Amendment federal protection.[9] Finally, mid-twentieth-century school desegregation also involved the expansion of the political realm to include psychological claims about subjective experience as evidence of the "fact" of unequal conditions. Under *Brown*, the shame students felt in a particular school became relevant to questions of political equality.

Arendt's critique of social adjustment and psychological belonging as political projects and her general attachment to separate spheres and the hierarchies she countenanced within the "private" and the "social" have rendered her an

[9] Robert C. Morris, *Reading,' Riting, and Reconstruction: The Education of Freedmen in the South, 1861–1870* (Chicago: University of Chicago Press, 2010).

awkward ally in egalitarian social struggle. Arendt both narrows the content of the "political" and then deems it the only realm in which equality matters.[10] Arendt's critique of Marx and her refusal to see poverty as a political question have disqualified and complicated her work for scholars and activists committed to social and economic equalities. The first wave of feminist reception of *The Human Condition* read it as "male-stream," wrongheaded in its claims to "protect" the laboring and pregnant body and women's domestic work behind a boundary of shame.[11] It is unsurprising that many feminists have interpreted Arendt's lament that the body has become public and political as inhospitable to women's mid-twentieth-century emergence from the private sphere as collective subjects willing to tell "private" stories of violence and misery – stories that, to use Arendt's own words, "every century before had hidden in darkness and shame."[12] This latter point speaks to the role shame has historically played in "respectability politics" and "dissemblance," which are especially germane to the publicity the US media granted to girls who unapologetically and unashamedly confronted violent white mobs to demand their educations.[13]

Although much of Arendt's critique of the modern age does not focus on shame per se, it results from her persistent articulation of a boundary of shame that has prevented some bodies and some questions from entering (legitimately) into the gaze of public judgment and the sphere of political action. That is to say, her underlying conception of shame and the nostalgia it involves helps to explain why – until recently – her work has been so poorly received by scholars and activists focusing on social class and the "identity politics" of gender, sexuality, and race. "Hidden away were the laborers who 'with their bodies minister to the [bodily] needs of life,' and the women who with their bodies guarantee the physical survival of the species," Arendt notes in her description of the premodern world for which she appears to long.[14] As has been rehearsed in much of the literature of the 1980s, 1990s, and early 2000s, feminist, LGBT, and antiracist work has been primarily focused on the project of visibility – of bringing into light the struggles and injustices that traditional conceptions of public and private have enclosed in shame. The "personal is political" sums up the rallying cry of this generation of scholarly and activist work, and it is easy to see how it is fundamentally at odds with Arendt's political theory and vision of politics.

10 Arendt, *On Revolution*; Arendt, *The Human Condition*.

11 For an overview of the first wave of reception, see Mary Dietz, "Feminist Receptions of Hannah Arendt," in *Feminist Interpretations of Hannah Arendt* ed. Bonnie Honig (University Park: Pennsylvania State University Press, 1995), 17–50.

12 Arendt, *On Revolution*, 38.

13 On "respectability politics" and "dissemblance" see Darlene Clark Hine, "Rape and the Inner Lives of Black Women in the Middle West," *Signs* 14, no. 4 (1989): 912–920; Evelyn Brooks Higginbotham, *Righteous Discontent* (Cambridge, MA: Harvard University Press, 1993); Michele Mitchell, "Silences Broken, Silences Kept: Gender and Sexuality in African-American History," *Gender & History* 11, no. 3 (1999): 433–444.

14 Arendt, *The Human Condition*, 72.

More recently, feminist political theorists have sought to bridge this divide by creatively interrogating the boundary of public and private and focusing on modes of action rather than the particular identity or content of a political actor or political claim. In one reformulation, for example, an issue like "domestic" violence – not clearly suitable to politics in an orthodox account of Arendt – could be made political by the deployment of political language and criteria. A political claim involves more than stating "this happened to me and therefore it is political," and requires a keen awareness of the different ways that claims are shaped in public and private realms. Another reads the "pariah as hero" as a way of politicizing the political outsider who is not normally seen as central to or even ready for full political action and the gaze of the public it involves. Far from *hiding* identity-based injuries and the bodies that endure them, these recuperative projects provide a frame in which formally private issues can nonetheless demand and receive the political attention for which scholars of "private" injustice have called.[15]

Yet in spite of these efforts, Arendt's boundaries push back against or at least call for a different way through the question of politicizing "private" injuries or overcoming one's identity-based shame. Linda Zerilli has offered a feminist defense of Arendt's (implied) critique of the "personal is political" by emphasizing how feminist politics has mistakenly taken up politics as a means to a specific, preordained political end.[16] By this logic, when women enter into politics as victims, for example, to secure domestic violence legislation or abortion rights protection, they are held captive by a vision of politics as a means to a particular end and unable to embrace Arendt's signature conception of politics as a realm of freedom that involves spontaneity, improvisation, and surprise. To extend this line of reasoning, Arendtian shame protects "private" issues not because they are "dirty" or "disrespectable," but because they are so vulnerable that their spokespeople cannot let go of the particular political direction they want to secure. Politicizing personal injuries ends up treating politics as a problem to be solved rather than as an opportunity to appear in public with others and unite around a common object or concern. Related to Arendt's insistence on keeping the intimate private, when one's private injury is the basis of one's public claim she also becomes open to attacks on her character and the questioning of her motivations. Genuine political questions never emerge because the issue is framed through the lens of a private injury that the victim wants solved.

A generous reading of Arendtian shame as consistent with feminist politics would identify personal as well as political benefits from keeping such issues

[15] Patricia Boling, *Privacy and the Politics of Intimate Life* (Ithaca: Cornell University Press, 1996); Bonnie Honig, "The Arendt Question in Feminism," in *Feminist Interpretations of Hannah Arendt*, ed. Bonnie Honig (University Park: Pennsylvania State University Press, 1995), 1–16; Jennifer Ring, "The Pariah as Hero: Hannah Arendt's Political Actor," *Political Theory* 19, no. 3 (1991): 433–452.

[16] Zerilli, *Feminism and the Abyss of Freedom*.

private or nonpolitical and affording them and their subjects the protection they deserve.[17] To the extent that one could ground an antirape or antiharassment feminist politics in Arendtian ideas, the decision to publicize the topics of intimate violence, for example, would need to be detached from the experiential claims of particular testifying subjects; similarly, the solution to these injuries would need to be open for discussion and contestation and not something that is pushed through with an agenda. And in the end, an orthodox reading of Arendtian shame still renders intimate violence as essentially nonpolitical and something to be resolved through the family in the private sphere.

Manu Samnotra's recent work on the personal and political value of Arendt's conception of shame provides another opening for feminists and others seeking to reclaim some of Arendt's insights about shame and borders of intimacy while also mobilizing Arendt for a politics that is sensitive to injury.[18] Samnotra acknowledges the more standard reading of Arendtian shame as a brake against hubristic self-fashioning of the kind we have seen in previous chapters. Yet moving beyond this reading, Samnotra invokes Arendt to suggest that even the worst forms of shame – those based upon one's identity (e.g., as Jewish, gay, immigrant, African American) – can have ethical and political value and are to be dwelled in rather than escaped through the flight of assimilation. (It is this path of assimilation and flight from the reality of racial difference that Arendt believes motivates the NAACP's school desegregation.) Describing Arendt's account of Rahel Varnhagen, the eighteenth-century Jewish salonnière, Samnotra notes that it was Rahel's shame of being Jewish that gave her consciousness of the unjust world; she was able to reflect upon her shame and understand the injustices shaping it. He writes: "[T]he personal courage demanded of Rahel required her to constantly place herself in situations that reminded her of the shame of being Jewish." By this account, Rahel *engaged* her shame rather than fled from it. Rahel's diary was a document of her shame, and this is why Arendt represents Rahel's life as "slow, cluttered, static, curiously oppressive" in its character. This documentation of shame through the diary, in Samnotra's reading, gave "Rahel ... some coherence and meaning [with respect] to her experiences." By listening to and being aware of her own shame, Rahel was able to gain perspective on her life and the social and political world in which she lived. "This awareness" of her shame and of her situation, notes Samnotra, "arises in the inner recesses of thought and not in the fashionable salons, nor in the thrust and parry of politics."[19] There is a consistency here between Samnotra's position and some of the work in Gay

[17] This is Elshtain's position and why she roots her defense of shame in Arendt's insistence on the need for shame to protect the private and intimate from the harsh gaze of the public. See Elshtain, *Democracy on Trial*, 37–64.

[18] Manu Samnotra, "'Sensitive to Shame': Hannah Arendt on Becoming Worldly," *Constellations* 21, no. 3 (2014): 338–350.

[19] Samnotra, "Sensitive to Shame," 343.

Shame discussed in Chapter 1. Ellis Hanson exemplifies this ambivalence, noting that "shame is my curse and my oldest friend."[20] Yet it also squares with the caution about politicizing personal suffering, as Samnotra's Arendt still asks the shame-ridden to reckon with her shame in "the inner recesses of thought" rather than going public to declare it and ask for recognition or response. Because the emotion of shame is debilitating and makes one feel vulnerable, these critiques suggest that politics is not the appropriate place for reckoning with your shame or seeking to move beyond it.

School Desegregation and Social Climbing

Vying for notoriety with Arendt's coverage of the Eichmann trial for *The New Yorker*, which led to her falling out with many of her friends and colleagues, the essay "Reflections on Little Rock" has been extraordinarily controversial. Unlike *Eichmann in Jerusalem*, whose critics have come around or softened over the years, "Little Rock" has largely been read and analyzed as evidence of Arendt's misunderstandings, bad faith, and latent racism.[21] It is certainly not a resource for the multitude of democratic theorists who invoke Arendtian texts and tropes to recuperate a robust vision of "action" and "freedom." Two recently published anthologies on Arendt reflect its avoided status among scholars closely engaged with her work. "Little Rock" receives only passing engagement and does not appear in either index.[22] And no wonder: the essay includes Arendt's defense of states' rights on the question of school desegregation, levies an extended and unsympathetic critique of *Brown* and the NAACP legal strategy that produced it, and claims that forcing white children into integrated schools infringes on the rights of white parents to educate their children as they see fit. Among those who have so much as a passing familiarity with its content, there is a sense that Arendt is both morally wrong and deeply ignorant about the politics of race and education in the United States.

Arendt's biographer, Elizabeth Young-Bruehl, provides some sympathetic context for Arendt's concerns in "Little Rock" and Jean Bethke Elshtain notes

[20] Ellis Hanson, "Teaching Shame," in *Gay Shame*, eds. David M. Halperin and Valerie Traub (Chicago: University of Chicago Press, 2009), 132–164: 138.

[21] See Michael Hanchard, "Contours of Black Political Thought: An Introduction and Perspective," *Political Theory* 38, no. 4 (2010): 510–536; Allen, "Law's Necessary Forcefulness"; Danielle S. Allen, *Talking to Strangers: Anxieties of Citizenship since Brown v. Board of Education* (Chicago: University Of Chicago Press, 2004); Anne Norton, "Heart of Darkness: Africa and African Americans in the Writings of Hannah Arendt," in *Feminist Interpretations of Hannah Arendt*, ed. Bonnie Honig (University Park: Pennsylvania State University Press, 1995), 247–262; Kathryn T. Gines, *Hannah Arendt and the Negro Question* (Bloomington: Indiana University Press, 2014).

[22] Roger Berkowitz, Thomas Keenan, and Jeffrey Katz, eds., *Thinking in Dark Times: Hannah Arendt on Ethics and Politics* (New York: Fordham University Press, 2009); Seyla Benhabib, ed., *Politics in Dark Times: Encounters with Hannah Arendt* (New York: Cambridge University Press, 2010).

that Arendt's concerns could be extended to object to mandatory sex education in school or the "war on drugs" that has children reporting their parents' drug use, but as far as I am aware no one at the time the essay was published or in the contemporary landscape of political theory and legal studies has defended Arendt's position and rationale on school desegregation.[23] Scholarly disagreement about *Brown v. Board* (1954) as it was argued and decided notwithstanding, most are inclined to agree with Ralph Ellison, who famously explained that "Hannah Arendt is way off ... in her reflections on Little Rock." Ellison went on to argue that Arendt failed to understand the concept of sacrifice – central to Black political thought and Black family life: "[Arendt] has no conception of what goes on in the parents who send their kids through these lines. The kid is supposed to be able to go through ... he's supposed to have mastered those tensions, and if he gets hurt then this is one more sacrifice."[24] Danielle Allen has extended Ellison's concept of sacrifice to argue for a concept of "democratic sacrifice" as essential to life in a democratic, plural public, arguing that children and the schools they attend are essential parts of the democratic experience. More recently, Michael Hanchard has drawn on Elsa Barkley Brown's account of Black families in Richmond, Virginia during Reconstruction – who saw the family unit, including children, as essential to political action and the development of political platforms and the pursuit of freedom – to argue that Arendt fundamentally misunderstands traditions of Black families and child involvement in the United States.[25] Hanchard emphasizes how Arendt's naturalization of a formal adult-child separation erases the collective, family-centered Black political tradition as an alternative framework to liberal bourgeois values. The period of Reconstruction is also part of the US story that Arendt misses.[26] More damningly, Anne Norton and Kathryn Gines read the essay as symptomatic of Arendt's anti-Black philosophy and read Arendt, both because of "Little Rock" and also what she has written beyond it, irredeemable on questions of racial equality.[27]

Let us map the contours of Arendt's argument and try to make sense of the essay on its own terms. Arendt wrote "Reflections on Little Rock" in 1957 to criticize the mandatory desegregation of southern schools after *Brown*. It was

[23] Elisabeth Young-Bruehl, *Hannah Arendt: For Love of the World* (New Haven: Yale University Press, 1977), 308–318; Jean Bethke Elshtain, "Commentary: Political Children," *Childhood* 3 (1996), 11–28: 18.

[24] Robert Penn Warren interview with Ralph Ellison, original transcript, February 25, 1964. Tape #1, p. 26, Warren, "Who Speaks for the Negro? An Archival Collection, http://whospeaks.library.vanderbilt.edu/interview/ralph-ellison.

[25] Hanchard, "Contours of Black Political Thought"; Elsa Barkley Brown, "Negotiating and Transforming the Public Sphere," *Public Culture* 7 (1994), 107–116.

[26] Jill Locke, "Little Rock's Social Question: Reading Arendt on School Desegregation and Social Climbing," *Political Theory* 41, no. 4 (August 1, 2013): 533–561.

[27] Anne Norton, "Heart of Darkness: Africa and African Americans in the Writings of Hannah Arendt"; Gines, *Hannah Arendt and the Negro Question*.

initially written for *Commentary*, whose editors refused to publish it. *Dissent* agreed to do so in 1959, by which point the Court had strengthened the central holding of *Brown* and decided *Cooper v. Aaron* (1958), which ruled that the Arkansas state government could not impede the Little Rock school district's integration plan. Arendt explained that she wrote the essay in response to a newspaper photo of an African American girl who was being harassed by a mob of white students as she walked – accompanied by a white friend of her father – away from the school she was hoping to attend. The essay is titled "Reflections on Little Rock," but there is only a passing mention of the specifics of the high-profile desegregation of Central High School.[28] "Little Rock" thus operates as a signifier as much as an actual place, as Arendt wrote to judge the role of the federal government and the use of education to remedy legal and social discrimination against African Americans in the aftermath of slavery, rather than to evaluate the specifics of what happened in Arkansas. She further developed her criticisms of the "wide-spread, uncritical acceptance of a Rousseauean ideal in education" in "The Crisis in Education" (1958), a clarificatory response to some of the early criticisms she encountered when trying to publish "Little Rock," most specifically the point that she "did not take into account the role education plays ... in the political framework of this country."[29]

Arendt's claims in "Little Rock" turn on an application of the spheres of human activity (private, social, and public) that she is developing simultaneously in *The Human Condition* (1958). If scholars and popular critics have found anything redeeming in this essay, it has been Arendt's powerful case to protect the sacred character of the private sphere, which is evident in her indictment of antimiscegenation laws – an indictment that has been resurrected in the fight for (same sex) marriage equality.[30] (Marriage, Arendt argued, is a private and intimate association that deserves protection from the state; any state that dictates whom and under what conditions a person can marry she

[28] Arendt titles her essay "Reflections on Little Rock" but she does not discuss the specifics of the case other than through a brief reference to Governor Faubus. Moreover, the photo to which she appears to refer does not correspond clearly with the newspaper image from Little Rock. Danielle Allen argues that Arendt has confused the Little Rock and Charlotte, North Carolina, photos on the grounds that the Charlotte photo includes the angry mob described by Arendt. According to Allen, the newspaper article to which Arendt refers is more likely a story about Dorothy Counts. Rebecca de Schweinitz notes that Dorothy Counts's parents withdrew her from the "integrated school" after three days to protect her, a point that is saturated with irony considering Arendt's indictment of absent Black parents who neglected their children's safety. Allen, *Talking to Strangers*, 197 n1; De Schweinitz, *If We Could Change the World*, 109.

[29] Arendt, "Reflections on Little Rock and Reply to Critics," 232.

[30] Roger Berkowitz, "Solitude and the Activity of Thinking," in *Thinking in Dark Times: Hannah Arendt on Ethics and Politics*, ed. Roger Berkowitz, Jeffrey Katz, and Thomas Keenan (New York: Fordham University Press, 2009), 237–248. Andrew Sullivan, "Why Gay Marriage Is Good for America," *Newsweek*, July 18, 2011, http://www.newsweek.com/andrew-sullivan-why-gay-marriage-good-america-68453.

describes as tyrannical.) She locates schools in the more ambiguous realm of the social – not private and hidden, but public and visible, yet not fully political – and sees the social as voluntary in character. The social includes the "public" activity of children, who are not yet prepared to live politically, and so – here begging the question – schools are social because they are the realm of children. It is the protection of the private and the enforcement of equality in the political and legal realms (in the Arendtian sense) that Arendt believes should be the NAACP's focus, rather than the voluntary sphere of society. Arendt's argument speaks to what legal scholars call "parental association liberty" – the right for parents to dictate the terms of their children's associational lives, a right that has been relevant in scholarly work on children's schooling.[31]

Rather than take up the right for adults to marry freely, the NAACP (and the Court that responded to it) first addressed social discrimination – the ability of individuals to associate with whomever they choose. Yet for Arendt, the concept of society does not make sense without discrimination; to recall Tocqueville's observations about nineteenth-century America, she sees society as composed of voluntary associations that gain their meaning and (positive) power from the fact that individuals freely enter into them and they are located in a sphere beyond government authority. As long as integrated social groups are not forbidden, that is, so long as parents would be free to form an integrated school if they desired, she has no objection to social segregation – even when it maps onto an axis of relative social power and powerlessness.[32] Arendt emphasizes in her "Reply to Critics" that the damage of social exclusion comes less from being excluded from a particular group per se than from trying to gain access to a voluntary association and being (inevitably) denied admission. To return to her concern about the effects of the desegregation policy on children, her argument suggests that however much the NAACP briefs and the *Brown* decision turn on a concern with the mental well-being and the psychological state of African American children attending "colored" schools, their mental state was harmed far more by "pushing, or rather being pushed [by

[31] See Seana Shiffrin, "What's Really Wrong with Compelled Association?," *Northwestern University Law Review* 99, no. 2 (2005): 839–888.

[32] Arendt clarifies this point in a March 30, 1959, letter to Matthew Lipman, lecturer in philosophy at Columbia College of Columbia University. In response to Lipman's point that government-sanctioned segregation constituted government interference "with the social life of the child," Arendt writes that racial segregation is "the kind of social life which the child now leads," and therefore protecting it cannot be read as interference. She continues, "It would be another matter if we had an integrated school in the South, under the auspices and with the consent of both, black and white parents. If the government should intervene [and prohibit it], it would indeed prohibit integration" and interfere. Here Arendt, like many who defend segregated schools on the grounds of the schools' voluntary character, reveals her lack of familiarity with post-civil War school integration, which Jim Crow *abolished*. I want to thank Patchen Markell for drawing my attention to this letter. Hannah Arendt to Matthew Lipman, March 30, 1959, "*Dissent* – 1958–1972, n.d.," Hannah Arendt Papers, Manuscript Division, Library of Congress, Washington, DC.

the NAACP] into pushing, one's way out of one group and into another." She continues, imagining herself as a Black mother, "The Supreme Court ruling," as we can gather from the photo Arendt describes, "has put my child into a more humiliating position than it had been in before."[33] For Arendt, psychological harm and social maladjustment do matter for how we live in the world, but they are exacerbated when they become politicized and force citizens – especially children – into hostile territory.

This focus on social advancement and social adjustment enables Arendt to read school desegregation as about gaining acceptance in society with the support of the federal government, and not about simple economic necessity, intellectual growth, or preparation for citizenship, all of which would be legitimate on her terms. It is perhaps because of the power of this frame in Arendt's imaginary that she reads race and racial difference through the lens of social fact – a lens that contradicts the analysis of racial ideology and race thinking that she had identified in *The Origins of Totalitarianism*. Against the logic of *Brown*, "Little Rock" – consistent with Arendt's impatience for political solutions to social unease or association – presents segregated schools as an effect of social difference and a natural, social inclination among people who are different or separate in terms of their factual makeup.[34] Arendt would later write passionately about the need to respect the "stubborn" character of facts and the dangers of destroying the facts of the world, as she links the preservation of factual truth to the preservation of the world that people share in common.[35] This preoccupation with facts and the denial of them through lies and deception is part of her critique of Jewish assimilation.[36] Her emphasis on the "visibility" and facticity of skin color as something that "'appear[s]' in public"[37] suggests that she sees the desire of African Americans to be protected in the right "[to] be admitted to schools of their choice" (*Brown*) as an erasure of the fact of color, which presumably carries the same risks as the denial of the facts of Jewishness and the rich history its social facts represent.[38] It is no wonder that she sees social climbing as a perverse means to assuage psychological injury, given that she understands it to involve joining a social group that requires you to renounce the facts of who you are.

33 Arendt, "Reflections on Little Rock and Reply to Critics," 244.
34 Ibid., 234.
35 Hannah Arendt, "Truth and Politics," in *The Portable Hannah Arendt*, ed. Peter Baehr (New York: Penguin Classics, 2000), 545–575.
36 Arendt, *Rahel Varnhagen*.
37 Arendt, "Reflections on Little Rock and Reply to Critics," 233–234.
38 This point may be too generous. Arendt does not treat African and African American history as worthy of preservation in the way that she fears the loss of the Jewish history through assimilation. Arendt's characterization of Afrocentric education in "On Violence" is particularly disturbing on this question. Anne Norton's essay "Heart of Darkness" emphasizes this point with powerful examples culled from a variety of Arendt's texts. See Hannah Arendt, *Crises of the Republic: Lying in Politics, Civil Disobedience, on Violence, Thoughts on Politics and Revolution* (New York: Harcourt Brace Jovanovich, 1972), 80, 96; Anne Norton, "Heart of Darkness: Africa and African Americans in the Writings of Hannah Arendt."

Moreover, extending her concern about the humiliation of pushing "one's way out of one group and into another" where one is unwanted, Arendt legitimately fears the violence that African American students would experience at the hands of a defensive and angry white mob.[39] This is at least part of what motivates her preoccupation with visible, "factual" racial difference – her concern that African American students would be seen and marked as different and vulnerable in a racial economy that was anything but neutral in spite of the Court's colorblind jurisprudence. Here Arendt anticipates contemporary criticisms of colorblind remedies to US racism and the *Brown* decision, in particular.

Girl Heroes, Absent Fathers

In spite of Arendt's blind spots with respect to US racial politics and the limitations of her analysis in "Little Rock," there is no reason to doubt the sincerity of her worry about the physical safety of the students in the front lines of the struggle for equal schools. Indeed, her insistence that Black children should enjoy the protections and innocence of a traditional (white) childhood indicates her reading of African Americans as full persons.[40] Her preoccupation with protecting black youth is evident in her scathing indictment of Little Rock's "law-abiding [white] citizens" who "left the streets to the mob" and failed to help "the girl" who had been asked to perform this heroic march to the white school gate. Although by her own account she avoided the US South,[41] Arendt would have been acutely aware of the extent of anti-Black violence and the backlash against *Brown*. Documentation of white attacks on African Americans for desegregating white neighborhoods in response to the liberalization of housing laws; attacks on Black adults and children riding buses; bombings of clergy homes; and "random" violence against Black children – especially girls[42] – filled the *New York Times* headlines from 1956 to 1957.[43] This knowledge and the highly visible nature of this particular image of "the

[39] Arendt, "Reflections on Little Rock and Reply to Critics," 244.

[40] I am grateful to Michael Hanchard for this point. For a terrific analysis of the racial and gendered constructions of childhood "innocence," see Robin Bernstein, *Racial Innocence: Performing American Childhood from Slavery to Civil Rights* (New York: New York University Press, 2011).

[41] Arendt, "Reflections on Little Rock and Reply to Critics," 232.

[42] Black women are also referred to as "Negro girls" in the US media at the time, but my focus is on school-age girls. There is coverage of "Negro girls" referring to seamstresses, opera singers, and so on, but what interests me is what appears to be a disproportionate emphasis on African American girls gaining entrance to schools. Whether this is because girls were more likely victimized or because the media covered it, I do not know, but it warrants further exploration. Rachel Devlin (Associate Professor of History, Rutgers University) is currently writing a book about the disproportionate number of girls in school desegregation cases.

[43] For example, "Tallahassee Law on Buses Is Defied; Negroes Ride in White Seats" reports "several whites" beating "Ollie Mae Collins, a 15-Year-Old Negro Girl," *New York Times*, December 25, 1956; "Bombing in Alabama Injures 5, Wrecks Negro Minister's Home: BLAST RIPS HOME OF BUS BIAS FOE," describes the Christmas bombing of Reverend Shuttlesworth's home,

girl" must have been part of what compelled her to write about the need for adults to protect children from the diseases of racism and racially motivated violence and assume responsibility for a world that would welcome all children. Some desegregation efforts were implemented without the violence and obstruction[44] that characterized Little Rock's Central High School, but a significant number of news stories focused on children being harassed and denied entrance by whites.[45] Given this media attention and Arendt's strong views of public and private spheres and her belief that the intimacy of the family should be protected behind a boundary of shame, it's not surprising that Arendt would have been appalled to see African American children facing the white mob without protection or escort from their parents, the district, or the NAACP.[46] But the Little Rock case, as with violence against African Americans in the United States more broadly, shows the limits of Arendt's political theory of the family, which she derives in one context and attempts – misguidedly – to apply to another that is incommensurate with her initial case.

Let me specify what I am reading as Arendt's political theory of the family, which is on display in "Crisis in Education" and "Little Rock."[47] Arendt understands children as essentially vulnerable and therefore best left out of politics, which she interprets as the exclusive work of adults. Schools, which are public but categorized by her as social because she locates them in the voluntary realm of civil society, are the portal between the family's home and the common world. Schools should *prepare* the child for entry in the world but they are not the world itself. Children, as strangers to the world, should not be required to go to schools that call into question the values of their parents. Children are not yet ready to navigate conflict over worldly matters with adults, whose job

New York Times, December 26, 1956; "Threat to Ohio Negroes; Ku Klux Klan Cross Is Burned on Family's Front Lawn" depicts the cross-burning on the lawn of a Black family who integrated a neighborhood. *New York Times*, August 16, 1956; "MISSOURI SCHOOL TENSE; White Students Try to Gang Negroes in New Flare-Up," reports that "White students tried to block the way of five Negroes at.the high school today in a new flareup of racial tension." *New York Times*, January 18, 1957.

44 See, for example, "INTEGRATION GAIN IS FOUND IN TULSA; School-Sponsored Activities Include Negroes–But Lag Is Seen After Classes," *New York Times*, May 22, 1957; "Charleston, W.Va., Integrates Schools with Little Difficulty; SCHOOL BIAS ENDS IN A BORDER CITY, System Saves $250,000 Operating Smoothly, Chosen for Ability," *New York Times*, May 15, 1957.

45 See, for example, "Clinton Whites Toss Eggs at Negro Girls," *New York Times*, November 28, 1956; "Violence Shuts Clinton School; Minister Beaten as Teenagers Invade Building as Negroes Return to Classrooms," *New York Times*, December 5, 1956.

46 Given that Arendt writes *The Human Condition* at the same time that she writes "Reflections on Little Rock" and "Crisis in Education," it is also quite possible that her witnessing of the events in Little Rock shapes the ways in which she conceptualizes borders of private, social, and public and the relationship thereof. It is unfortunate that Arendt never wrote about the mob mentality of Southern racism.

47 Arendt's preoccupations with children also appear in her essay "Rosa Luxemburg (1871–1919)" in *The Patable Hannah Arendt*, ed. Peter Baehr (New York: Penguin Classics, 2000): 419–437.

it is to care for them. Arendt recounts her exasperation with this inversion of adult/child authority here:

> [T]he most startling part of the whole business was the Federal decision to start integration in, of all places, the public schools. It certainly did not require too much imagination to see that this was to burden children, black and white, with the working out of a problem which adults for generations have confessed themselves unable to solve. I think no one will find it easy to forget the photograph reproduced in newspapers and magazines throughout the country, showing a Negro girl, accompanied by a white friend of her father, walking away from school, persecuted and followed into bodily proximity by a jeering and grimacing mob of youngsters. The girl, obviously, was asked to be a hero – that is, something neither her absent father nor the equally absent representatives of the NAACP felt called upon to be.... The picture looked to me like a fantastic caricature of progressive education which, by abolishing the authority of adults, implicitly denies their responsibility for the world into which they have borne their children and refuses the duty of guiding them into it. Have we now come to the point where it is the children who are being asked to change or improve the world? And do we intend to have our political battles fought out in the school yards?[48]

Rather than starting integration in the public schools, Arendt believed the NAACP should have focused its attention on the *adult* question of interracial marriage, prioritizing the striking of these bans, which represent a totalitarian invasion of the private sphere by the state. This battle would have had her full support. But by politicizing both the lives of children and the schoolyards on which they played, the NAACP strategy took the easy way out, resisting the heroic fight for equal marriage standing and deferring real political struggle to children. Arendt saw this as a total abdication of adult responsibility. And while she judges Black and white adults as guilty, Arendt reserves a specific animus for Black parents, conjured in her choice of the trope of the "absent father" and her own effort, in the "Reply to [her] Critics," to substitute her judgment for an African American mother's.

The school desegregation plan as Arendt understood it violated an essential, world- and child-preserving triangular relationship among the child, the adult, and the world. For Arendt, one of the fundamental reasons adults invest in the world and engage in politics is for the sake of children. Arendt understands adults as reentering the world from their unworldly love in order to care for the world their child will grow into and inherit. Hence the child is a bridge between the parents and also a bridge between the home and the world. She writes: "Through the child, it is as though the lovers return to the world from which their love had expelled them."[49] The adult's job is therefore to care for and educate children for the world – to "assume joint responsibility for the world." If one cannot assume this responsibility, she says matter-of-factly, he or she "should not have children and must not be allowed to take part in

[48] Arendt, "Reflections on Little Rock and Reply to Critics," 236.
[49] Arendt, *The Human Condition*, 242.

educating them."[50] Thus the absent father, which I take to mean the father who refuses to play the role of proper adult vis-à-vis his own children as well as the adult nonparent who refuses to assume responsibility for the world, must leave the care of children and their education to *those who do*. This is for the sake of the world as much as for the child: "The world, too," she writes, "needs protection to keep it from being overrun and destroyed by the onslaught of the new that burst upon it with each new generation."[51] This means that the world cannot handle the idealistic, immature, untutored child with her visions of lofty social equality; nor can it handle the negligence of the adult who acts like a child in failing to take responsibility for the world. The adult's job in this triangle is to care for and educate children for the world, which is always "out of joint," and to nurture the child without turning her into a world of her own.[52]

To reemphasize, Arendt locates the child and the family in which it is raised (primarily) in the private realm so that she or he can grow into the hard work of citizenship. She writes: "the child must be protected against the world ... children need the security of darkness to grow at all."[53] All human beings need privacy and darkness, but children need it especially. They are not yet ready for the demands of public life, nor are they ready to bear responsibility for the state of the world. Arendt's children are "apprentice citizens" who are becoming habituated to the world under the protection of their parents and other adults in their communities.[54] They must be led by adult authorities and not asked to lead. The girl who is asked to be a hero is denied this protected stage of apprenticeship. The adult cannot accompany the child everywhere, but can provide the child with a protective covering. In a 1964 interview, Arendt recalls with fondness the ways in which her mother protected her from anti-Semitic remarks by contacting authorities if the remarks came from teachers and armoring Arendt with dignity and self-composure for confronting anti-Semitic taunts by youth.[55] What her mother refused to do was to put her child (Arendt)

[50] Hannah Arendt, "The Crisis in Education," in *Between Past and Future: Eight Exercises in Political Thought* (New York: Penguin, 1993), 173–196: 189.

[51] Ibid., 186.

[52] Ibid., 192, 186.

[53] Ibid, 186.

[54] Elshtain, "Commentary: Political Children," 27.

[55] Arendt reflects on her own mother's effort to protect her even when she was out of sight and in the schoolyard: "[A]ll Jewish children encountered anti-Semitism. And it poisoned the souls of many children. The difference with us was that my mother was always convinced that you mustn't let it get to you. You have to defend yourself! When my teachers made anti-Semitic remarks ... I was told to get up immediately, leave the classroom, come home, and report everything exactly. Then my mother wrote one of her many registered letters; and for me the matter was completely settled. I had a day off from school, and that was marvelous! But when it came from children, I was not permitted to tell about it at home. That didn't count. You defended yourself against what came from children. Thus these matters never were a problem for me. There were rules of conduct by which I retained my dignity, so to speak, and I was protected, absolutely protected, at home." Arendt, "'What Remains? The Language Remains': A Conversation with Gunter Gaus," in *The Portable Hannah Arendt*, ed. Peter Baehr (New York: Penguin Classics, 2000), 3–23: 9.

in situations she knew would be dangerous and humiliating. Hence her objection to school desegregation: the child is put into an "even more humiliating position" than she was in when she attended the inferior, segregated schools that prompted the Court's therapeutic remedies. Young-Bruehl clarifies: "What [Arendt] hoped for other's children was what she had had herself; time for a good education before the *Judenfrage* ('Jewish Question') was personally posed in her life and before she, as a Jew, had to choose politics."[56]

Elshtain notes that Arendt wants to "protect[] ... the first natality in order to make possible the second," which is a helpful way of clarifying Arendt's political investment in child protection.[57] Natality, for Arendt, refers to that spontaneous birth that occurs when the citizen enters the public realm, engaging in the doing and speaking of political action in the company of other adults who are – in spite of whatever social inequalities might remain – politically equal.[58] The "first natality" is, of course, childhood, the incubatory stage during which the child gets his or her bearings, comes to develop a sense of self – as Arendt was able to do in her own family, in spite of threats of anti-Semitism in the world beyond it – and prepares for the challenging and even threatening work of public citizenship. It is in part because Arendt understands politics as risky and threatening to one's sovereign control over his or her body, (which she believes is anathema to politics), that she insists on a foundational, protective childhood behind "four walls."[59] To the extent that the child has a public life, it exists at school – an intermediary space between home and public, "the institution that we interpose between the private domain of home and the world in order to make the transition from the family to the world possible at all."[60] School, according to Arendt, is political in the sense that it has political implications, but education should not be politicized. Rather, it should reflect the values (which she presumes to be coherent) of the family and governed through the authority of adults, specifically teachers. Perhaps in part because Arendt understands the political realm as a site of nonsovereignty and full equality, to the point that everything in this sphere of action can be open to question and reformulation, she insists on protecting pre- or nonpolitical spheres as sites of traditional authorities.

Arendt never mentions Hitler Youth or how fascism, more generally, mobilized children in the name of the nation (fatherland), yet it appears to frame the background of her understanding of the family's appropriate relationship to politics and the dangers of involving children in politics and nation-building.[61] One could argue that part of the reason Arendt's critique of school desegregation

[56] Young-Bruehl, *Hannah Arendt: For Love of the World*, 318.

[57] Elshtain, "Commentary: Political Children," 14.

[58] Arendt, *The Human Condition*, 9, 177–178.

[59] The trope of "four walls" recurs throughout Arendt's work; see especially *The Human Condition*, 52, 71. On sovereignty as anathema to freedom, see Arendt, "What Is Freedom?," 455.

[60] Arendt, "The Crisis in Education," 188–189.

[61] Elshtain connects the concerns of "Little Rock" to the role of Hitler Youth. Elshtain, "Commentary: Political Children," 18–19.

feels so tin-eared is because the theory on which it is based emerged from Arendt's observations of European children's involvement in totalitarian movements. Indeed, Arendt's account of "absent fathers" fits better and is much more understandable when applied to this European context. During World War II, many men died leaving their children fatherless. As has been widely documented, youth movements were a central part of twentieth-century totalitarian ideology.[62] Some have argued that there is a direct link between an absent father, a casualty of wartime, and children's vulnerability to organizations like Hitler Youth and the ideology of rebuilding the nation with children at the helm.[63] With this in mind, Arendt's indictment of "absent fathers" perhaps reads as less of a precursor to the trope that is canonized in the Moynihan Report on "The Negro Family: The Case for National Action" (1965).[64]

Given this context of youth participation in European totalitarianism and Arendt's memory of her own youth as relatively free from politics, Arendt appears to have already developed a political theory of the family before she laid her eyes on the heroic girl in the *New York Times*. What we see in "Little Rock," therefore, is an application of Arendt's more general political theory of the family to a situation that does not fully fit the context in which she derived it. Shifting from the European to the US frame, we can see that Arendt's political theory of the family, which she presents as universal, common sense, and even *natural*, is anything but. However problematic and risky it may have been to "begin with the schools" with respect to desegregation, as I will show in the next section, it is far more problematic and dangerous to resurrect the United States' *traditional* borders of adult authority and public/private division in the name of protecting children.

The Presence of the Past

As in much of her other work, Arendt's writings about children's education redound with anxieties about ruptures with the historical past, in these cases how school desegregation and progressive, child-centered learning have erased traditional parental and adult authority. Arendt presents the "Little Rock" moment as new because by involving children and asking them to lead the way, the NAACP disrespects the value of adult authority and is cowardly in doing so. Perhaps more accurately, the actual problem from an Arendtian perspective is that the NAACP's adult leadership puts children on the front lines

62 Lynn H. Nicholas, *Cruel World: The Children of Europe in the Nazi Web* (New York: Vintage, 2006); Gerhard Rempel, *Hitler's Children: The Hitler Youth and the SS* (Chapel Hill: University of North Carolina Press, 1989).

63 Peter Loewenberg, "The Psychohistorical Origins of the Nazi Youth Cohort," *The American Historical Review* 76, no. 5 (1971): 1457–1502. I am grateful to Brady Brower for this point and directing me to Loewenberg's work.

64 See The US Department of Labor: http://www.dol.gov/dol/aboutdol/history/webid-meynihan .htm.

of the struggle while adults strategize where they shall go and under what circumstances. The hard work of face-to-face negotiation across races – at least in Arendt's telling – is deferred to youth.

The "Little Rock" moment is also new because it defies historical (not simply Greek and Roman but also Madisonian and Jeffersonian) borders between what counts as "public" and "private" and, in so doing, calls into question the social and moral value of the experience of shame. That is to say, if shame is typically understood as a brake or a boundary that limits what one can say and do, the evisceration of this boundary eliminates one of the mechanisms limiting human behavior. Like the twentieth-century trend in US education more generally, school desegregation indulged in Rousseauean ideas about authenticity and nature in which shame becomes an emotion to overcome rather than heed. To recall Wendy Brown's lament about the "steady slide ... toward therapeutic discourse," Arendt reads the newness as cause for political concern.[65] Hence Arendt's cataloging of the problems with school desegregation assumes a tone of both social critique and mourning of eviscerated lost ways. She suggests that adults *used to* understand their roles vis-à-vis care for children but this role has changed so much that common-sense understandings of the specific spheres and duties of children and adults have become erased and even inverted. Children are not to be thrust into the gaze of the public and the violence and judgment present there because they need "security and darkness to grow at all."[66] When children are forced out of this sphere of security and darkness or allowed to leave without adult intervention, Rousseauean transparency has won and we can very well say that *shame is dead*.

This fear of the world being overrun and destroyed by the onslaught of the new links up with the critique Arendt would eventually level against the French Revolution and reflects her long standing objection to Rousseau's naturalism. Rousseau's famous paeans to "natural man" and "natural goodness" and the sentiments of the primitive heart are not enough for world-sustaining, Arendtian politics. For Arendt, the civic persona is defined by the existence of a mask that protects one's inner self from the harsh gaze of the public.[67] Rousseau's conception of "progress" takes man back to an idealized conception of nature, reading the artifacts and masks of the civic persona and the law as hiding our natural selves away in shame. The child signifies nature and natural goodness for both Rousseau and Arendt, but their interpretations of the significance of this observation are radically opposed. Rousseau wants to retrieve – or, more accurately, cultivate – a natural, childlike goodness as a tonic for the pains of modernity and its artifice. By stark contrast, Arendt insists upon artifice as essential to and

[65] Brown, *States of Injury*, 75.

[66] Arendt, "The Crisis in Education," 186.

[67] Hannah Arendt, *On Revolution*, 98. See also Norma Claire Moruzzi, *Speaking through the Mask: Hannah Arendt and the Politics of Social Identity* (Ithaca: Cornell University Press, 2000).

constitutive of the political world, believing that the demands of modernity require works of civic fabrication, human-made and human-sustained institutions and artifacts. Hence whereas Rousseau would insist that "whoever blushes is already guilty,"[68] indicating that the good man has childlike innocence, Arendt reads shame felt in the gap between one's inner thoughts and public presentation as essential. The idea that children and the family's commitments must be on full display before an audience of neighbors and teachers, and that no sentiment or private opinion ought to be hidden away in shame is anathema to Arendt's understanding of what politics involves. And it resonates deeply with the more contemporary iterations of The Lament.[69]

Arendt's fears about totalitarian regimes requiring citizens to perform their loyalty to state ideology and to invest their children in the movement – allowing no room for divisions between public and private selves or hypocrisy and inconsistency – are well-founded. She writes persuasively about the need to protect inner thoughts from the gaze of the public. But her particular investment in the borders of public and private, like her idealized conception of "childhood" itself, lacks a specific explanation of the ways in which these borders and categories are historically and socially constituted by and constitutive of received political and social norms. Beyond a general account of the shift from the ancient to modern age, Arendt does not acknowledge that what one counts as public, private, worthy of publicity, or better off hidden in shame, reflects normative investments. Arendt fails to acknowledge that the "public" and "private" are never simply described, but rather constituted through proclamations of what ought to be revealed and what ought to be concealed – what belongs in which sphere and why.

The failure of Arendt's "universal" theory of the family to translate to "Little Rock" makes its particularity very clear. A local-control and anti-Rousseauean argument against German fascism cannot be parlayed into Jim Crow. She prefaces "Reflections on Little Rock" with a plea with her readers to take her sympathy with African Americans as a given, but then goes on to invoke states' rights and parental control of education in ways that resemble segregationist arguments of the era. "Our children ... are [now] the property of the federal government" was a common segregationist complaint that resonates with Arendt's critique of the NAACP and the Warren Court. In a similarly Arendtian vein, white supremacists described their children as "helpless pawns in a frightening struggle." To seize the moral high ground of parental authority and castigate Black parents, prosegregationist groups formed "Mother's Leagues" that capitalized on traditional ideas about motherhood and parental care, establishing white supremacy itself as the proper family because it protected white children and kept them out of the "race mixing" of politics and

[68] Rousseau, *Emile*, 217.

[69] See especially Nagel, "Concealment and Exposure," 23–24.

the public.[70] Rebecca De Schweinitz notes the supremacist politics of parental protection: "Many white parents … explained their resistance to integration in terms of … natural parental desires and obligations to protect their children and provide them with the rights of childhood."[71] In this spirit, "one man … likened adult protest leaders to bad mothers" who did not know how to care for their children.[72]

Furthermore, Arendt misses the degree to which segregationists and white supremacists did not keep their children out of politics. Nor was white children's protected status the result of their parents' good judgment and knowledge of what was fit and unfit for their children. The state provided protection for white children, and this state investment in white children's innocence and security was, in fact, constituted against the threat of fully enfranchised, full-standing African Americans as adult citizens in their own right. That is to say, white children's "protection" from any form of egalitarian contact with youth of color was the product of a highly coordinated and meticulously maintained campaign that used a terrorizing combination of the US Constitution, state law, vigilante lynch mobs, market economics, and political disfranchisement to secure white supremacy and white authority. It is precisely this combination and the power it yielded that explains the reasons why students of color had been barred from the gleaming largesse, social and economic power, and academic rigor signified in Central High School. A nostalgic ideology of "parental protection" with a federalist structure that was content to defer security measures to the states had given us the white mob that attacked Eckford. It could not be resurrected to protect her.

More specifically, the ideology of parental protection, buttressed by state power, went hand in hand with what segregationists believed to be sexually shameful. As Ida B. Wells explained in the context of the late-nineteenth century, Gunnar Myrdhal in 1944, and has been updated and retheorized in the work of African American literature, history, and critical race theory throughout the past century, interracial sex was the primary thing that white parents sought to "protect" their children from.[73] Mid-twentieth-century battles over school desegregation were no exception. Ultimately, white supremacists feared that school desegregation would pave the way for sex outside of the bounds of white supremacy. Interracial sex had, of course, occurred for centuries as white men's systematic rape of African American women as a weapon of white supremacy. Southern white police used rape to quell the political equality

70 De Schweinitz, *If We Could Change the World*, 124.

71 Ibid., 123.

72 Ibid., 219.

73 Ida B. Wells, *Southern Horrors and Other Writings; The Anti-Lynching Campaign of Ida B. Wells, 1892–1900*, ed. Jacqueline Jones Royster (Boston, MA: Bedford/St. Martin's, 1996); Gunnar Myrdal and Sissela Bok, *An American Dilemma: The Negro Problem and Modern Democracy* (New Brunswick, NJ: Transaction Publishers, 1995); Ida B. Wells-Barnett, *On Lynchings* (Amherst, NY: Humanity Books, 2002).

authorized by Reconstruction and the social equality that emerged through a robust, postwar civil society of free African Americans. These cases and countless others also clarify the ways in which interracial sex itself is not the taboo the segregationists framed it to be.[74] Although some ardent segregationists would have no doubt criticized rape and sexual violence by whites against African American women, quelling it did not become a rallying point. In the Jim Crow era, white men regularly visited the "colored" railcar to assault African American women. James Weldon Johnson recalled that "It was the custom for white men to go into that ['colored'] car whenever they felt like doing things that would not be allowed in the 'white' car."[75] Quelling the violence and racial hatred was left to "unashamed citizens" – activists such as Johnson, Wells, Rosa Parks, Fannie Lou Hamer, and other African American women and men who sought to "protect" their daughters, sisters, neighbors, nieces, and themselves – as well as the Black public sphere – by deploying the media and whatever state apparatuses and civil institutions were available to publicize and criminalize white sexual violence.

Hence many whites would go to almost any length to debar interracial love and friendship and saw school desegregation as the front lines of their battle for racial purity. Many white parents and clergy believed that a strong sense of shame – a restraint and brake that involved students imagining themselves being judged by others – needed to be cultivated in children with the goal of sexual regulation. Just as Black children were taught deference to whites of all ages, white children were tutored in the shameful and civilization-destroying power of interracial love and sex.[76] Alabama State Senator Walter C. Givhans described *Brown* as a plot "to open the bedroom door of our white women to Negro men."[77] Givhans's fear, repeated throughout segregationist pamphlets, editorials, and speeches, was that without the regulative work of shame made manifest through segregation, white boys and Black girls, white girls and Black boys (and white boys and Black boys, Black girls and white girls, though this was not the particular moral panic of the time) would see each other as moral and sexual equals and "race mixing" would ensue. "Don't wait for your daughter to be raped by these Congolese," warned one pamphlet.[78] The idea that interracial love and friendship were something to be prized or legitimized

[74] Hannah Rosen, *Terror in the Heart of Freedom: Citizenship, Sexual Violence, and the Meaning of Race in the Postemancipation South* (Chapel Hill: University of North Carolina Press, 2009).

[75] Blair Kelley, *Right to Ride: Streetcar Boycotts and African American Citizenship in the Era of Plessy v. Ferguson* (Chapel Hill: University of North Carolina Press, 2010), 39.

[76] Jennifer Lynn Ritterhouse, *Growing Up Jim Crow: How Black and White Southern Children Learned Race: How Black and White Southern Children Learned Race* (Chapel Hill: University of North Carolina Press, 2006).

[77] Jane Dailey, "Sex, Segregation, and the Sacred after Brown," *The Journal of American History* 91, no. 1 (June 1, 2004), 119–144: 120.

[78] De Schweinitz, *If We Could Change the World*, 124.

marked the death of shame, once and for all. This breach would go against the metaphysical "order of things," as the taboo was divinely sanctioned by white pastors and preachers who invoked biblical teachings to justify segregation. The "most common argument of the dissenters [against school desegregation] was in fact theological: integration encouraged miscegenation, which contradicted divine Word." And while the mid-century NAACP stayed away from the inflammatory issue of interracial dating and sex, there is no question that most proponents of equal schooling wanted to lift miscegenation bans and the shame enforcing them, as well.[79] A world of desegregated schools would teach children that there is no shame in calling racial borders into question and loving across them. Segregationists sought to control interracial love and any questioning of racial "truth" by conjuring the classic tropes of The Lament – bodies improperly out of order and shameless and hubristic political activity that sought to overturn custom, tradition, and divine will.[80]

Because the feeling of shame is inextricably linked to sex and sexuality and has been understood across disciplines as a regulative emotion that delimits appropriate and legitimate sex (see previous chapters for full discussion), segregationists appealed to the regulative work of shame and its cognates (like sexual modesty) to challenge *Brown* and the broader movement of which it was a part. As Jennifer Ritterhouse documents in her study of childhood racial socialization, customs and manners were the primary way in which both Black and white children learned and produced racial difference and its significance.[81] Given this, it is unsurprising that supremacists feared the erosion of institutions like segregated schools that would support and enforce racial lessons preached in the pulpit and learned at home. As they told hyperbolic and harrowing tales of civilizational decline, they parroted Rousseau's famous lament about the rise of public women: "Everything is changed."[82] True to Rousseauean paradox (see Chapter 3), Rousseau's praise of the transparent and unashamed bonding among men was made possible by feminine *pudeur* (shame), a necessary brake that kept women in place and from stepping out of line. Similarly, and showing the ways in which the logic of shame supports an ideology of sexual and racial difference, southern white community cohesion and homogeneity required the visible – that is, publicly known and recognizable – civic invisibility of African Americans that segregation guaranteed. This civic invisibility or visible invisibility was the ground on which "whiteness" stood.

The limitations of a nostalgic conception of shame as a means of protecting African American boys and girls come into even sharper relief when we consider the role the shame of interracial sex played in lynching campaigns

[79] Dailey, "Sex, Segregation, and the Sacred after Brown," 126.

[80] Mississippi Senator Theodore G. Bilbo states a common Southern view, well-documented by Jane Dailey: "Miscegenation and amalgamation are sins of man in direct defiance with the will of god." Dailey, "Sex, Segregation, and the Sacred after Brown," 125.

[81] Ritterhouse, *Growing Up Jim Crow*.

[82] Rousseau, *Politics and the Arts*, 89.

enacted in the name of protecting white women and girls' purity, and the ways in which an ideology of shame and modesty made it difficult for African American women and girls to publicize their own sexual victimization by white men. Much more can be (and has been) said about this, but it is worth emphasizing that whites justified lynchings of African Americans through narratives of white women's sexual innocence and Black boys' and men's sexual predation. This was true in the prominent cases of the Scottsboro Boys and Emmett Till, as well as the thousands of less well-known lynching victims.[83] Reconstruction-era and early twentieth Century antilynching activists pointed out that whites often lied to cover up or account for consensual sex, or concocted stories of sexual encounters to ensure the victimization of Black men. Simply stating that white women and Black men engaged in consensual sex was itself scandalous; an editorial by an African American newspaper editor that said as much is generally understood to have triggered the massive riot of 1898 in Wilmington, North Carolina, that destroyed the biracial political coalition that had unseated formal rule by white supremacists.[84] White hysteria about interracial sex also served as justification for eliminating African American economic competition and shutting down political opposition.[85]

The denial of consensual interracial sexual relations and the promotion of a mythology of rapacious Black men who target white women literally whitewashed the sexual violence perpetrated with impunity by white men during slavery and its aftermath.[86] For example, in what became known as the Memphis Riot (1866), white police and small businessmen used rape to intimidate newly free African Americans who were establishing a Black public sphere. "The violence began," explains Hannah Rosen, "as a clash over a festive gathering of African Americans [Black Union soldiers, freedwomen, and children]" who were celebrating the Union victory, offering tributes to Abraham Lincoln, and engaging in the construction of a free community with rights to public space.[87] The soldiers attempted to protect the women and children present, but were outgunned by the Memphis police and vigilante groups. Predictably, the state blamed the Black Union soldiers for the violence and cast the police and vigilantes as protectors of decent, white Southerners. Incensed by the violence,

[83] Patricia A. Schechter, *Ida B. Wells-Barnett and American Reform, 1880–1930* (Chapel Hill: University of North Carolina Press, 2001), 147.

[84] Glenda Elizabeth Gilmore, *Gender and Jim Crow: Women and the Politics of White Supremacy in North Carolina, 1896–1920* (Chapel Hill: University of North Carolina Press, 1996), 105; Schechter, *Ida B. Wells-Barnett and American Reform, 1880–1930*, 115, 127.

[85] Ida B. Wells, *Crusade for Justice: The Autobiography of Ida B. Wells* (Chicago: University of Chicago Press, 1970), 64. I am grateful to Lawrie Balfour for this point. See also Lawrie Balfour, "Ida B. Wells and 'Color Line Justice': Rethinking Reparations in Feminist Terms," *Perspectives on Politics* 13, no. 3 (2015): 680–696.

[86] Rosen, *Terror in the Heart of Freedom*, 76; Schechter, *Ida B. Wells-Barnett and American Reform, 1880–1930*, 118–120.

[87] Ibid., 63–64.

more than one hundred free African American women refused to hide their stories in shame, and spoke out before a Freedmen's Bureau commission and a military commission to detail the police raids and sexual violence designed to shut down the emerging Black public sphere. However much contemporary feminists have bristled at a confessional and testimonial politics, in this particular political context, as Rosen notes, "African American women testifying that they had been raped was a radical act within the context of southern state law and tradition that had negated the possibility that black women could be raped....When black women represented their experience of coerced sexual intercourse with white men as a violation of their will, they asserted a claim to the status of 'woman' and 'citizen.'"[88] Although no immediate consequences for the police came about at the time, the stories of sexual violence publicly challenged white supremacists' monopoly on the discourse of shame and concealment of sexual matters.

Some of these bold and unapologetic efforts to tell the truth of sexual violence were met with cries of civilizational decline and the need to resurrect shame and modesty as part of a respectable Black sensibility. Wells's antilynching campaign was caught in the cross hairs of this dynamic, as her work had emphasized the refusal to hide sexual violence and the lies told about it out of shame, modesty, and respectability. Wells had no patience for paeans to great civilization that needed preserving, asking "What does 'civilization' mean if it is racially construed?"[89] But "respectability politics," framed through its own version of The Lament, nonetheless emerged to challenge and publicly shame Wells and her boldness. A combination of W.E.B. Du Bois's emerging significance in the movement and "respectable" women's groups, specifically the National Association of Colored Women (NACW), which preached "Homes, more homes, better homes, purer homes" buffered Wells's practices of unashamed citizenship that resisted the terms of shame and shaming. Wells was accused of fomenting civilizational decline as both she and her radically democratic work were pathologized as "beyond the pale," disrespectful of the borders and boundaries of shame, and needing to be moderated, braked, and contained. Patricia Schechter elaborates:

> [Wells] was described as unsexed and supersexed, unladylike and too feminine, a paragon and a prostitute, a "black" woman and a "mulattress," a martyr and a savior. Black women stepped up to the opportunities she created, but because Wells-Barnett's work proved as provocative as it was empowering, the NACW sought to mediate and channel her impact. The combination of Wells-Barnett's boldness and vulnerability mobilized African American women to band together for mutual support and draw more tightly defined, reliable standards of feminine behavior under the rubric of racial uplift, middle-class respectability, and dignified ladyhood.[90]

[88] Ibid., 77.
[89] Schechter, *Ida B. Wells-Barnett and American Reform, 1880–1930*, 119.
[90] Ibid., 118.

It became increasingly difficult for Wells to tell the story of rape as respectability politics of various forms gained traction. Soon the NACW and the NAACP took on a strategy of racial uplift that involved self-presentation of virtue, rather than detailed accounts of sexual violence, and a bourgeois politics of shame emerged within African American politics.

This bourgeois preoccupation with shame and respectability is, on its face, a far cry from the kind of shame and protection of the private sphere motivating Arendt in her essay on "Little Rock" or her broader corpus of work. Yet Arendt's failure to acknowledge both the force of sexual violence as part of the discourse of shame in the United States and the tradition of shame as a piece of respectability politics give her work, once again, a troubling resemblance to the work of social conservatives (both white and African American) who sought to quiet the unruly clash of issues of identity, social belonging, and sexual violence with the proper, official work of politics in the public sphere. Wells's unapologetic and unashamed politics, by contrast, calls the public/private divide and the entire mantle of US civilization to task for its implication in sexualized and racialized violence. As with other variations of unashamed citizenship that The Lament both obscures and pathologizes, Wells's work does not provide a clear-cut solution or blueprint for the direction politics must take once it interrogates the object and terms of a nostalgic politics of shame. It does, however, take as its starting point the need to publicize the violence that had been hidden in shame and the subjective dimensions of shame's experience. Wells's lifting of the veil of shame and civility authorized an unruly, democratic politics far more revolutionary than the Jeffersonian ideal Arendt celebrates. It does not fall prey to the fear that "social" politics must always be means-end and programmatic in its orientation. Anyone retrieving the United States lost traditions, panicking about the death of shame or civilizational decline, or romanticizing the "revolutionary spirit" of Jefferson should have to contend with Wells and more recent historians' analyses of what was countenanced in the name of these sacred borders and the shame that enforced them.

Equality without Lament

As should be clear, Arendt's critique of school desegregation and the general state of US education in the 1950s functions as yet another example of the phenomenon I call The Lament. Recall that The Lament is a temporal story of civilizational decline – a nostalgic invocation of an imagined past in which the boundaries and requirements of shame regulated behavior in ways that maximized human dignity and protection. A central feature of this nostalgic longing for a world in which shame regulated behavior is the belief that some things must be concealed and hidden. In Elshtain's classic account, "Shame and its felt experience as it surrounds our body's functions, passions and desires requires symbolic forms, veils of civility that conceal some activities and aspects of ourselves even as we boldly and routinely display and reveal other sides of ourselves when we take part in public activities in the light of day for all to see."[91] As I have been arguing throughout this book, The Lament often appears as a sincere effort to protect democracy and its politics but does so while enforcing inegalitarian reforms and practices. Arendt's nostalgia for a past with borders of shame that both protect the "private" and generate a robust, political "public" is a response to what she reads as excessive egalitarianism in the school desegregation effort. This excessive character pertains to its extension of properly political ideas about equality into the realm of the schools, which Arendt includes in (civil) society, and which she reads – following Tocqueville – as being essentially voluntary and discriminatory.

To put it in more straightforward Arendtian terms, Arendt laments the confusion of the ethos of the political realm – equality – with the ethos of the social realm – discrimination. She criticizes the effort to equalize the social realm because it ruptures the past: the new progressive preference to use education as a tool of social mobility – for "teach[ing] the underprivileged the rules of the game," which "no revolutionary ever thought [was] his task."[92] Moreover, by politicizing education (that is, trying to make it equal), the Court and the NAACP strategy that pressures it use the law and the federal government to address problems of student shame and low self-esteem, psychic injures that must be nurtured and assuaged through the work of parents and communities and lie far beyond the scope of legitimate government. Arendt prefers a resuscitation of authoritative practices in which parents, rather than children, know what is best and lead political fights about issues that pertain to adults, as a way to protect children and prepare them to grow into democratic citizens in their own right.

But good faith aside, Arendt's turn to the past and its protective shame and borders of public and private is misplaced and ultimately incapable of delivering the kind of protection and world-building she seeks to cultivate. This is clear in the troubling overlap between Arendt's complaint and the complaint of segregationists. As the examples show, a racist and misogynistic discourse of shame and honor, private and public, upheld, nurtured, and justified both racial difference and white-supremacist violence against African American adults and children. "Little Rock" as an expression of The Lament *is* a shaming practice. It performatively shames African Americans, who are disallowed by the conditions of slavery and Jim Crow from comporting with the appropriate spheres of activity and boundaries of protection Arendt deems essential. Without access to the formal public sphere, African American citizens (including children) created counterpublics, robust sites of political engagement that

[91] Elshtain uses identical language about the death of shame to describe the rise of political children and the rise of gay liberation – both are examples of the loss of protective "veils of civility" that are central to her politics of shame. See Elshtain, *Democracy on Trial*, 55 and "Political Children," 14.

[92] Arendt, *On Revolution*, 62.

nonetheless defied her strict borders secured by shame.[93] Indeed, although The Lament is a response to a therapeutic discourse of authenticity and social equality, the racial and sexual history of an ideology of shame and civility in the United States provides a helpful context for understanding the "therapeutic turn," the appeal of a politics of recognition that calls into question artificial hierarchies and identities, and the emergence of both "pride" movements such as Black Power as well as Martin Luther King Jr.'s plea for a world (from public to private to social) in which one is "no longer ashamed of being Black."[94] Recent work that acknowledges the role shame plays in queer world-building may exceed and call into question the politics of recognition and the goal of being "no longer ashamed," but it is decidedly non-nostalgic for shame as general social code and order.[95] The tradition of shame in the United States cannot be decoupled from the racial and sexual work it has performed.

I see three significant objections to my argument thus far. I want to outline and clarify my response to them as a way of further sharpening my argument here and in the book in general. I will then offer some final reflections on this particular case of egalitarianism and set the stage for the book's conclusion.

The first, and most obvious, response to the argument I lay out here is that shame can be used for good. That is to say, I am reading and focusing on "bad" shame or "negative" shame – the shame of the bigot and the shame of the racist. Instead of looking at "bad" shame, I should look at the good, progressive, and egalitarian work that shame can perform. Along these lines, one could rightly point out that activists in the civil rights movement – like other egalitarian struggles (e.g., gay liberation and feminism) – have used shame as a political tactic to "call out" and shame those who shame them. Hence we have the person protesting inequality carrying the sign that reads, "Shame on You!" Moreover, the language of shame (and its absence) can be a useful way of rallying the grassroots and making moral arguments. The lawyers who defended the Scottsboro Boys, the nine boys who were wrongly accused of raping two white women on a train in Alabama in 1931, appealed to shame as a protective cover for children and childhood. Prosecutors tried the boys as men, a tactic their defenders said denied them the right to childhood innocence. "These 'nine negro children grow[ing] to young manhood in jail,' defenders argued, represented the 'shame of America.' "[96] The shame was trying these boys as men, denying them the benefits of childhood innocence, especially in an era where even their fathers lacked standing as full adults. De Schweinitz notes,

[93] Hanchard, "Contours of Black Political Thought."

[94] Martin Luther King, Jr., "Where Do We Go from Here?".

[95] As Michael Warner notes, "This is the problem with any conservative ... stance on sexual morality: What we have to conserve is barbaric." Warner, *The Trouble with Normal*, 5. See also, more generally, David M. Halperin and Valerie Traub, eds., *Gay Shame*.

[96] De Schweinitz, *If We Could Change the World*, 9.

"many white southerners considered the idea of a separate state of childhood for blacks impossible, since, according to racist philosophies, blacks lived in a perpetual state of childhood.... [B]lack men could attain the status of men only when they seemed to threaten white womanhood and ... under such conditions, black boys were denied their true status as children."[97]

The problem was, to put it simply, that these lamentations about the "shame of America" and the "shameless" prosecutors who would charge boys as men – to say nothing of the "shameless" whites who manufactured the story about the boys on the train in the first place – fell on deaf ears. This moral framework of shame may have provided the defense a sense of moral righteousness, but its influence has paled in comparison to lamentations about the death of a traditional conception of shame that regulates social order in favor of whites. That is to say, as I emphasized in the previous chapter's discussion of John Quincy Adams's shaming of Andrew Jackson and Jackson's project of Indian Removal, both of which were justified in the language of civilizational preservation, claims about the death of shame "stick" to some bodies more than others. They do not always perform the moral regulation that antiracist or antisexist proponents seek. Perhaps because of shame's roots as an aristocratic ethos that gets parlayed and updated into bourgeois respectability framed against an undifferentiated working class, and because shame directs us to fixed identities and norms of order that have *not been egalitarian*, shame seems poorly suited to securing egalitarian norms and outcomes and is more often successfully deployed as a brake against them. Elsa Barkley Brown writes about the ways in which African American men deployed narratives of shamelessness and civilizational decline against barbarous whites in the face of Reconstruction's decimation, trying to shame whites into living up to their allegedly refined civilization.[98] But this effort failed to the extent that whites, like Adams who lost the election but won the cultural war, had inoculated themselves against discourses of civilizational decline with respect to their own "barbaric" behavior. Similarly, African American strategies of respectability failed to confer the protections shame and civility would suggest.[99] The narratives of shamelessness and incivility fail to adhere to white bodies in the same way they adhere to the bodies of Others, just as practices of respectability did not confer recognition to African American men, women, and children. The discourse of shame, bound up with an ideology of civility and civilization, has been secured by whites and white men, in particular, for their own protection. The very idea of preserving civilization against barbarism therefore

[97] Ibid., 10.

[98] Elsa Barkley Brown, "Negotiating and Transforming the Public Sphere," 139–140.

[99] See Erin Alane Boade, "The Limits of Civility in the Civil Rights and Black Power Movements: Three African-American Women's Autobiographies," PhD Dissertation, December 2009, http://repositories.lib.utexas.edu/handle/2152/23444.

functions as a protective shield to insulate and naturalize white, European, and masculine violence.[100]

When whites or other elites disavow their power and privilege in response to being shamed by civil rights or other antiracist or antisexist activists, it is tempting to read their transformation as evidence of moral accounting, reflection, and the decision to do the right thing.[101] Yet as Arendt herself insists, and on this point I agree, politics and political change is not about moral reflection translated into a particular social policy.[102] Politics is about conflict, struggle, and pressure. To be sure, it involves moral vision and claims-making and that work can sustain activists. But as Charles Payne emphasizes so well, civil rights and racially egalitarian victories resulted from day-to-day organizing and hard-fought, sometimes bloody activism and political pressure rather than moral change in the hearts of whites or national leaders.[103] It is the pressure of direct action and the occupation of white space that triggers change, not a moral awakening on the part of whites and other elites. To return to a point from the Gay Shame movement, shame cannot be counted on and it is not felt equally: a shaming campaign offers no guarantee that its targets will respond in a particular way.

The second potential apprehension I want to address relates to the strategy to begin the civil rights struggle in the schools. That is, even if it is wrong to invoke a traditional boundary of shame as a protection, perhaps Arendt is right to argue that this naturalized, child-led and child-centered approach to social change left African American children extremely vulnerable to both physical violence and psychological trauma, and NAACP leaders should have considered alternative civil rights strategies.[104] In a rarefied context, Arendt has a point – one that might be extended to pro-choice or pro-life parents who ask their children to fight the battle for their side of the reproductive rights wars.[105] But in the context of the sheer lack of personal and psychological safety that many African American children experienced – especially in the South, but not exclusively there, the idea that an alternative civil rights strategy could

[100] See Bailyn, *The Barbarous Years*; Cañizares-Esguerra, *Puritan Conquistadors*.

[101] See Elizabeth Anderson, "Social Movements, Experiments in Living, and Moral Progress: Case Studies from Britain's Abolition of Slavery," The Lindley Lecture, University of Kansas, February 11, 2014, http://kuscholarworks.ku.edu/handle/1808/14787.

[102] This point recurs throughout Arendt's work; see especially "What Is Freedom?" "Truth and Politics," and her discussion of the lost "revolutionary spirit" in *On Revolution*.

[103] Charles Payne, "Debating the Civil Rights Movement: The View from the Trenches," in *Debating the Civil Rights Movement*: 1945–1968, ed. Steven Lawson and Charles Payne (Lanham, MD: Rowman & Littlefield, 2006), 115–135: 132–135. See also Charles Payne, *I've Got the Light of Freedom: The Organizing Tradition and the Mississippi Freedom Struggle* (Berkeley: University of California Press, 2007).

[104] Allen emphasizes the ways in which Eckford was traumatized by her first day at Central High School. Allen, *Talking to Strangers*, 33–34.

[105] Some feminists have criticized pro-life activists for "using" their children to make a point about fetal rights. Elshtain, "Commentary: Political Children," 22.

have protected the children from violence reads as both misplaced and myopic. Mississippi whites lynched a fourteen-year-old boy, Emmett Till, for allegedly failing to obey the norms of Southern racial deference in 1955.[106] Children whose parents have worked assiduously to tutor them in "respectability" have not been spared white supremacist violence. So long as the state protects white parents' conception of what protection of white children involves and requires, proper borders of shame among African Americans and sparing Black youth the struggle of politics will not deliver the relief Arendt imagined. The mid-twentieth century United States – as remains true in the early twenty-first – was a dangerous place for African American children and adults; there was no initial idealized state that was lost when Daisy Bates and the NAACP put children on the front lines of the movement in Little Rock or anywhere else.[107]

The final concern relates to the second, and is also germane to Arendt's argument in "Little Rock" as well as other strategies to politicize children's suffering. I speak here of the NAACP's Rousseauean gamble of presenting children as "natural" and "innocent"*human beings* worthy of white pity and charity as they sought what every child wants: an education and a sense of belonging and self-esteem. By using the therapeutic language of psychological trauma and low self-esteem, school desegregation was, in this view, about accommodating difference – a forerunner to multiculturalism – and not about political citizenship.[108] The "media presented the struggle for civil rights in terms that highlighted sentimental notions of childhood."[109] The optics of African American children's suffering appeared and reappeared in national and international media. But this sentimentality and childhood innocence was double-edged. Focusing on "treating" African American children as sentimental objects of care and concern was radically different from reading them and their parents as citizens with full rights and standing. Martin Berger's account of photos of police brutality against African Americans during the civil rights era makes this point, as well.[110] There are good reasons to be apprehensive about political movements based upon idealized notions of childhood.[111]

[106] For a rich account of the Emmett Till case and its significance for American conceptions of childhood, see De Schweinitz, *If We Could Change the World*, 91–103.

[107] The United States is still dangerous for youth and adults of color. At the time this book goes to press, the Unietd States is in the midst of a consciousness-raising about the preponderance of police violence against African American adults and children. For a recent overview, see Melvin L. Rogers, "Introduction: Disposable Lives," *Theory & Event* 17, no. 3 (2014), http://muse.jhu.edu/journals/theory_and_event/v017/17.3S.rogers.html.

[108] See Daryl Michael Scott, *Contempt and Pity: Social Policy and the Image of the Damaged Black Psyche, 1880–1996* (Chapel Hill: University of North Carolina Press, 1997); Daryl Michael Scott, "Postwar Pluralism, Brown v. Board of Education, and the Origins of Multicultural Education," *The Journal of American History* 91, no. 1 (2004): 69–82.

[109] De Schweinitz, *If We Could Change the World*, 12.

[110] Martin A. Berger and David J. Garrow, *Seeing through Race: A Reinterpretation of Civil Rights Photography* (Berkeley: University of California Press, 2011).

[111] De Schweinitz, *If We Could Change the World*, 249–250.

I agree with aspects of this final point and see the risks of sentimentalized accounts of inequality that can be resolved or minimized through compassion and charity. Documentation of suffering orphans and victims of drought and famine, for example, tend to appear as objects of pity rather than subjects in their own right or citizens in the making.[112] Allen provides a helpful counter-interpretation to reading school desegregation through the lens of compassion as she emphasizes the political and citizenship-building character of school desegregation and asks us to see Eckford and others as democratic citizens in the making, rather than objects of white pity and compassion.[113] Eckford and the Little Rock Nine thus emerge as unashamed citizens who punctured norms of civility that had sought to secure their silence and shame. On this point, it is worth returning to one of Arendt's chief concerns, which she raises as she is imagining herself as a Black mother: the claim that the NAACP has put her child in a more humiliating position than she was in before. However humiliating second-class schools may have been, Arendt maintains that pushing – or appearing to push – your way into a place where you are not wanted involves a particularly acute level of humiliation, and it is this kind of humiliation she imagines Eckford (or perhaps Counts, given the confusion about the photograph) suffering through because of the toxic combination of *adults'* cowardice and high-minded ideas about reform.

Yet if we consider the images of both Eckford and Counts, it is not clear that the heroic girls are humiliated at all.[114] Naturally it is beyond the scope of this project or my knowledge to be able to document the inner feelings of either girl as she faces down the white mob. And in some sense that is beside the point. But one should I pause before reading these young women as wrought with shame and humiliation for being exposed as social climbers, as Arendt reads them to be. To the contrary, their goals appear neither to be renouncing the facts of who they are nor joining white society, the ills of which are readily apparent to them long before this particular moment. Rather, both Eckford and Counts look determined to secure the education to which they are entitled as citizens of the United States.[115] That they are harassed while trying to secure this education is not a failing of them or their parents, but of the whites

[112] See Karen Zivi, "The Politics of Compassion in the Age of AIDS," in *W Stands for Women: How the George W. Bush Presidency Shaped a New Politics of Gender*, eds. Michaele Ferguson and Lori Marso, (Durham, NC: Duke University Press, 2007), 41–62; Richard Boyd, "Pity's Pathologies Portrayed Rousseau and the Limits of Democratic Compassion," *Political Theory* 32, no. 4 (2004): 519–546.

[113] Allen, *Talking to Strangers*.

[114] Dorothy Counts personally thanked Danielle Allen for presenting her desegregation fight in heroic terms. Personal communication with Danielle Allen, June 2, 2015.

[115] Dorothy Counts and Elizabeth Eckford both appeared on the front page of the *New York Times* on September 5, 1957. Allen, *Talking to Strangers*, 197 n1.

involved in the protests and in the state and federal governments that deny equal education and personal security.[116]

Moreover, to return to the particulars of Arendt's lament, had the NAACP effort focused on the fight for full public and private standing for African American adults – voting and interracial marriage rights with schooling following, it is *possible* that the outcome might have been different and the change would have been more properly political (in the Arendtian sense) and less therapeutic and sentimental in character. But the violent history of white supremacist attacks on Reconstruction's egalitarianism suggests otherwise. Lifting bans on interracial marriage was an early part of the NAACP's strategy in the twentieth century, and there were a few brief exceptions during Reconstruction to the 300-year ban on interracial marriage. But the issue was generally understood as insurmountable in mid-century. This climate meant that the NAACP had to minimize any link between equal education and the logical possibility that it would lead to interracial sex and marriage. Justice John Marshall Harlan II noted that the Court could only take on "one bombshell at a time."[117] On the question of voting rights, given what we know about the violence of the disfranchisement campaign following Reconstruction and what occurred in the 1960s voter registration effort, there is no reason to believe children would have been safer as a result of a 1950s voting rights campaign. Fantasies of the curative powers of shame and civility would both fail to protect African American youth and also be deployed to criminalize and victimize them.

[116] On the subject of denial of African American security and safety, see Naomi Murakawa, *The First Civil Right: How Liberals Built Prison America* (New York: Oxford University Press, 2014).

[117] Dailey, "Sex, Segregation, and the Sacred after Brown," 127.

Conclusion

Is Shame Necessary?

The title of a new book asks, "Is shame necessary?"[1] The mere posing of such a question, of course, gives the answer: "Yes!" Following contemporary trends in moral and political philosophy, the author argues that shame has been too quickly abandoned by those who do not understand its essential value, and shame must be revitalized for the good of all. In this particular case, the author focuses on environmental devastation as evidence of a dangerous shamelessness that can be corrected with an influx of healthy shame. But, as I hope I have shown throughout this book, the impulse to pose such a question and answer it with healthy affirmation could be extended to any number of crises in late-modern democracy: police brutality, income disparity, torture of detainees, disfranchisement, delays in federal emergency response, achievement and resource gaps in public education, and so on.

"Is shame necessary? Yes!" is a variant of The Lament That Shame Is Dead. Like it, the rhetorical question appears to address these problems (and promises to address more) through a process of moral awakening whereby people struggle, both alone and together, to live up to in practice their shared theoretical commitments to clean air, public safety, an educated citizenry, free and fair elections, and so on. As the story goes, these all seem to be things that "we" can agree about in spite of "our" disagreements and diversity. That is, "we" would be fine were it not for the shameless few who have gotten in the way of collective self-governance through common principles. The shameless have derailed the project of democracy with their individualistic desires to serve only themselves and those with whom they are most closely allied. A lack of shame is an appealing diagnosis for what ails any given community. Shame then is both solace and cure.

[1] Jacquet, *Is Shame Necessary?*.

Although I have been generally skeptical of The Lament's explanatory and political power, much of what I have catalogued thus far has to do with a recurring nostalgia for a lost ethos of shame with respect to relatively marginalized and powerless peoples trying to claim space in public for themselves and politicize the terms of their exclusion and domination. Rejecting some of the shaming practices expressed through The Lament, that is, the shaming of the "weak" by the "strong," might not mean rejecting *all* shaming practices or eliminating the need for shame as a recuperative and restorative tonic for social and political ills. One could still, it would seem, marshal The Lament against the people and organizations that commit genuine harm to the public. We would then gather together and lament that shame is dead when it comes to things good democrats want to change. The intentions and heart of the speaking subject of The Lament and the object of her lamentation would be what matters.

I want to push this point further by reflecting on the allure of a politics of shame and shaming that involves capturing shame for "good" ends by way of two linked democratic crises that mark the specific historical moment in which this book goes to press: the connection of racial, economic, and social inequality with both police violence, specifically against African Americans and racial and ethnic minorities, and environmental devastation and the denial thereof. I then reiterate a point I have been making throughout the book: unapologetic and unashamed political action, rather than moral awakening, is the best path through these conflicts. This is the path of unashamed citizenship discussed in the previous chapters. I close by reappraising the Greek ethos of *aidōs*, reflect on whether it is as "dead" as The Lament suggests, and offer some preliminary thoughts about its afterlife and implications for radically democratic politics today.

Let me again acknowledge the legitimacy of concerns about the poor character of people who promote and defend technologies and practices that are scientifically shown to deplete natural resources and contribute to the warming of the earth's core, only then to deny that such changes are taking place and those who profile, brutalize, ticket, arrest, indict, and incarcerate ethnic minorities and citizens of color. To the extent that one is in the business of assessing others' moral character, one can't avoid thinking: these people come up very short.

But the problems that shame and other fantasies of moral awakening are typically called upon to resolve are not as straightforward as the "shamelessness" diagnosis suggests. Reading our most pressing circumstances as failures of shame and resurrecting shame as the "solution" to the inequalities, injustices, and calcifications of power and privilege plays into a fantasy about shame's regulative power as a moral guide that can be deployed against what ails us. This fantasy is tied to a highly individualistic account of moral agency as a lever for changing collective social dynamics. It reads inequalities and injustices as moral failings of people with bad hearts who need to be shamed into proper moral and political action. To invoke Lani Guinier and Richard

Torres's critique of ethical solutions to political problems, the preoccupation with revitalizing shame "not only locates the problem in the individual but it locates the remedy there as well." To continue in this vein: "All that is necessary to overcome racism [or police brutality, economic exploitation, or environmental devastation]" is to feel shame and act on it.[2] This emphasis on individual ethical reflection and its transformative powers runs throughout the contemporary reappraisals of shame's indispensability for social and political change.

Moreover, settling the difference between "good" and "bad" or "true" and "false" forms of shame is not as simple as the typological accounts suggest. Segregationists and white supremacists may very well believe with all of their hearts that interracial love and friendship are harmful in terms of the effects they bring to children of all races. Settling the moral rules that would ground any typology of "good" and "bad" is not likely to resolve the problems the typologies seek to address. It is precisely the desire for moral high ground and the prize of a "true" account of what is shameful that motivates so many of the ideologies and movements unashamed citizens seek to disrupt.

And furthermore, The Lament and the general diagnosis of shamelessness as the culprit to what ails us obscures the context in which these egregious acts emerge and are exercised. Framing problems with respect to environmental devastation and police brutality, for example, in terms of the presence or absence of shame, erases the larger forces in motion. The "death of shame" diagnosis does not account for the birth and protection of the automobile industry; the national investment in and reliance on fossil fuels; the lack of funding for alternative energies; the police department quotas to stop, frisk, ticket, and detain; the bankrolling of city budgets through aggressive policing of minor offenses among citizens of color; the mandates of federal crime policy; the redlining of real estate; the resegregation of the public schools; the cheap availability of guns on the street; the arrival of surplus military weapons and equipment in local police departments; and other overlapping, often contradictory, structural and incentivized policies that create a value structure that often shames people into compliance with the very acts we would summon shame to repair. To play out the example in a bit more detail, the police officer who listens to her conscience and resists the policies handed down by the chief of police may be publicly shamed for doing so. She might internalize this shame for failing to live up to the expectations of solidarity and trust within the department. The logic of shame provides no clear path for her to do the "right thing" because the problems of police violence exceed the individual decision making and moral consciousness of this particular officer. Her ethical deliberation involves competing factors: a sense of herself as a female police officer who has taken an oath to "serve and protect"; a promise to herself not to "make trouble" or quit; a need to pay a mortgage to provide for her family; a need for vacation time

[2] Lani Guinier and Gerald Torres, *The Miner's Canary: Enlisting Race, Resisting Power, Transforming Democracy* (Cambridge, MA: Harvard University Press, 2003), 43.

to spend with ailing parents; a desire to avoid the social, psychological, and economic penalties of resisting her chief's orders'; and finally the word of her nagging conscience that says the chief's orders have taken police power *too far*. This is not to say she bears no responsibility for following the chief's orders.[3] But she is not the locus of the problem of police violence. Most importantly, fortifying her sense of shame will not transform the practices in question.

Summoning The Lament to address the depravities many democratic citizens find egregious paradoxically indulges in some of the antiegalitarian nostalgia for rule by elites whose manners, mores, and capacity to preserve civilization are supposedly intact. Recall that I have argued that The Lament is a nostalgic longing for an imagined past in which shame and civility regulated social and political life. The Lament, by my account, emerges at a fevered pitch when "new arrivals" or democratic parvenus puncture the political and social order either through the expansion of who counts as a citizen with standing, what counts as a political claim, or a reorganization of the social order that extends and radicalizes democratic egalitarian commitments. With this in mind, I invoked the examples of Andrew Jackson, who a generation prior would not have been eligible to vote, being elected to the White House; the Cynics' occupation of the public sphere in the name of the poor and unpropertied; the entrance of people of the "literary low life," the *declassés*, to the borders of the "republic of letters"; and the mandatory desegregation of public schools. Each of these disturbances and transformations of the social order is met with a version of the cry that Shame Is Dead!

What would it mean to see the failures of environmental regulation, policing, and the economy as failures of shame on the part of the people at the helm of these institutions and industries? Lags in gender and racial parity notwithstanding, the composition of most institutions and industries has relatively greater diversity than a generation ago. Characterizing the devastating failures of these institutions to serve "the people" properly as evidence of the death of shame backs into a nostalgic and redemptive story about the moral probity of the fathers and sons of the original ruling class. This is the Burkean fantasy of aristocratic *politesse*, whereby elites who had inherited power did not behave in such gauche and crass ways because their status was intact. The old elites, this story goes, were good stewards of the nation and the earth. The present crisis results from the new arrivals who lack ties to the past, present, and future. This story deflects attention away from the structural and legal changes in the economy and industry and toward the bad character of the new leadership. It glosses over ways in which old elites and the socio-economic-political apparatus in which they dwelled set in motion a set of institutional, economic, and political

[3] For an extended discussion of these "burdens of responsibility," see Jade Larissa Schiff, *Burdens of Political Responsibility: Narrative and the Cultivation of Responsiveness* (New York: Cambridge University Press, 2014).

conditions and imperatives that frame contemporary democratic crises. And it lays blame at the feet of democracy's new arrivals whose bad hearts and minds make them the generation to lack the moral compass of shame.

Beyond redeeming elites of the past, The Lament also obscures and pathologizes the radically democratic work of those people who – alone and together – expose the ways in which the discourse and rhetoric of shame naturalizes and endorses invisibilities, dominations, and inequalities. These unashamed citizens do not fear appearing disrespectable and do not heed ideologies of shame and civility. They are not afraid of behaving in ways that will be decried as fomenting civilizational decline. They recognize the very scandal of their being in the world as speaking subjects and political actors, and they exploit this scandal in order to unsettle the symmetry between regimes of power and domination and moral and aesthetic appeals to civility and shame. And they are skeptical of those who appeal to shame and civility as regulative ideals because they understand – from their own experience or from solidarity with others – the political work these appeals perform.

Unashamed citizens are not simply trying to overcome their own shame and live in a perfect, ideal state where no one ever has a bad feeling or negative emotion about themselves. They do not look to erase the ethical antennae their shame provides. But you rarely hear them waxing nostalgic for the decline of civility and shame. In the vast majority of feminist work that deals with shame, for example, much of which is written by queer feminists and feminists of color, there is not much good to be said about it. More often, shame is omnipresent, in the woodwork, self-defining, perhaps an "old[] friend" and "bedrock" but not something needing revitalization.[4] Gloria Anzaldúa writes of the grip of *verguenza* (shame) – "being afraid that [her] friends would see [her] momma, would know that she was loud," and of the ways in which she and her siblings learned the art of "hiding [their] 'lonches' *papas con chorizo* behind cupped hands and bowed heads, gobbling them up before the other kids could see."[5] Nostalgia toward or a romanticization of the grip of shame is conspicuously absent. More often shame is something to be negotiated, managed, and striven to be overcome even if one knows shame will always linger. One's radical activism may originate in shame but is also imagined as a way through it. Politics in this spirit does not seek to revitalize or recultivate shame to resolve the social and political crises of one's time. Feminists' political proclamations often take up the language of moral righteousness and use shaming tactics but deploy them to create space for unsettling received mores and norms that shame and silence.

And no wonder: We have been waiting a very long time for a moral awakening that ushers in a community of equals. To return to the examples of police

[4] Hanson, "Teaching Shame," 138; Warner, *The Trouble with Normal*, 35.

[5] Gloria Anzaldúa, "*La Prieta*," 42.

brutality, if elites and rank-and-file members of the police force have a moral transformation and remedy the brutality that has been part and parcel of police practice at least since Reconstruction, there will be great rejoicing.[6] But given these historical patterns and the emergence of police power in the context of white desire to control, exploit, and extract labor from free African Americans, faith in and hope for a moral transformation triggered by collective shame seems misplaced. To the contrary, political work against racially motivated and differentiated police power, in keeping with the practice of unashamed citizenship, pressures, agitates, exposes, obstructs, occupies, writes, speaks out, and refuses to hide in shame. These strategies have recently come to life under the aegis of Black Lives Matter, but they are part of a longstanding tradition of African American resistance to "legal" and extra-judicial violence.

The negative responses to protests against extra-judicial violence in Ferguson, Missouri, Baltimore, Maryland, and all around the United States repeat the logic of The Lament as a narrative of civilizational decline that conceals the legitimately democratic and political character of unashamed citizens' struggles and pathologizes the movement and the people participating in it as "beyond the pale." As the network of activists organized under the banner of Black Lives Matter coordinate, strategize, take up the work of critiquing state power, and lay their bodies down to stop the traffic of ordinary life, their critics invoke the terms of The Lament. These citizens are *taking things too far*. They are shameless and uncivilized. Their intersubjective networks, creative politicking, artistic engagement, rhetorical flourish, and communication strategies are ignored as they are rendered unfiltered, unanchored, shameless threats with no connection to the past, institutions, or the future. They are told to focus on *all lives*. They are reminded they must obey the law even as its illegitimacy is their *raison d'être*. They are told that any property damage is evidence they are unfit for self-rule and only proves that the use of force is necessary. The Lament and the ideal of shame as a regulative code here again switches and deflects the focus away from the violence of the police department or vigilante and toward the shameless and uncivilized "behavior" (rather than "politics") of the activists.[7] Activists are expected to maintain civility and decorum as the police department engages in systematic brutalization and, among other outrages, the Grand Jury fails to indict Darren Wilson. Miscarriages of justice persist.

In the moral panic and the fear of social disturbance that operates in The Lament, the violence of the police and the violence of the protesters become equivalent. Or worse still, the former is justified and naturalized as preserving

[6] On the reiterative nature of police violence against African Americans since Reconstruction, see Khalil Gibran Muhammad, *The Condemnation of Blackness: Race, Crime, and the Making of Modern Urban America* (Cambridge, MA: Harvard University Press, 2011); Murakawa, *The First Civil Right*; Michelle Alexander, *The New Jim Crow: Mass Incarceration in the Age of Colorblindness* (New York: The New Press, 2012).

[7] On the legal force of vigilantism, see Jennet Kirkpatrick, *Uncivil Disobedience: Studies in Violence and Democratic Politics* (Princeton, NJ: Princeton University Press, 2008).

order and civility and the latter is pathologized as at odds with democratic politics and practice.[8] From the perspective of The Lament, each new attempt at citizen insurrection of police power only serves as further evidence of shamelessness and civilization destruction, which in turn justifies – rather than minimizes – increased state violence. As with the Jacobins' pathologizing of *pudeur*-defying women as destroyers of the republic who "trample[] on the virtues of [their] sex," the unashamed tactics of Black Lives Matters become crimes unto themselves. The stakes are high, civilization hangs in the balance, the so-called shameless must be punished – often with death.

But the unashamed citizens of Black Lives Matter, like those citizens who struggle against wealth inequalities and environmental devastation in movements like Idle No More, an indigenous peoples' movement in Canada that links indigenous sovereignty and environmental rights, are not untethered and isolated individuals who refuse to share the world with others. To the contrary, as I hope the framework of unashamed citizenship helps to show, they are part of a history of radically democratic citizenship that resists and disavows the terms of shame and civility and the "civilizations" they are deployed to preserve.

Idle No More focuses on the Canadian government's interest in extracting oil and gas from the tar sands that are on First Peoples' lands. Like other unashamed citizens, their entrance on the political stage by definition commingles the personal and the political, the political and the therapeutic, the social and the political.[9] They seek to cultivate, rather than destroy, plurality. And, like the Cynics, the literary low life, the pariahs of the periods surrounding the French Revolution, and the youth on the front lines of school desegregation, they do so not as isolated individuals but as part of a peer group invested in the world as much as, if not more than, their own psychological health. Unashamed citizens across time and place show the ways in which meaningful democratic political struggle always involves those "remainders" and "excesses" that lie outside of the formal bounds of public activity and speech. For Black Lives Matter and Idle No More to comport with the terms of politics laid out in The Lament, they would have to strip themselves of the productive extra-political elements that give their movements such political and democratic force. They

[8] Naomi Murakawa makes this point about the equivalent (or often greater) concern about Black violence than about white violence. "Eddie Glaude and Naomi Murakawa in Conversation," Public Event, Labyrinth Books, Princeton, New Jersey, March 12, 2015.

[9] Brooke Jarvis, "Native-Led Protest Movement Takes on Canadian Government," *Rolling Stone*, February 4, 2013. http://www.rollingstone.com/politics/news/idle-no-more-native-led-protest-movement-takes-on-canadian-government-20130204. For scholarly analyses of Idle No More, see L. Jane McMillan, Janelle Young, and Molly Peters, "Commentary: The 'Idle No More' Movement in Eastern Canada," *Canadian Journal of Law and Society/La Revue Canadienne Droit et Société* 28, no. 3 (2013): 429–431; Terry Wotherspoon and John Hansen, "The 'Idle No More' Movement: Paradoxes of First Nations Inclusion in the Canadian Context," *Social Inclusion* 1, no. 1 (2013): 21–36.

would be left trying to properly balance the right amount of shame with the right amount of equality; to be appropriately deferential to the differences that shame secures. That would be very much beside the point of crafting a world in which African Americans, First Peoples, and others perennially cast as threats to civilization were seen as capable of self-determination and not dominated in the name of Anglo and European rule.

Moreover, contemporary movements that politicize the ways in which shame, civility, and "civilization" are used to stigmatize, marginalize, and pathologize people at the margins of formal social and political power show the precariousness of a sharp divide between "political" work and "therapeutic" work. These movements show, as has been evident in the work of unashamed citizens explored throughout the book, the therapeutic dimensions of political action itself. Perhaps ironically, this is something that some of the theorists – from Aristotle to Arendt – who defend a strict separation between the "political" and other realms of life seem to have understood. For what does it mean that "man is by nature a political animal" and that "men *are* free ... as long as they act, ... for to *be* free and to act are the same" if not that participating in public, world-affecting work with a peer group "whose destiny [one] share[s]" is psychologically transformative and essential to living fully as a person?[10] It makes little sense to speak of unashamed citizens or unashamed citizenship as evidence that shame (or politics) is dead. Unashamed citizens engage the world as actors on the stage of politics.

With this in mind, let us return for a moment to the concept of *aidōs* with which I began in the Introduction. The Greeks did not have separate terms for guilt or shame, but *aidōs* captures a sense of measuring oneself in relation to the values of others that you approve of and share – values that you want to measure yourself against, as well. I have argued that The Lament judges people in late-modernity as lacking these values and the capacity for self-judgment. By contrast, Bernard Williams, in his discussion of *aidōs* in Greek tragedy and poetry, claims that our contemporary ethical decision making is not so different from that of the Greeks. Rather, he insists that *aidōs* is alive and well. *Aidōs* is an apt description of how people make ethical decisions, and it looks nothing like the willful deliberation of modern moral philosophy. When people organize to protest against environmental devastation, the denial of climate change, policy brutality, the carceral state, and other plagues of late-modern inequalities, they do not act in a vacuum. Their claims and movements have a history that includes processes of domination and resistance. These contexts generate values and commitments that work as touchpoints for present and future organizing. By this account shame is not in fact "dead" at all, but a highly political and emotionally charged idea that is disavowed, invoked, and negotiated in moments of democratic struggle.

[10] Aristotle, *The Politics* (1253a2); Arendt, "What Is Freedom?," 445–446; Arendt, *Rahel Varnhagen*, 251.

When people lament that shame is dead, perhaps they are not really lamenting the death of *aidōs*. Perhaps they are pining for something they never had: a moral rule that governed collective life in ways that appeared to serve everyone with outcomes of which we approved. Lamentations for *aidōs* are really longings for clear guidelines for *others'* ethical action that always turn out the way *we* want them to. And so, when people act in ways that seem irrational and incomprehensible because they do not affirm "our" values, it is tempting to declare them shameless and to say that shame is dead. Williams's study reminds us that *aidōs* can never be the guide for politics that The Lament invests in it. Citizens in democratic Athens resisted the dictates of *aidōs* because it was tied to a very particular, elite social order – one they sought to refuse and replace. The Cynics doubled down on this resistance, calling into question all social conventions that were tied in any way to an inegalitarian state. But, in doing so, they did not generate a politics without any common concern or values; to the contrary, democratic or cosmopolitan (or a motley assortment of the two) values replaced aristocratic ones. That their implementation and extension was flawed and imperfect is much of the story of democratic politics.

Rather than read *aidōs* as a stabilizing supplement to the unruliness of democracy, we can read it as a way of understanding how people, both alone and together, weigh ethical decision making and account for their own actions before others. It has no clear outcomes or guarantees. It is deeply attached to the specifics of identity both in terms of how someone understands themselves and how she or he is understood by others. But this identity is not static or singular, and so ethical deliberation often involves weighing competing identities of being a son or a daughter, a father or a mother, a citizen, a soldier, a doctor, a craftsman, an Athenian, a foreigner, and so on. What to do is not automatic. No wonder shame has been such a contested guide to political problems, as it provides no clear path through them. Appeals to ethics to solve or soften the problems of politics have tremendous appeal. The same can be said for political procedures that promise just outcomes that everyone can supposedly accept. But the more pressing political conflicts of any given moment are also *effects* of ethical rules and political procedures and therefore entangled in them. The problems remain. Politics, of course, also has no guarantees. But unlike moral rules and procedures, it enables the people who have been fodder for lamentations about civilizational decline and the death of shame to emerge from the shadows of shame, make claims for themselves, and participate in the building of a world.

How might we resist participating in the "death of shame" and the slide toward therapeutic discourse? My final answer is twofold: First, whatever shame is, so long as we are arguing about what it entails and means, it isn't dead. Second, if the disavowals of shame and the breaches of what we believe shame secures make philosophers and political theorists uncomfortable, we can certainly point out the dangers of a politics that invokes therapeutic language to imagine a world without shame. We can also choose not to provide its philosophical defense. But if we're talking about how the dream of a life free from shame circulates at the level of political activity – and I think that is the real question here – we would do better to accept psychological-political entanglements as intimately and inextricably tied to a democratic politics that is committed to a full-bodied idea of equality.

As long as people who have been historically excluded and dominated enter the stage of politics as citizens or potential citizens, their self-representations and demands for freedom will put others on the defensive. These others may, in turn, invoke the language of authenticity and the need to be unashamed as a way of securing their power rather than conceding it. Thus we have the oppressed Christian Right, beleaguered white pride groups, and men who have been injured by feminism. This is much of the story of modern politics. We can spin out its moral, we can imagine alternative scripts and responses, we can pine for the days before *ressentiment*, when only elites participated in public life and it supposedly did not occur to nonelites to resent this fact. But the on-the-ground antagonisms between the political and the therapeutic come with the territory of democracy under the conditions of full enfranchisement. These antagonisms play out as modern political drama.

Rather than summon political theory to close the door on these robust acts of citizenship, we might turn a sympathetic and contextual eye toward them. It may be the task of theorists to interpret the world, but it is the business of everyday actors to engage in and change it.

Bibliography

Abdel-Nour, Farid. "National Responsibility." *Political Theory* 31, no. 5 (October 1, 2003): 693–719.

Adorno, Theodor W. *Jargon of Authenticity*. Evanston, IL: Northwestern University Press, 1973.

Agel, Jerome. *The Radical Therapist: Therapy Means Change, Not Adjustment: The Radical Therapist Collective*. New York: Ballantine Books, 1971.

Ahmed, Sara. *The Cultural Politics of Emotion*. New York: Routledge, 2004.

Alexander, Michelle. *The New Jim Crow: Mass Incarceration in the Age of Colorblindness*. New York: New Press, 2012.

Allen, Danielle S. "Law's Necessary Forcefulness: Ralph Ellison vs. Hannah Arendt on the Battle of Little Rock." *Oklahoma City University Law Review* 26 (2001): 857–895.

Talking to Strangers: Anxieties of Citizenship since Brown v. Board of Education. Chicago: University of Chicago Press, 2004.

The World of Prometheus: The Politics of Punishing in Democratic Athens. Princeton, NJ: Princeton University Press, 2000.

Allgor, Catherine. *Parlor Politics: In Which the Ladies of Washington Help Build a City and a Government*. Charlottesville, VA: University of Virginia Press, 2000.

Andrew Sullivan, "Why Gay Marriage Is Good for America."*Newsweek*, July 18, 2011. http://www.newsweek.com/andrew-sullivan-why-gay-marriage-good-america-68453.

Anzaldúa, Gloria. *The Gloria Anzaldúa Reader*. Durham, NC: Duke University Press, 2009.

Appiah, K. Anthony. "Cosmopolitan Patriots." In *For Love of Country?*, edited by Martha Nussbaum and Joshua Cohen, 21–29. Boston: Beacon Press, 1996.

"Global Citizenship." *Fordham Law Review* 75, no. 5 (2006): 2375–2391.

Cosmopolitanism: Ethics in a World of Strangers. New York: W. W. Norton, 2007.

"Identity, Authenticity, Survival." In *Multiculturalism and the Politics of Recognition*, edited by Amy Guttman, 149–164. Princeton, NJ: Princeton University Press, 1994.

Arendt, Hannah. *Crises of the Republic: Lying in Politics, Civil Disobedience, on Violence, Thoughts on Politics and Revolution*. New York: Harcourt Brace Jovanovich, 1972.

On Revolution. New York: Penguin Books, 1990.

RahelVarnhagen: The Life of a Jewess. Edited by Liliane Weissberg. Translated by Richard Winston and Clare Winston. Baltimore: Johns Hopkins University Press, 1997.

"Reflections on Little Rock and Reply to Critics." In *The Portable Hannah Arendt*, edited by Peter Baehr, 231–246. New York: Penguin Classics, 2000.

"The Crisis in Education." In *Between Past and Future: Eight Exercises in Political Thought*, 173–196. New York: Penguin, 1993.

The Human Condition. Chicago: University of Chicago Press, 1958.

The Jewish Writings. New York: Random House, 2008.

"Truth and Politics." In *The Portable Hannah Arendt*, edited by Peter Baehr, 545–575. New York: Penguin Classics, 2000.

"What Is Freedom?" In *The Portable Hannah Arendt*, edited by Peter Baehr, 438–461. New York: Penguin Classics, 2000.

Aristotle, *The Politics*. Translated by Ernest Barker. New York: Oxford University Press, 1995.

Bailyn, Bernard. *The Barbarous Years: The Peopling of British North America: The Conflict of Civilizations, 1600–1675*. New York: Alfred A. Knopf, 2012.

Balfour, Lawrie. "Ida B. Wells and 'Color Line Justice': Rethinking Reparations in Feminist Terms." *Perspectives on Politics* 13, no. 3 (2015): 680–696.

Barber, Benjamin R. *A Place for Us: How to Make Society Civil and Democracy Strong*. New York: Hill and Wang, 1998.

Aristocracy of Everyone. New York: Ballantine Books, 1992.

Bartky, Sandra Lee. *Femininity and Domination: Studies in the Phenomenology of Oppression*. New York: Routledge, 1990.

Basch, Norma. "Marriage, Morals, and Politics in the Election of 1828." *Journal of American History* 80, no. 3 (December 1, 1993): 890–918.

Bates, Daisy. *The Long Shadow of Little Rock: A Memoir*. Fayetteville: University of Arkansas Press, 2007.

Bax, Ernest Belfort. *Jean-Paul Marat: The People's Friend*. G. Richards, 1901.

Beauvoir, Simone de. *The Second Sex*. Translated by Constance Borde and Sheila Malovany-Chevallier. New York: Alfred A. Knopf, 2010.

Benhabib, Seyla, ed. *Politics in Dark Times: Encounters with Hannah Arendt*. New York: Cambridge University Press, 2010.

"The Pariah and Her Shadow: Hannah Arendt's Biography of Rahel Varnhagen." *Political Theory* 23, no. 1 (February 1, 1995): 5–24.

Bercovitch, Sacvan. *The American Jeremiad*. Madison: University of Wisconsin Press, 1978.

Berger, Martin A. *Seeing through Race: A Reinterpretation of Civil Rights Photography*. Berkeley: University of California Press, 2011.

Berkowitz, Roger. "Solitude and the Activity of Thinking." In *Thinking in Dark Times: Hannah Arendt on Ethics and Politics*, edited by Roger Berkowitz, Jeffrey Katz, and Thomas Keenan, 237–248. New York: Fordham University Press, 2009.

Berkowitz, Roger, Jeffrey Katz, and Thomas Keenan, eds. *Thinking in Dark Times: Hannah Arendt on Ethics and Politics*. New York: Fordham University Press, 2009.

Berlant, Lauren. *Cruel Optimism*. Durham, NC: Duke University Press, 2011.

"Trauma and Ineloquence." *Cultural Values* 5, no. 1 (2001): 41–58.

Berlant, Lauren, and Warner, Michael. "Sex in Public." *Critical Inquiry* 24, no. 2 (1998): 547–566.

Berlant, Lauren, Najafi, Sina, and Serlin, David. "The Broken Circuit: An Interview with Lauren Berlant." *Cabinet*, no. 31 (2008).

Bernstein, Robin. *Racial Innocence: Performing American Childhood from Slavery to Civil Rights*. New York: New York University Press, 2011.

Bewes, Timothy. *Cynicism and Postmodernity*. London: Verso, 1997.

Billerbeck, Margarethe. "The Ideal Cynic from Epictetus to Julian." In *The Cynics: The Cynic Movement in Antiquity and Its Legacy*, edited by R. Bracht Branham and Marie-Odile Goulet-Cazé, 203–221. Berkeley: University of California Press, 2000.

Boade, Erin Alane. "The Limits of Civility in the Civil Rights and Black Power Movements: Three African-American Women's Autobiographies." PhD Dissertation, University of Texas-Austin. December 2009.

Boling, Patricia. *Privacy and the Politics of Intimate Life*. Ithaca: Cornell University Press, 1996.

Botting, Eileen Hunt. *Family Feuds: Wollstonecraft, Burke, and Rousseau on the Transformation of the Family*. Albany: SUNY Press, 2006.

Boyd, Richard. "Pity's Pathologies Portrayed: Rousseau and the Limits of Democratic Compassion." *Political Theory* 32, no. 4 (August 1, 2004): 519–546.

Branham R. Bracht. "Nietzsche's Cynicism: Uppercase or Lowercase." In *Nietzsche and Antiquity: His Reaction and Response to the Classical Tradition*, edited by Paul Bishop, 170–81. Suffolk, UK: Camden House, 2004.

"Defacing the Currency: Diogenes' Rhetoric and the Invention of Cynicism." In *The Cynics: The Cynic Movement in Antiquity and Its Legacy*, edited by R. Bracht Branham and Marie-Odile Goulet-Cazé, 81–104. Berkeley: University of California Press, 2000.

Brown, Elsa Barkley. "Negotiating and Transforming the Public Sphere: African American Political Life in the Transition from Slavery to Freedom." *Public Culture* 7 (1994): 107–146.

Brown, Gregory S. "The Self-Fashionings of Olympe de Gouges, 1784-1789." *Eighteenth-Century Studies* 34, no. 3 (Spring 2001): 383–401.

Brown, Wendy. *Edgework: Critical Essays on Knowledge and Politics*. Princeton, NJ: Princeton University Press, 2005.

Politics Out of History. Princeton, NJ: Princeton University Press, 2001.

States of Injury. Princeton, NJ: Princeton University Press, 1995.

Cairns, Douglas L. *Aidōs: The Psychology and Ethics of Honour and Shame in Ancient Greek Literature*. New York: Oxford University Press, 1993.

Cañizares-Esguerra, Jorge. *Puritan Conquistadors: Iberianizing the Atlantic, 1550–1700*. Palo Alto, CA: Stanford University Press, 2006.

Carpenter, Dale. *Flagrant Conduct: The Story of Lawrence v. Texas: How a Bedroom Arrest Decriminalized Gay Americans*. New York: W. W. Norton, 2012.

Chaloupka, William. *Everybody Knows: Cynicism in America*. Minneapolis: University of Minnesota Press, 2001.

Cogan, Jacob Katz. "The Look Within: Property, Capacity, and Suffrage in Nineteenth-Century America." *The Yale Law Journal* 107, no. 2 (November 1, 1997): 473–498.

Cole, John R. *Between the Queen and the Cabby: Olympe de Gouges's Rights of Woman*. Montreal: McGill-Queen's University Press, 2011.
Combahee River, Collective. *Combahee River Collective Statement: Black Feminist Organizing in the 70s and 80s*. New York: Kitchen Table/Women of Color Press, 1986.
Cott, Nancy F. "Passionlessness: An Interpretation of Victorian Sexual Ideology, 1790–1850." *Signs* 4, no. 2 (December 1, 1978): 219–236.
Public Vows: A History of Marriage and the Nation. Cambridge, MA: Harvard University Press, 2002.
Counts, Ira Wilmer, Ernest Dumas, Will Campbell, and Robert S. McCord. *A Life Is More Than a Moment: The Desegregation of Little Rock's Central High*. Bloomington, IN: Indiana University Press, 2007.
Dailey, Jane. "Sex, Segregation, and the Sacred after Brown." *The Journal of American History* 91, no. 1 (June 1, 2004): 119–144.
Dalton, Susan. *Engendering the Republic of Letters: Reconnecting Public and Private Spheres in Eighteenth-Century Europe*. Montreal: McGill-Queen's University Press, 2003.
"Gender and the Shifting Ground of Revolutionary Politics: The Case of Madame Roland." *Canadian Journal of History* 36, no. 2 (2001): 259–282.
Darnton, Robert. *The Great Cat Massacre: And Other Episodes in French Cultural History*. New York: Basic Books, 2009.
"The High Enlightenment and the Low-Life of Literature in Pre-Revolutionary France." *Past & Present*, no. 51(May 1, 1971): 81–115.
Derrida, Jacques. *Of Grammatology*. Translated by Gayatri Chakravorty Spivak. Baltimore: Johns Hopkins University Press, 1998.
De Schweinitz, Rebecca. *If We Could Change the World: Young People and America's Long Struggle for Racial Equality*. Chapel Hill: University of North Carolina Press, 2011.
Desmond, William D. *The Greek Praise of Poverty: Origins of Ancient Cynicism*. Notre Dame, IN: University of Notre Dame Press, 2006.
Cynics. Berkeley: University of California Press, 2008.
Dietz, Mary. "Feminist Receptions of Hannah Arendt." In *Feminist Interpretations of Hannah Arendt*, edited by Bonnie Honig, 17–50. University Park: Pennsylvania State University Press, 1995.
duBois, Page. *Slaves and Other Objects*. Chicago: University of Chicago Press, 2008.
Dudley, Donald R. *A History of Cynicism – From Diogenes to the 6th Century A.D.* London: Methuen & Company, 1937.
Echols, Alice. *Daring to Be Bad: Radical Feminism in America, 1967–1975*. Minneapolis: University of Minnesota Press, 1989.
Elias, Norbert. *The Civilizing Process, Volume One: The History of Manners*. Oxford: Blackwell, 1978.
Elshtain, Jean Bethke. "Commentary: Political Children." *Childhood* 3 (1996): 11–28.
Democracy on Trial. New York: Basic Books, 1995.
Espejo, Paulina Ochoa. *The Time of Popular Sovereignty: Process and the Democratic State*. University Park: Pennsylvania State University Press, 2011.
Euben, J. Peter. *Corrupting Youth*. Princeton, NJ: Princeton University Press, 1997.
Platonic Noise. Princeton, NJ: Princeton University Press, 2003.
The Tragedy of Political Theory. Princeton, NJ: Princeton University Press, 1990.
Euripides. *Medea, Hippolytus, Heracles, Bacchae: Four Plays*. Indianapolis: Hackett, 2012.

Fanon, Frantz, trans. Richard Philcox. *The Wretched of the Earth*. New York: Grove Press, 2004.
Farrar, Cynthia. *The Origins of Democratic Thinking: The Invention of Politics in Classical Athens*. Cambridge; New York: Cambridge University Press, 1988.
Felman, Shoshana, and Dori Laub. *Testimony: Crises of Witnessing in Literature, Psychoanalysis and History*. New York: Routledge, 1991.
Foster, Thomas A. *Sex and the Founding Fathers: The American Quest for a Relatable Past*. Philadelphia: Temple University Press, 2014.
Foucault, Michel. *Fearless Speech*. Edited by Joseph Pearson. Los Angeles, CA: Semiotext(e), 2001.
The History of Sexuality. Translated by Robert Hurley. New York: Pantheon Books, 1978.
France, Peter. *Politeness and Its Discontents: Problems in French Classical Culture*. New York: Cambridge University Press, 2006.
Frank, Jason A. *Constituent Moments: Enacting the People in Postrevolutionary America*. Durham, NC: Duke University Press, 2009.
Gelbart, Nina Rattner. "The Blonding of Charlotte Corday." *Eighteenth-Century Studies* 38, no. 1 (2004): 201–221.
Geuss, Raymond. *Public Goods, Private Goods*. Princeton, NJ: Princeton University Press, 2001.
Gilmore, Glenda Elizabeth. *Gender and Jim Crow: Women and the Politics of White Supremacy in North Carolina, 1896–1920*. Chapel Hill: The University of North Carolina Press, 1996.
Gines, Kathryn T. *Hannah Arendt and the Negro Question*. Bloomington, IN: Indiana University Press, 2014.
Goodman, Dena. *The Republic of Letters: A Cultural History of the French Enlightenment*. Ithaca: Cornell University Press, 1996.
Gordon-Reed, Annette. *The Hemingses of Monticello: An American Family*. New York: W. W. Norton, 2009.
Thomas Jefferson and Sally Hemings: An American Controversy. Charlottesville: University of Virginia Press, 1997.
Gottesman, Alex. *Politics and the Street in Democratic Athens*. New York: Cambridge University Press, 2014.
Gross, Larry P. *Up from Invisibility: Lesbians, Gay Men, and the Media in America*. New York: Columbia University Press, 2001.
Guinier, Lani, and Gerald Torres. *The Miner's Canary: Enlisting Race, Resisting Power, Transforming Democracy*. Cambridge, MA: Harvard University Press, 2003.
Gurstein, Rochelle. *The Repeal of Reticence: America's Cultural and Legal Struggles Over Free Speech, Obscenity, Sexual Liberation, and Modern Art*. New York: Hill and Wang, 1999.
Halperin, David M. and Valerie Traub, eds. *Gay Shame*. Chicago: University of Chicago Press, 2009.
Halsall, Robert. "Sloterdijk's Theory of Cynicism, Ressentiment and Horizontal Communication." *International Journal of Media & Cultural Politics* 1, no. 2 (2005): 163–180.
Hamilton, Alexander, James Madison, and John Jay. *The Federalist Papers*. New York: Penguin Classics, 1987.

Hanchard, Michael. "Contours of Black Political Thought: An Introduction and Perspective." *Political Theory* 38, no. 4 (August 1, 2010): 510–536.

Hansen, Mogens Herman. *The Athenian Democracy in the Age of Demosthenes: Structure, Principles, and Ideology*. Norman: University of Oklahoma Press, 1999.

Hanson, Ellis. "Teaching Shame." In *Gay Shame*, edited by David M. Halperin and Valerie Traub, 132–164. Chicago: University of Chicago Press, 2009.

Harris-Perry, Melissa V. *Sister Citizen: Shame, Stereotypes, and Black Women in America*. New Haven: Yale University Press, 2011.

Hartog, Hendrik. *Man and Wife in America: A History*. Cambridge, MA: Harvard University Press, 2000.

Higginbotham, Evelyn Brooks. *Righteous Discontent*. Cambridge, MA: Harvard University Press, 1993.

Hine, Darlene Clark. "Rape and the Inner Lives of Black Women in the Middle West." *Signs* 14, no. 4 (July 1, 1989): 912–920.

Homer. *The Iliad*. Translated by Richmond Lattimore. Chicago: University of Chicago Press, 1951.

Honig, Bonnie. "Antigone's Laments, Creon's Grief: Mourning, Membership, and the Politics of Exception." *Political Theory* 37, no. 1 (February 1, 2009): 5–43.

"The Arendt Question in Feminism." In *Feminist Interpretations of Hannah Arendt*, edited by Bonnie Honig, 1–16. University Park: Pennsylvania State University Press, 1995.

hooks, bell. *Sisters of the Yam: Black Women and Self-recovery*. Cambridge, MA: South End Press, 1993.

Howe, Daniel Walker. *What Hath God Wrought: The Transformation of America, 1815–1848*. New York: Oxford University Press, 2009.

Illouz, Eva. *Saving the Modern Soul: Therapy, Emotions, and the Culture of Self-help*. Berkeley: University of California Press, 2008.

Jacquet, Jennifer. *Is Shame Necessary? New Uses for an Old Tool*. New York: Pantheon, 2015.

Janara, Laura. *Democracy Growing Up: Authority, Autonomy, and Passion in Tocqueville's Democracy in America*. Albany: State University of New York Press, 2002.

Johnson, David E., and Johnny Ray Johnson. *A Funny Thing Happened on the Way to the White House: Foolhardiness, Folly, and Fraud in Presidential Elections from Andrew Jackson to George W. Bush*. Lanham, MD: Taylor Trade, 2004.

Johnston, Steven. *Encountering Tragedy: Rousseau and the Project of Democratic Order*. Ithaca: Cornell University Press, 1999.

Kale, Steven. *French Salons: High Society and Political Sociability from the Old Regime to the Revolution of 1848*. Baltimore: Johns Hopkins University Press, 2005.

"Women, Salons, and the State in the Aftermath of the French Revolution." *Journal of Women's History* 13, no. 4 (2002): 54–80.

Kasimis, Demetra. "The Tragedy of Blood-Based Membership: Secrecy and the Politics of Immigration in Euripides's *Ion*." *Political Theory* 41, no. 2 (April 1, 2013): 231–256.

Kasson, John F. *Rudeness and Civility: Manners in Nineteenth-Century Urban America*. New York: Hill and Wang, 1991.

Kaufman, Gershon, and Lev Raphael. *Coming Out of Shame: Transforming Gay and Lesbian Lives*. New York: Main Street Books, 1996.

Kelley, Blair. *Right to Ride: Streetcar Boycotts and African American Citizenship in the Era of Plessy v. Ferguson*. Chapel Hill: University of North Carolina Press, 2010.

Kelly, Christine A. "Whatever Happened to Women's Liberation? Feminist Legacies of '68." *New Political Science* 22, no. 2 (2000): 161–175.

Kennedy, Kristen. "Cynic Rhetoric: The Ethics and Tactics of Resistance." *Rhetoric Review* 18, no. 1 (1999): 26–45.

Kerber, Linda K. "Separate Spheres, Female Worlds, Woman's Place: The Rhetoric of Women's History." *The Journal of American History* 75, no. 1 (1988): 9–39.

"The Republican Mother: Women and the Enlightenment – An American Perspective." *American Quarterly* 28, no. 2 (1976): 187–205.

King Jr., Martin Luther. "Where Do We Go From Here?" Delivered at the Eleventh Annual SCLC Convention, Atlanta, GA, August 16, 1967. http://mlk-kpp01.stanford.edu/index.php/encyclopedia/documentsentry/where_do_we_go_from_here_delivered_at_the_11th_annual_sclc_convention.

Kirkpatrick, Jennet. *Uncivil Disobedience: Studies in Violence and Democratic Politics*. Princeton, NJ: Princeton University Press, 2008.

Kruks, Sonia. *Retrieving Experience: Subjectivity and Recognition in Feminist Politics*. Ithaca: Cornell University Press, 2001.

Laertius, Diogenes. *Lives of Eminent Philosophers, Volume II, Books 6–10*. Translated by R. D. Hicks. Cambridge, MA: Loeb Classical Library, 1925.

Lange, Lynda, ed. *Feminist Interpretations of Jean-Jacques Rousseau*. University Park: Pennsylvania State University Press, 2002.

Lanier, Carlotta Walls Lisa Frazier Page and Bill Clinton. *A Mighty Long Way: My Journey to Justice at Little Rock Central High School*. New York: Random House, 2010.

Lasch, Christopher. *The Culture of Narcissism*. New York: Warner Books, 1979.

Lawson, Steven and Charles Payne, eds. *Debating the Civil Rights Movement, 1945–1968*. Lanham, MD: Rowman & Littlefield, 1998.

Lebron, Christopher J. *The Color of Our Shame: Race and Justice in Our Time*. New York: Oxford University Press, 2013.

Letzter, Jacqueline and Robert Adelson. "French Women Opera Composers and the Aesthetics of Rousseau." *Feminist Studies* 26, no. 1 (2000): 69–100.

Levine, Ellen S. *Freedom's Children: Young Civil Rights Activists Tell Their Own Stories*. New York: Puffin, 2000.

Lewis, Jan. "The Republican Wife: Virtue and Seduction in the Early Republic." *The William and Mary Quarterly* 44, no. 4 (1987): 689–721.

Leys, Ruth. *From Guilt to Shame: Auschwitz and After*. Princeton, NJ: Princeton University Press, 2009.

Lilti, Antoine. *The World of the Salons: Sociability and Worldliness in Eighteenth-Century Paris*. New York: Oxford University Press, 2015.

Lippmann, Walter, Clinton Rossiter, and James Lare. *The Essential Lippmann: A Political Philosophy for Liberal Democracy*. Cambridge, MA: Harvard University Press, 1982.

Locke, Jill. "Aristocratic Mourning: Tocqueville, John Quincy Adams, and the Affairs of Andrew Jackson." In *Feminist Interpretations of Alexis de Tocqueville*, edited by

Jill Locke and Eileen Hunt Botting, 125–150. University Park: Pennsylvania State University Press, 2009.
"Hiding for Whom? Obscurity, Dignity, and the Politics of Truth." *Theory & Event* 3, no. 3 (1999).https://muse.jhu.edu/journals/theory_and_event/v003/3.3locke .html.
"Little Rock's Social Question: Reading Arendt on School Desegregation and Social Climbing." *Political Theory* 41, no. 4 (2013): 533–561.
"Shame and the Future of Feminism." *Hypatia* 22, no. 4 (2007): 146–162.
"The Color of Our Shame: Race and Justice in Our Time." *Contemporary Political Theory* 14, no. 3 (2015): e50–e53.
Loewenberg, Peter. "The Psychohistorical Origins of the Nazi Youth Cohort." *The American Historical Review* 76, no. 5 (1971): 1457–1502.
Long, A.A. "The Socratic Tradition: Diogenes, Crates, and Hellenistic Ethics." In *The Cynics*, edited by R. Bracht Branham and Marie-Odile Goulet-Cazé, 28–46. Berkeley: University of California Press, 1996.
Lorde, Audre. *A Burst of Light: Essays*. Ithaca, NY: Firebrand Books, 1988.
Lotz, Christian. "From Nature to Culture?Diogenes and Philosophical Anthropology." *Human Studies* 28, no. 1 (2005): 41–56.
Luxon, Nancy. *Crisis of Authority: Politics, Trust, and Truth-Telling in Freud and Foucault*. New York: Cambridge University Press, 2013.
Manion, Jennifer C. "Girls Blush, Sometimes: Gender, Moral Agency, and the Problem of Shame." *Hypatia* 18, no. 3 (2003): 21–41.
"The Moral Relevance of Shame." *American Philosophical Quarterly* 39, no. 1 (2002): 73–90.
Markell, Patchen. *Bound by Recognition*. Princeton, NJ: Princeton University Press, 2003.
Marso, Lori. *(Un)Manly Citizens: Jean-Jacques Rousseau's and Germaine de Staël's Subversive Women*. Baltimore: Johns Hopkins University Press, 1999.
Marszalek, John F. *The Petticoat Affair: Manners, Mutiny, and Sex in Andrew Jackson's White House*. Baton Rouge: Louisiana State University Press, 2000.
Martin, Mike W. *From Morality to Mental Health: Virtue and Vice in a Therapeutic Culture*. New York: Oxford University Press, 2006.
Mason, Haydn Trevor. *The Darnton Debate: Books and Revolution in the Eighteenth Century*. Voltaire Foundation, 1998.
Mazella, David. *The Making of Modern Cynicism*. Charlottesville: University of Virginia Press, 2007.
McGee, Micki. *Self-help, Inc.: Makeover Culture in American Life*. New York: Oxford University Press, 2005.
McGuire, Danielle L. *At the Dark End of the Street: Black Women, Rape, and Resistance–A New History of the Civil Rights Movement from Rosa Parks to the Rise of Black Power*. New York: Alfred A. Knopf, 2011.
McMahon, Darrin M. "The Counter-Enlightenment and the Low-Life of Literature in Pre-Revolutionary France." *Past & Present*, no. 159 (1998): 77–112.
McMillan, L. Jane, Janelle Young, and Molly Peters. "Commentary: The 'Idle No More' Movement in Eastern Canada." *Canadian Journal of Law and Society / La Revue Canadienne Droitet Société* 28, no. 3 (2013): 429–431.
Mitchell, Michele. "Silences Broken, Silences Kept: Gender and Sexuality in African-American History." *Gender & History* 11, no. 3 (1999): 433–444.

Moles, John. "Cynic Cosmopolitanism." In *The Cynics: The Cynic Movement in Antiquity and Its Legacy*, edited by R. Bracht Branham and Marie-Odile Goulet-Cazé, 105–120. Berkeley: University of California Press, 2000.
Moore, Patrick. *Beyond Shame: Reclaiming the Abandoned History of Radical Gay Sexuality*. Boston: Beacon Press, 2004.
Morefield, Jeanne. *Empires Without Imperialism: Anglo-American Decline and the Politics of Deflection*. New York: Oxford University Press, 2014.
Morris, Robert C. *Reading, 'Riting, and Reconstruction: The Education of Freedmen in the South, 1861–1870*. Chicago: University of Chicago Press, 2010.
Moruzzi, Norma Claire. *Speaking through the Mask: Hannah Arendt and the Politics of Social Identity*. Ithaca: Cornell University Press, 2000.
Moskowitz, Eva. *In Therapy We Trust: America's Obsession with Self-Fulfillment*. Baltimore: Johns Hopkins University Press, 2001.
Muhammad, Khalil Gibran. *The Condemnation of Blackness: Race, Crime, and the Making of Modern Urban America*. Cambridge, MA: Harvard University Press, 2011.
Murakawa, Naomi. *The First Civil Right: How Liberals Built Prison America*. New York: Oxford University Press, 2014.
Myrdal, Gunnar. *An American Dilemma: The Negro Problem and Modern Democracy*. New Brunswick, NJ: Transaction, 1995.
Nagel, Mechthild. "Beyond the Pale: Reflections on the Vulnerability of Black Life in the United States." In *Diversity, Social Justice, and INclusive Excellence: Transdisciplinary and Global Perspectives*, edited by Seth N. Asumah and Mechthild Nagel, 69–92. Albany: SUNY Press, 2014.
Nagel, Thomas. "Concealment and Exposure." *Philosophy & Public Affairs* 27, no. 1 (1998): 3–30.
Nathans, Benjamin. *Beyond the Pale: The Jewish Encounter with Late Imperial Russia*. Berkeley: University of California Press, 2004.
Nicholas, Lynn H. *Cruel World: The Children of Europe in the Nazi Web*. New York: Vintage, 2006.
Norton, Anne. "Heart of Darkness: Africa and African Americans in the Writings of Hannah Arendt." In *Feminist Interpretations of Hannah Arendt*, edited by Bonnie Honig, 247–262. University Park: Pennsylvania State University Press, 1995.
Nussbaum, Martha. *Hiding from Humanity: Disgust, Shame, and the Law*. Princeton, NJ: Princeton University Press, 2004.
"Patriotism and Cosmopolitanism." In *For Love of Country?*, edited by Joshua Cohen and Martha Nussbaum, 3–20. Boston: Beacon Press, 2002.
Ober, Josiah. *Mass and Elite in Democratic Athens: Rhetoric, Ideology, and the Power of the People*. Princeton, NJ: Princeton University Press, 1991.
The Athenian Revolution. Princeton, NJ: Princeton University Press, 1998.
"Ohio Man Ordered to Hold Sign Saying He Is a Bully." *USATODAY*. April 12, 2014. http://www.usatoday.com/story/news/nation/2014/04/12/ohio-bully-sign/7635449/.
Owsley, Harriet Chappell. "The Marriages of Rachel Donelson." *Tennessee Historical Quarterly* 36, no. 4 (December 1, 1977): 479–492.
Parkinson, Gavin. "The Delvaux Mystery: Painting, the Nouveau Roman, and Art History." *Nottingham French Studies* 51, no. 3 (2012): 298–313.
Parsons, Lynn Hudson. "'A Perpetual Harrow upon My Feelings': John Quincy Adams and the American Indian." *The New England Quarterly* 46, no. 3 (1973): 339–379.

The Birth of Modern Politics: Andrew Jackson, John Quincy Adams, and the Election of 1828. New York: Oxford University Press, 2011.

Payne, Charles. "The View from the Trenches." In *Debating the Civil Rights Movement: 1945–1968*, edited by Steven Lawson and Charles Payne, 115–135. Lanham, MD: Rowman & Littlefield, 2006.

I've got the Light of Freedom: The Organizing Tradition and the Mississippi Freedom Struggle. Berkeley: University of California Press, 2007

Perl, Harriet, and Gay Abarbanell. *Guidelines to Feminist Consciousness Raising*. Los Angeles, CA: H.M. Perl, 1979.

Pitkin, Hanna. *The Attack of the Blob: Hannah Arendt's Concept of the Social*. Chicago: University of Chicago Press, 1998.

Plato, *Protagoras*. Translated by N. Denyar. Cambridge: Cambridge University Press, 2008.

Popiel, Jennifer J. *Rousseau's Daughters: Domesticity, Education, and Autonomy in Modern France*. Lebanon: University of New Hampshire Press, 2008.

Povinelli, Elizabeth A. *The Cunning of Recognition: Indigenous Alterities and the Making of Australian Multiculturalism*. Durham, NC: Duke University Press, 2002.

Pownall, Frances. "From Orality to Literacy: The Moral Education of the Elite in Fourth-Century Athens." *Mnemosyne Supplementum* 6, no. 280 (2007): 235–289.

Probyn, Elspeth. *Blush: Faces of Shame*. University of Minnesota Press, 2005.

Putnam, Robert D. *Bowling Alone: The Collapse and Revival of American Community*. Simon & Schuster, 2000.

Raaflaub, Kurt. "Aristocracy and Free speech in the Greco-Roman World." In *Free Speech in Classical Antiquity*, edited by Ineke Sluiter and Ralph Rosen, 41–61 Leiden: Brill, 2004.

Rancière, Jacques. *Hatred of Democracy*. London: Verso, 2007.

Rawls, John. *A Theory of Justice*. Cambridge, MA: Belknap Press of Harvard University Press, 1971.

Remini, Robert V. *Andrew Jackson: The Course of American Freedom, 1822–1832*. Baltimore: Johns Hopkins University Press, 1998.

John Quincy Adams. New York: Times Books, 2002.

The Life of Andrew Jackson. New York: Harper Perennial Modern Classics, 2010.

Rempel, Gerhard. *Hitler's Children: The Hitler Youth and the SS*. Chapel Hill: University of North Carolina Press, 1989.

Reynolds, David S. *Waking Giant: America in the Age of Jackson*. New York: Harper, 2008.

Rieff, Philip. *The Triumph of the Therapeutic: Uses of Faith after Freud*. New York: Harper & Row, 1966.

Ring, Jennifer. "The Pariah as Hero: Hannah Arendt's Political Actor." *Political Theory* 19, no. 3 (1991): 433–452.

Ritterhouse, Jennifer Lynn. *Growing Up Jim Crow: How Black and White Southern Children Learned Race*. Chapel Hill: University of North Carolina Press, 2006.

Robbins, Bruce. "Cosmopolitanism: New and Newer." *Boundary* 2 34, no. 3 (2007): 47–60.

Rochefoucauld, La. *Maxims*. New York: Penguin, 1981.

Roediger, David R. *The Wages of Whiteness: Race and the Making of the American Working Class*. New York: Verso, 1999.

Rogers, Melvin L. "Introduction: Disposable Lives." *Theory & Event* 17, no. 3 (2014). http://muse.jhu.edu/journals/theory_and_event/v017/17.3S.rogers.html.

"David Walker and the Political Power of the Appeal." *Political Theory* 43, no. 2 (2015): 208–233.

Rogin, Michael Paul. *Fathers and Children: Andrew Jackson and the Subjugation of the American Indian*. New Brunswick, NJ: Transaction, 1975.

Rose, Nikolas S. *Governing the Soul: The Shaping of the Private Self*. New York: Routledge, 1990.

Rosen, Hannah. *Terror in the Heart of Freedom: Citizenship, Sexual Violence, and the Meaning of Race in the Postemancipation South*. Chapel Hill: University of North Carolina Press, 2009.

Rosenblatt, Helena. *Rousseau and Geneva: From the First Discourse to the Social Contract, 1749–1762*. New York: Cambridge University Press, 1997.

Rousseau, Jean-Jacques. *Emile: Or, on Education*. Translated by Allan Bloom. New York: Basic Books, 1979.

First and Second Discourses, Together with Replies to the Critics and Essay on the Origin of Languages. New York: Harper and Row, 1986.

La Nouvelle Héloïse: Julie, or the New Eloise: Letters of Two Lovers, Inhabitants of a Small Town at the Foot of the Alps. Translated by Judith H. McDowell. University Park: Pennsylvania State University Press, 1990.

Politics and the Arts: Letter to M. D'Alembert on the Theater. Translated by Allan Bloom. Ithaca: Cornell University Press, 1968.

The Confessions. Translated by J.M. Cohen. New York: Penguin Books, 1953.

The Social Contract. Translated by Maurice Cranston. New York: Penguin Classics, 1968.

Samnotra, Manu. "'Sensitive to Shame': Hannah Arendt on Becoming Worldly." *Constellations* 21, no. 3 (2014): 338–350.

Sartre, Jean-Paul. *Being and Nothingness*. Translated by Hazel E. Barnes. New York: Washington Square Press, 1993.

Saxonhouse, Arlene W. *Free Speech and Democracy in Ancient Athens*. New York: Cambridge University Press, 2006.

Saxton, Alexander. *The Rise and Fall of the White Republic: Class Politics and Mass Culture in Nineteenth-Century America*. New York: Verso, 2003.

Schechter, Patricia A. *Ida B. Wells-Barnett and American Reform, 1880–1930*. Chapel Hill: University of North Carolina Press, 2001.

Schiff, Jade Larissa. *Burdens of Political Responsibility: Narrative and the Cultivation of Responsiveness*. New York: Cambridge University Press, 2014.

Scott, Daryl Michael. *Contempt and Pity: Social Policy and the Image of the Damaged Black Psyche, 1880–1996*. University of North Carolina Press, 1997.

"Postwar Pluralism, *Brown v. Board of Education*, and the Origins of Multicultural Education." *The Journal of American History* 91, no. 1 (2004): 69–82.

Scott, Joan W. *Only Paradoxes to Offer: French Feminists and the Rights of Man*. Cambridge, MA: Harvard University Press, 1997.

Sedgwick, Eve Kosofsky. *Epistemology of the Closet*. Berkeley: University of California Press, 2008.

Sellers, Charles Grier. "Andrew Jackson versus the Historians." *The Mississippi Valley Historical Review* 44, no. 4 (March 1, 1958): 615–634.

The Market Revolution: Jacksonian America, 1815–1846. New York: Oxford University Press, 1992.

Shabbir Amanullah, Sabu K. Oomman, and Soumitra Shankar Datta. "'Diogenes Syndrome' Revisited." *German Journal of Psychiatry* 12 (2009): 38–44.

Shea, Louisa. *The Cynic Enlightenment: Diogenes in the Salon*. Baltimore: Johns Hopkins University Press, 2009.

"Shields, Brooks on Gates' Legacy, Gingrich Campaign 'Meltdown,' Weiner Fallout." PBS NewsHour' June 10, 2011.

Shields, Mark. "Does Wall Street Know No Shame?," 2009. http://www.creators.com/opinion/mark-shields/-does-wall-street-know-no-shame.html.

Shiffrin, Seana. "What's Really Wrong with Compelled Association?" *Northewestern University Law Review* 99, no. 2 (2005): 839–888.

Shulman, George. *American Prophecy: Race and Redemption in American Political Culture*. Minneapolis: University of Minnesota Press, 2008.

Sloterdijk, Peter. *Critique of Cynical Reason*. Minneapolis: University of Minnesota Press, 1988.

Sluiter, Ineke. "Communicating Cynicism: Diogenes' Gangsta Rap." In *Language and Learning: Philosophy of Language in the Hellenistic Age*, edited by Dorothea Frede and Brad Inwood, 139–163. New York: Cambridge University Press, 2005.

Smart, Annie. *Citoyennes: Women and the Ideal of Citizenship in Eighteenth-Century France*. Lanham, MD: University of Delaware Press, 2011.

Snyder, Claire R. *Citizen-Soldiers and Manly Warriors: Military Service and Gender in the Civic Republican Tradition*. Lanham, MD: Rowman & Littlefield, 1999.

Sparks, Holloway. "Dissident Citizenship: Democratic Theory, Political Courage, and Activist Women." *Hypatia* 12, no. 4 (1997): 74–110.

Stanley, Sharon A. *The French Enlightenment and the Emergence of Modern Cynicism*. New York: Cambridge University Press, 2014.

Starobinski, Jean. *Jean-Jacques Rousseau: Transparency and Obstruction*. Translated by Arthur Goldhammer. Chicago: University of Chicago Press, 1988.

Stein, Arlene. "The Forum: Therapeutic Politics – An Oxymoron?" *Sociological Forum* 26, no. 1 (2011): 187–193.

Stelzig, Eugene L. *The Romantic Subject in Autobiography: Rousseau and Goethe*. Charlottesville: University of Virginia Press, 2000.

Stott, Andrew. *Comedy*. New York: Routledge, 2014.

Strong, Tracy B. *Jean Jacques Rousseau: The Politics of the Ordinary*. Lanham, MD: Rowman& Littlefield, 2002.

Sullivan, Andrew. *Virtually Normal: An Argument about Homosexuality*. New York: Vintage Books, 1996.

Sullivan, Shirley Darcus. *Psychological and Ethical Ideas: What Early Greeks Say*. Leiden: Brill, 1995.

Tarnopolsky, Christina H. *Prudes, Perverts, and Tyrants: Plato's Gorgias and the Politics of Shame*. Princeton, NJ: Princeton University Press, 2010.

Taylor, Charles. *A Secular Age*. Cambridge, MA: Belknap Press of Harvard University Press, 2007.

"The Politics of Recognition." In *Multiculturalism: Examining the Politics of Recognition*. Edited by Amy Gutmann, 25–74. Princeton, NJ: Princeton University Press, 1994.

The Ethics of Authenticity. Cambridge, MA: Harvard University Press, 1992.

Taylor, Gabriele. *Pride, Shame, and Guilt: Emotions of Self-assessment*. Oxford: Clarendon Press, 1985.

Tocqueville, Alexis de. *Journey to America*. New Haven: Yale University Press, 1959.

The Old Regime and the French Revolution. Translated by Stuart Gilbert. New York: Anchor, 1983.
Democracy in America. Translated by Gerald Bevan. New York: Penguin Classics, 2003.
Tompkins, Kyla Wazana. *Racial Indigestion: Eating Bodies in the 19th Century.* New York: New York University Press, 2012.
Trouille, Mary Seidman. *Sexual Politics in the Enlightenment: Women Writers Read Rousseau.* Albany: SUNY Press, 1997.
Usher, M. D. "Diogenes' Doggerel: Chreia and Quotation in Cynic Performance." *The Classical Journal* 104, no. 3 (February 1, 2009): 207–223.
Villa, Dana. *Socratic Citizenship.* Princeton, NJ: Princeton University Press, 2001.
Warner, Michael. *The Trouble with Normal: Sex, Politics, and the Ethics of Queer Life.* New York: Free Press, 1999.
Wells, Ida B. *Crusade for Justice: The Autobiography of Ida B. Wells.* Chicago: University of Chicago Press, 1970.
Southern Horrors and Other Writings; The Anti-lynching Campaign of Ida B. Wells, 1892–1900. Edited by Jacqueline Jones Royster. Boston, MA: Bedford/St. Martin's, 1996.
Wells-Barnett, Ida B. *On Lynchings.* Amherst, NY: Humanity Books, 2002.
Wilentz, Sean. *Andrew Jackson: The 7th President, 1829–1837.* New York: Macmillan, 2007.
Williams, Bernard. *Shame and Necessity.* Berkeley: University of California Press, 1993.
Williams, Patricia J. *Alchemy of Race and Rights: Diary of a Law Professor.* Cambridge: Harvard University Press, 1992.
Wingrove, Elizabeth Rose. *Rousseau's Republican Romance.* Princeton, NJ: Princeton University Press, 2000.
Wood, Kirsten E. "'One Woman so Dangerous to Public Morals': Gender and Power in the Eaton Affair." *Journal of the Early Republic* 17, no. 2 (1997): 237–275.
Woodward, Kathleen. "Traumatic Shame: Toni Morrison, Televisual Culture, and the Cultural Politics of the Emotions." *Cultural Critique*, no. 46 (2000): 210–240.
Wotherspoon, Terry, and John Hansen. "The 'Idle No More' Movement: Paradoxes of First Nations Inclusion in the Canadian Context." *Social Inclusion* 1, no. 1 (2013): 21–36.
Wright, Katie. "Theorizing Therapeutic Culture: Past Influences, Future Directions." *Journal of Sociology* 44, no. 4 (2008): 321–336.
Young-Bruehl, Elisabeth. *Hannah Arendt: For Love of the World.* New Haven: Yale University Press, 1977.
Zerilli, Linda. *Feminism and the Abyss of Freedom.* Chicago: University of Chicago Press, 2005.
Signifying Woman: Culture and Chaos in Rousseau, Burke, and Mill. Ithaca: Cornell University Press, 1994.
Zivi, Karen. *Making Rights Claims: A Practice of Democratic Citizenship.* New York: Oxford University Press, 2011.
"The Politics of Compassion in the Age of AIDS." In *W Stands for Women: How the George W. Bush Presidency Shaped a New Politics of Gender*, edited by Michaele Ferguson and Lori Marso, 41–62. Durham, NC: Duke University Press, 2007.
Žižek, Slavoj. *The Sublime Object of Ideology.* New York: Verso Books, 1989.

Index

Lightning Source UK Ltd.
Milton Keynes UK
UKHW01f0018250718
326237UK00001B/33/P

9 781107 635906